SUSTAINABILITY STRATEGY

SUSTAINABILITY STRATEGY

Paul Martin & Miriam Verbeek

THE FEDERATION PRESS
2006

Published in Sydney by:
The Federation Press
PO Box 45, Annandale, NSW, 2038
71 John St, Leichhardt, NSW, 2040
Ph (02) 9552 2200 Fax (02) 9552 1681
E-mail: info@federationpress.com.au
Website: http://www.federationpress.com.au

This book is published with the support of Land & Water Australia.
GPO Box 2182, Canberra, ACT, 2601
Level 2, UNISYS Building,
91 Northbourne Avenue, Turner, ACT, 2612
Ph (02) 6257 3379 Fax (02) 6257 3420
E-mail: public@lwa.gov.au
Website: http://www.lwa.gov.au

The opinions expressed in the book represent those of the authors and not necessarily those of Land & Water Australia and its Board.

National Library of Australia
Cataloguing-in-Publication entry

Martin, Paul V.
Sustainability Strategy.

Bibliography.
Includes index.
ISBN 1 86287 555 3.

1. Industrial management – Environmental aspects – Australia. 2. Social responsibility of business – Australia. I. Verbeek, Miriam. II. Title.

658.4080994

© The Federation Press

This publication is copyright. Other than for the purposes of and subject to the conditions prescribed under the Copyright Act, no part of it may in any form or by any means (electronic, mechanical, microcopying, photocopying, recording or otherwise) be reproduced, stored in a retrieval system or transmitted without prior written permission. Enquiries should be addressed to the publishers.

Typeset by The Federation Press, Sydney, NSW.
Printed by Southwood Press Pty Ltd, Sydney, NSW.

Preface

This book has one purpose: to assist people who are committed to sustainability to design and implement resource management strategies that will work. We intend that it help community and agency members of catchment management and natural resource agencies, policy makers, and activists for sustainability by giving them command of the underlying concepts of sustainability strategy, supported by many examples from around the world of both successful and less successful strategies.

Why is this book needed? There is a great deal of attention focused on particular instruments, such as regulation or incentives or tradeable rights. Often it seems that the only component of natural resource management is to select the right instrument, but clearly this is very far from correct. There are too many examples of regulations, market incentives, education, or property rights failing to deliver what their advocates promised, or to believe that any instrument is guaranteed to work. Unless decision-makers have a clear understanding of how these different approaches work, and the situations in which they are likely to be effective, it is hard to design behaviourally-focused, integrated strategies. This book will provide both the underlying conceptual understanding and many illustrative examples which will make it possible for readers to tackle this challenging design issue.

A key feature of our approach is that we have outlined a fundamental model for understanding how resource-use decisions are made. We have then used this same model to explain how policed regulation, private legal action, tradeable market instruments, incentive schemes and information strategies work, and the limits to their effectiveness. In all cases we have provided a myriad of examples from Australia and around the world. This approach has caused us to question some of the commonly expressed conventional wisdom about, for example, the relative efficiency of market instruments, the paramount importance of property security for rights markets to work and the role of regulation.

To achieve our aim of assisting decision-makers at the sharp edge of sustainability, we have concentrated on explaining the fundamentals in a way that goes beyond particular disciplines, and we have provided 'how to' guidance. We aim to provide our readers with a comfortable understanding of what can (on the surface) seem to be extraordinarily complex concepts, so that they are able to consider the issues involved in redirecting natural resource-use behaviour towards more sustainable pathways.

We would like to thank the many people who have assisted in this endeavour. In the book you will find interviews with leading advocates of sustainability. Their practical wisdom provides a touchstone for action. We also thank the many people we have worked with over the past 20 years who are involved in front-line activism, government policy-making and strategy implementation, corporate sustainability, and particularly catchment management, for both the inspiration and the ideas that drove this book. Finally, to Federation Press and Land & Water Australia – thanks for the opportunity and the practical support that made this possible.

Paul Martin
Miriam Verbeek
November 2005

CONTENTS

Preface   v

Introduction
The 'big picture': Facing up to instutional reform   1

PART 1: CONCEPTS

Chapter 1
Strategy and sustainability   11

Chapter 2
Achieving behavioural change   27

PART 2: INSTRUMENT CHOICE

Chapter 3
Instruments and instrument choice   57

Chapter 4
Market forces and consumption   83

Chapter 5
Rights markets   109

Chapter 6
Property rights   132

Chapter 7
Strengthening private regulation   154

Chapter 8
Public regulation   167

Chapter 9
Influencing the rate of change   183

PART 3: IMPLEMENTATION

Chapter 10
High-level design considerations   207

Chapter 11
Implementation   220

References   258
Index   275

Introduction

The 'big picture':
Facing up to institutional reform

This book concentrates on explaining strategies for creating a sustainable Australia. It shows that there are many possibilities. This could lead to the misleading and comforting conclusion that we can do all we need to do within the framework of our existing institutions. Policies and institutions in a society work in much the same way as physical structures work in a physical system. They shape how the flows are directed, and as a result they are powerful in determining how that system works and the outcomes it produces.

It is hard believe that we can rapidly change our unsustainable resource use by throwing more money at the problem, by deploying market or regulatory instruments, or by securing improved scientific or management information, without radical change to institutions. Institutions, by their very nature, embed patterns of power and wealth in a society. Many who are powerful will oppose change to the institutions from which they benefit, until that change is unavoidable. Because resource exploitation is a basis of political and economic power in our society, there will be much resistance to demands for resource conservation.

Significant change to resource control always requires major institutional changes. Inevitably this creates social disturbance. The transition from monarchy to democracy involved bloody battles, as did the separation of church from state. The shifts from agrarian to industrial economies caused incredible social upheavals – Australia being the recipient of many people (both convicts and free settlers) who were the fall-out of that period. More recent examples are the information economy-led restructures in legal institutions, policy frameworks, market competition, and wealth allocation which are still taking place.

The desire to avoid disruption partly explains the enormous effort to find ways to use market mechanisms and voluntary arrangements to achieve sustainable use without forced resource reallocation. The chaotic implementation of sustainability policy shows the strains as the system tries to accommodate changes that do not fit well within structures designed largely to support ever-increasing production and consumption.

For instrument-based strategies to be fully effective – regardless of whether they are market or incentives based or regulatory in form – they must align with the institutions of society. Alignment will occur when institutions are easily able to implement the instruments of sustainability, without any conflict with culture or operating practice, and without the need for significant re-learning during implementation. Where there is a misalignment, turbulence and conflict are more likely and will play a far greater role in shaping the outcomes. The longer we delay taking necessary action towards reshaping our institutions, later adjustments will have to be more radical and there will be less time for innovation and adaptation.

Harnessing market capitalism is vital

A theme in this book is that market capitalism is pivotal to the achievement of sustainability. Competition that is not the enemy of sustainability, nor is capitalism. However, particular behaviours that society chooses to reward through these mechanisms need to be reconsidered. Institutional structures generate patterns of winners and losers, and thence patterns of behaviour and the outcomes. Society can harness competition to strengthen whatever pattern of contingencies it believes will yield optimal outcomes. For example, martial skills were rewarded in medieval Europe or 18th century Japan; bloodlines are valued in ancestral monarchies; and horse and cattle breeding expertise was prized 18th and 19th century Spain. The elevation of self-interested economic activity to the status of a paramount value is, in anthropological terms, a very recent aberration. It does not have to remain the key contingency which leads to personal reward.

In some tribal societies where resource limitations are part of everyday existence, custodial performance is a much-rewarded contingency and the source of political and financial power. Totemic rules often involve constraints on resource use, rights and preservation duties. There are powerful custodians, such as shamans or elders, to ensure that the natural capital is conserved. Community belief systems support this.

To put this in a modern context: those in a resource-conserving community who have the ability to protect and enhance natural resources, to use resources without depleting them, or are able to provide additional resources, would get rights to resources and this would become a key to 'win' within that society. Those who are unwilling or unable to conserve would find their access to resources diminished (just as those lacking wealth have their resource access capped in a capitalist society).

To be a sustainable society, we need to create both a custodial and productivity-oriented culture and behaviour. This requires that we consistently reward both economic performance and good custodianship and concurrently penalise resource users with loss of access when they are outcompeted in custodial performance.[1]

Overlaying a custodial culture on a capitalist culture will create a complex context with resulting uncertainty that will be unwelcome, particularly

---

1   The risk of loss of resource through failures in economic performance is already built into capitalist contingency structures.

by those who are currently most successful. Such a situation will test the resilience of decision-makers and the maturity of our political institutions.

A framework for innovation and market-focused reform

Any truly effective policy approach to sustainability must not only conserve, it must also stimulate significant innovation in economically productive resource use at many levels. It requires a shift to a technology- and services-intensive economy, reducing the strain on natural resources to produce wealth; more efficient use of natural resources in production; and more efficient consumption patterns. This will create greater economic value from the resources that we harness.

An effective approach would also stimulate significant innovation in the protection of resources that are not essential to efficient and profitable production, at four levels:

- Reducing perverse subsidies and preventing inadequately-priced spillover effects of both production and consumption.
- Reinvesting substantial resources in the protection and rehabilitation of environmental capital to allow future natural service benefits to flow. This would be achieved through both subsidies and market support schemes.
- Creating effective safeguards against undesirable uses of the environment, including:
  - unpriced or insufficiently-priced use of resources;
  - mismanagement or catastrophic accident;
  - cumulative incremental harm to the environment.
- Halting institutional failure by those agencies charged with protecting and/or rehabilitating our natural capital.

The approach would minimise reliance on government. Government's main role would be to maintain the integrity of the natural resource management system including:

- Managing population, industrial development, social support and other policy settings within a framework of sustainable resource use, not as independent considerations.
- Integrating a central emphasis on practical action on sustainability into all government communications and resourcing, and into resource use by government;
- Ensuring that the public have unambiguous information about the condition of our natural capital, the rate of its depletion, the implications of that depletion, and the directions for change that are required to ensure sustainability.

- Providing a strong regulatory safety net against failure of voluntary and market instruments, and against increased harm to the environment, and ensuring that this net strengthens if pressure on these resources increases.
- Ensuring that the agencies responsible for controlling resource-use activities are sufficiently resourced, with clear incentives and accountability, so that the underlying limits to use are respected.
- Regulating with integrity, which requires that funds available for implementation match the demands of implementation, and that as funds availability reduces, regulatory instruments are redesigned to be effective within available policing resources.
- Managing transaction costs in the mix of instruments that shape resource-use behaviour, by designing regulatory instruments that use transaction costs (including the default cost-of-failure of regulation) to discourage environmental harm and ensuring that transaction costs systematically discourage those activities that have the potential to harm the environment.

The approach should be designed so that those whose behaviour is being targeted can readily access and understand information. This requires:

- Reducing administrative complexity including rationalisation of the range of regulations and administrative and consultative bodies.[2]
- Redesigning processes using quality system concepts to minimise administrative complexity;
- Investing in transparency and providing real access to environmental, policy and regulatory information for the community;
- Providing full public accountability for outcomes relative to policy. This requires that natural resource policy have clear outcomes specified, measured and reported.

Innovation and investment in the delivery of social equity is also important. This requires that:

- We acknowledge that the operation of markets and the needs of sustainability can cause inequity, and adopt a firm commitment to social equity as a distinct aim of natural resource management;
- Social equity objectives for natural resource use be clearly defined, including specification of national goals for:

---

[2] For details on how this might be done, see Land & Water Australia report detailed in 'Fifty Million Australians: Can this be Sustainable?' (Martin and Vorbeck (2001) on which this book is based.

- embracing Aboriginal interests in natural resources,
- protecting access and use opportunities for all Australians, and
- the health, welfare and opportunities of disadvantaged communities, including regional towns and villages;
- We develop funding mechanisms associated, whenever possible, with market initiatives and economic opportunities through natural resource use, to provide an economic base for achieving social objectives; and
- We modify natural resource management instruments, both regulatory and market, to ensure that they do not add to the difficulty of achieving social equity goals.

There is already a great deal of exciting work being done around Australia by catchment committees, local government, State agencies and many thousands of committed volunteers. To date, they have not been efficiently supported. The present policy frameworks are sometimes irrational, poorly designed and inefficiently administered when compared to the infrastructures supporting wealth production. If we are serious about tackling the major threats to the future we hand to our children, it is time for those with policy power to engage in serious reform of the institutional structures, so that those who work at the sharp end of sustainability can get on with the job.

Moving toward institutional reform

There is no strategy for sustainability that avoids serious change to Australians' behaviour. Achieving change with minimal stress requires time. It is more cost-effective and less socially disruptive to make institutional change early, allowing society time to adopt innovations to deal with and prevent problems. Our choices are about the type of disruption we will accept, and when, not whether, we will change.

Adoption of four principles for institutional reform could speed the transition.

1. Make resource conservation a central behavioural contingency for business and society. This requires that proven resource custodianship performance becomes the key to winning more wealth, on a par with the more traditional approach to rewarding production performance. For example, winning government contracts should depend as much upon demonstrating good resource custodianship and environmental management as demonstrating financial capacity.
2. Make the signals that support custodianship much more powerful. This requires that confusion about the state of resources, the need to conserve, and the actions to be taken, be substantially reduced. This is less about monitoring than it is about more effective interpretation

and communication. This would also mean requiring scientific organisations which currently capture information about natural systems adopt a far more proactive approach – forecasting and communicating the future state of our resources, and the impacts this might have on society.

3. Use transaction costs to support custodianship. This would include ensuring that mechanisms for sustainability are made far more administratively efficient, through marked reforms of the legal regulatory structures, reduction of the inefficiencies in delivering environmental subsidies, and making it easier for entrepreneurs with beneficial innovations to achieve success in markets. A related initiative would be to ensure that the costs of transacting (or failures to transact) fall consistently on those whose actions deplete natural resources. Among other approaches, this would require design of regulation to transfer costs from government to potential or actual harm-doers, and the transaction costs of moving towards sustainability to be much reduced.

4. Maintain societal cohesiveness during a period of disruptive change. This requires building the capacity to cope with change, and to manage adverse effects in a manner that strengthens social capital. It requires conscious attempts to ensure that changes to resource consumption are not at the cost of the least advantaged. Particular attention would be paid to ensuring that resource-dependent economies (such as mining and farming towns) and Indigenous communities are treated generously, as a national priority, during the transition. It would mean moving from a case-by-case adjustment approach to a nationally-planned adjustment strategy.

Can we really be sustainable?

If you follow the popular scientific media you could have little doubt that we are on the cusp of another technological revolution. In recent times, scientists have altered their measurement of the speed of light – once considered the constant of the universe (and discovered that the speed of light was not constant in nature), experimentally proven that the intensity of gravity can be changed and focused, and teleported matter (a gas) by mirroring patterns of electrons in one place in another. Our relationship with the physical world is in flux.

The paths of innovation are dictated by the patterns of wealth and power. Institutional redesign can change these patterns and harness the capacity to innovate towards outcomes that will be valuable to society. Fundamental innovation is focused where the financial incentives are strong (like defence, transport, and manufacturing industry). No equivalent breakthroughs are promised in reducing our load on the earth, except as a by-product of commercial innovation. Sustainability requires an entrepreneurial shift.

Australia has achieved major transitions in the past. Australians, in a relatively short space of time, have transformed a continent, raised and equipped armies, created a relatively harmonious and diverse society, and responded to challenges of drought and flood. Australians have a capacity to do astounding things – when the national will is present, when leadership is strong, and when we create institutional frameworks to focus that capacity. It is not instrumental choices that make the difference, but strong commitment and an architecture for change that makes radical improvement possible.

Commerce has already provided a possible model for change. Without removing tariffs on goods, our national economy would have been uncompetitive and vulnerable in a globalising market. The removal of tariffs was inevitable, our choice was how we managed our accommodation of the transition. In the same way, the issue of sustainability needs to be grasped with courage and national commitment. The inevitable change is not something that can be avoided, nor will the social or economic outcomes will be improved by delay.

Australia's tariff removal strategy demonstrated four key elements in large-scale reform.

1. Government signalled unambiguously (with bipartisan support about the ends, though with difference views of means) that Australia would become a low-tariff economy, and that government leadership would be firm but supportive.
2. Government committed to timetables and targets for the transition, and ensured that there could be little doubt that transition was not negotiable, though sector specific programs were.
3. Industry and unions engaged in formulating sectoral transition plans. These plans established timetables and specific actions. Government partnered with industry and unions to develop training and incentive schemes so that change could occur with the minimum of injury to those who were prepared to embrace change, and with social safeguards for those who could not.
4. Irrevocable steps were taken to change the institutional structures to ensure that the transitions would be successful.

There was conflict. Businesses that had been secure behind tariff walls were forced to innovate rapidly or exit. Many people had their lives seriously disrupted. Industries found their fortunes diminished. However, other businesses found that they were able to reduce their costs and compete on world markets. Australia positioned itself with a relatively strong economy which is serving us well in the current period of international economic turmoil.

Achieving sustainability requires a similar approach and an equivalent strength of commitment. The end point is to have an economy and a society which are frugal in their demands on natural resources, and to reap the harvest of this in international competitiveness and the ability to withstand the shocks that will arise as the world undergoes a similar transition. There will be winners and losers and a great deal of scepticism. The end result will be a community that is better adapted and able to succeed in a much-changed context.

The evidence is that Australians are not yet making substantial progress towards sustainability. In most areas of environmental management – water use, salinity, fossil fuel consumption, emissions levels – we are failing badly. Pointing to small wins while incurring consistent losses is deluding ourselves.

There are many instrumental approaches involving markets or regulation or other supports that hold out hope for improvement. All depend for their effectiveness on the quality and integrity of underlying institutions. All depend ultimately on a pattern of resource allocation that makes custodianship no less important than economic exploitation. If we can align our institutions and our reward systems, then we have means at our disposal to pursue growth without prejudicing future generations. If we cannot, then instruments will be inefficient, conflict and confusion will be pervasive, and we will all lose.

This is not a debate about political right and left, or even rich and poor. It is about the world we intend to leave to our children – the physical world, and the state of security and social comfort that we want them to enjoy. This is more than enough reason to move determinedly and move early towards creating strong institutional arrangements and to foster a custodial culture alongside a commercial culture.

PART 1: CONCEPTS

Chapter 1

STRATEGY AND SUSTAINABILITY

Strategy

There are many alternative definitions of strategy. All suggest a conscious choice to shape the use of resources and to focus on achieving the highest priority aims. Many definitions emphasise choosing a formula that will work given the particular context, and quite a few concentrate on issues of power and competition.

For example, Bruce Henderson and Abe Zakon of a major international business consultancy, The Boston Consulting Group, express strategy by asking: 'In what direction will I take my company? Simply stated this question expresses the essence of strategy'. In a military terminology, strategy means: 'the employment of the battle as a means towards the attainment of the object of the war.'[1]

The key to strategy is not in the terminology, but the underlying principle. Strategy implies a conscious choice about the central formula driving both individuals and organisations, the *diamond hard piece of logic* that focuses its activities. This formula may be overt (like an official plan), or it may be reflected in behaviour rather than words. It can be a good formula, which means that it is appropriate for the environment in which it is used and contributes to success, or it can be a bad formula, which is inappropriate and increases the potential of failure.

How does strategy work? The true value in having a strategy is in the concentration of all available resources and energies of a team. We can see this in sport. The logic of a team game plan is that the probability of winning is increased if the plan is followed with no wastage of energy and resources. The outcome of strategy is team behaviour focused around a single 'formula for success'. The game plan or strategy is based upon evaluating the opposing team, the capabilities of your own, and variables like the playing surface or weather. Decisions are made about where and how to allocate limited team resources to best effect. The team then breaks the strategy down into a series of implementation actions, tactics, and roles.

The quality of the strategy can be assessed only once the team is on the field. The two tests of the strategy are:

1. Does the team follow the strategy? and
2. Does it work?

---

[1] Von Clausewitz, K, *On War*, Penguin, 1982 or available online at <www.clausewitz.com.cwzhome/on-war>.

If the core strategy is sound but the team does not follow it, it is a failure (even if victory is achieved). If everyone follows it but it does not work, it is also a failure. To ensure that the strategy has the best chance of working, strategists need information. They need to know what they and their allies want out of the campaign, the capability and goals of their opponents, and the context in which they are working, including the resources that might be available. 'Context' refers to the social and cultural, economic, political, and technological environment within which the strategy is acted out. It is often the context that has the greatest affect on outcomes.[2]

The context and the challenge

Australians' performance as custodians of our natural inheritance is well documented in two recent reports – *State of the Environment 2001* (Thom 2002) and *Future Dilemmas: Options to 2050 for Australia's population, technology, resources and environment* (Foran and Poldy 2002). The result of more than two decades of effort towards sustainability is not encouraging. *State of the Environment 2001* (SoE 2001) sums up (albeit in very mild terms):

> Despite some areas of significant improvement, Australians still have major challenges in the sustainable use of resources and in the maintenance of our natural and cultural heritage.[3]

By what logic could we continue down a pathway that places at risk the future richness of the Earth on which we and our children depend?

It is possible to distil the realities of why it is illogical at the personal level for people to concern themselves with sustainability. A thought experiment will serve to illustrate.

> Imagine that a group of young people and their parents ask you to assist them in a discussion. The children want to become workers for sustainability. The parents want them to have good lives and provide thriving grandchildren. One of the parents says: *All I want to know is that my child has a fair chance to make a reasonable living and be respected. Can you tell me, if my child works for sustainability as a career, is there a reasonable chance that he/she will be able to get rich from it, if they are very good at it? Is this something that those who are already rich and powerful will support because they value it, or will they see it as a threat and oppose it?* They ask you to compare it with other possible careers – restaurateur, lawyer, undertaker, dancer. What would you say to them?

Our economic and social systems depend upon production and consumption. The logic of the economic system is that it will efficiently reallocate resources to those who are the most efficient producers, and reward them with the ability to be the best-endowed consumers. Power is a reflection of

---

[2] In behavioural strategy, perception of context is no less important than the reality (and may vary markedly from that reality).
[3] See <www.ea.gov.au/soe/2001/overview.html#conditionoftheenvironment>.

the capacity to produce and to consume, or to control who can do so. The pursuit of power and wealth are inextricably linked, and achievement of these is understood as 'good'. The sanctity of private property is elevated, even in the Koran and the Bible. Wealth, power, and common morality align to support a consumption-focused social system. The indications for the future do not suggest radical change to this – sustainability issues will continue to be marginal to the mainstream of social and economic activity. Consequently, strategy must be realistic. Many current environmental proposals are based on wishes and dreams – essential to inspire change, but not a recipe for effective action.

Over-consumption is systemic

What would it take to change the fundamentals of our water consumption practices?

Australians use about 75% of diverted water on irrigated crops and pastures and about 20% for industrial and urban uses. They take about 80% of this diverted water from the surface. In total this is less than 5% of Australia's total surface water run-off, but in many regions, like the Murray Darling Basin, primary producers divert as much 80% of the surface water (Dunlop, Foran et al 2001), leading to serious harm to the environment and pressure on irrigators to reduce their water demands.

Given that farmers typically are conscious of the need to conserve water, why are they so relatively unsuccessful in doing so? The answer lies deeper in the infrastructures of farming such as the low price of farm products, the technologies that are available to them, and historical farming practices. Even with the greatest of good will, farmers are locked into a consumption-driven resource use system, with much of the benefit accumulating in the cities.

The focus on rural water demand hides the water demand effects of urban consumers.[4] To provide for the water needs of urban areas, governments isolate tracts of land from both economically productive and recreational uses for water catchment and storage. What is this water mainly used for? Drinking and consumption is a tiny percentage (potable quality uses are only about 10%). The bulk of urban water use goes to uses that are generated by pre-existing technologies and 'luxury' consumption activities: an average Australian household uses 250 kilolitres per year – approximately 30% higher than the OECD average. Flushing toilets, baths and showers and washing machines etc reflect our inherited technologies. European-style parks and gardens, swimming pools, water features and piped creeks reflect aesthetics and luxury. Industry uses water to manufacture a variety of products, with startling waste. All these features of everyday life reflect economic, social and cultural aspects of our society.

Writing for the Australian Bureau of Statistics, Lenzen (2002) calculates that consumers require is 0.2ML of water per capita per year, or 200,000 litres a year per person. This is only for 'direct water' – water for household and urban infrastructure needs. When embodied water demand is added, water consumption rates rise to between 0.6 and 1.1 ML per capita. 'Embodied water demand' is the water required for each dollar of commercial value.

---

4 Data taken from Australian Dept of Environment & Heritage Urban Water Use Statistics in Australia, available on-line at <http://www.deh.gov.au/water/urban/statistics.html#urban>.

Table 1.1: Embodied water intensities, selected goods and services Produced in Australia *(Lenzen, 2002)*

Product	Water intensity (Litres/$)
Rice (in the husk)	7,459
Seed cotton	1,600
Sugar cane	1,239
Dairy products	680
Wine	503
Vegetables and fruit	103
Clothing	90
Coal, ores and other mining products	30
Motor vehicles	15
Electronic equipment, TV, household appliances	16
Phone, Fax and mail	7
Education and health	7

Australia's largest city, Sydney, has a population of over four million. Its direct water demand is between 2.4–4.4 million ML per year. In 2001, Sydney Water Corporation delivered 600,000 ML of water from storages that hold 2.4 million ML. Water reserves fell to below 50% in the 1998 and 2004 droughts. In 2005 reserves fell below 40%. Sydney Water has contractual obligations to the NSW government to encourage Sydneysiders to reduce their water demand by 35%. Although consumption levels have fallen, the corporation has not yet been able to meet the target.

What would it mean if Sydney's population were to double? Mere encouragement through intermittent promotional programs hardly seems to be sufficient as a strategy to encourage sustainable practices in the face of our inherited economic and cultural attitudes to, and the 'benefits' of low water prices, ease of access, and the luxury of waste.

Strategy and sustainability

Worldwide, those fighting for sustainable environmental practices may win skirmishes, but there is little evidence of them winning the battle. A strategist would conclude that this is because the wrong strategies are being implemented given the resources available and the nature of the challenge.

Further delay in acting to reduce unsustainable environmental practices will lead to greater environmental depletion and greater cost. We need the fastest possible path to change, even if that change is incomplete. This book is predicated on the view that to wait for an ideal solution could result in such irreversible consequences that delay is not a viable option. What is necessary are mechanisms that place a 'drag' on the rate of depletion of the earth to reduce the scale of the challenge and to facilitate greater changes to societal behaviour. We need behaviour change strategies that work, regardless of *how* they work.

Why 'behavioural' strategy?

The way in which we use natural resources exists in a framework of decisions and relationships. For example, it is not possible to completely understand (and therefore manage) water use without understanding the actions of domestic consumers, the economics of industrial users, the decisions of governments, the vendors of whitegoods, the psychology of cleanliness, the pricing decisions of utilities, and a host of other decisions that together create a wasteful pattern of water use in Australia – the Earth's driest continent. Our consumption pattern is underpinned by complex motivations, information flows, incentives, beliefs, knowledge and goals.

While sustainability is about man's relationship to the natural world, from a management point-of-view, nature is almost irrelevant to sustainability strategy. If the aim is to change patterns of consumption, then three levels of human behaviour are issues to consider:

(a) individual consumption (or non-consumption);
(b) action by commercial, government and private organisations;
(c) action of society as a whole (or perhaps more accurately societies as a network).

Many research disciplines are concerned with human behaviour. A list would include psychology, marketing, economics, law and sociology. These disciplines use specialised language and concepts, and consider innate (internal) and environmental aspects of behaviour. Some are concerned with internal outcomes like emotions and beliefs, whereas others are concerned with the management of behaviour to create external outcomes like collective action or purchasing. Sustainability is primarily concerned with this latter kind.

Change the system to change the behaviour

Recent literature about economics and innovation systems highlight the concept of 'path dependence' and the role of institutional frameworks.[5] In society, people's actions are substantially shaped by a pattern of incentives, supports and penalties, resource structures and social expectations. The 'path' that is available to them is constrained, making any other path difficult to follow.

---

5 Institutions are the structures that shape patterns of interaction in a society. They may be tangible (like the courts or parliament) or they may be intangible such as embedded beliefs about property rights. We discuss institutions in more depth towards the end of this book.

How infrastructures embed consumption

Sometimes consumption choices are largely beyond the control of the consumer. This is particularly when infrastructures dictate what opportunities are available to satisfy requirements. The use of energy by Australians provides a good example.

Between 1990-91 and 1998-99 Australia's energy consumption increased by 23%. In 2001 Australians consumed more energy per capita than the average OECD consumers. The trend in OECD[6] countries is for a declining ratio of energy use to GDP. Australia's decline is less than that of other countries.

Households consume over half of the energy in Australia, with 25% used for transport. Dependence on the motor vehicle continues to grow even as there are indications that world oil production is declining (Hobbs 2000).

There are over 800,000 km of roads in Australia. Before the Second World War, public transport was the main means of transport. After the war, a national effort began to improve the road network. Road construction became a major industry. State departments of roads became well-resourced bureaucracies, with long-term plans for roadways throughout urban and rural areas.

Institutions and cultural attitudes developed around the motorcar. Cities such as Canberra and Perth, and newer suburbs of large cities, were developed to support access for the car. Dollar flows around the motor vehicle became financially important, and the votes of car-users became politically significant. The excise on petrol was dedicated to road construction. The number of vehicle registrations was adopted as an indicator of social wellbeing.

Reducing motor vehicle dependency would require changing attitudes to car ownership as a 'need' and a symbol of success; and reduction in the power or redirection of the goals of organisations that sponsor motor vehicle use and petrol consumption.

To achieve this there would have to be viable alternatives to the private vehicle. Public transport requires significant up-front investment to create complete and efficient networks that will attract patronage. Use will only grow once that network is proven to be efficient and to meet consumer needs.

Democracy itself may be a limiting factor. The majority of people travel by car. The pattern of government investment reflects this. In 2000, ABS figures show that the federal government allocated $1.2 billion for regional roads and $400 million for the national highway system on top of $1.6 billion a year allocation to the States. In addition, it provided $350 million towards Sydney's Western orbital and $293 million for an external Albury by-pass coupled with $70 million towards an internal boulevard. By contrast, it allocated only $250 million over four years to upgrading 'sub-standard' national rail tracks. This is demonstrative of the relative allocation of funds between road and public transport infrastructures.

Fundamental institutions (like democracy) and the investment in infrastructure naturally embed power and wealth structures and can limit the feasible choices of consumers. Achieving sustainability requires far more than a change in short-term consumer preference, or even the availability of technically viable solutions. It inevitably involves changes to the structures that allocate wealth and power, and to the infrastructure investments that are made as a result.

---

6 The Organisation for Economic Cooperation and Development (OECD) comprises 30 countries that share a commitment to democratic government and the market economy.

Barriers to change

Change in society is a complex process of negotiation. There are many players, with their own aims and agendas, and different stakes in the outcome. Many of these interests compete or are unclear. Beliefs and self-interest line up with scientific uncertainty to generate arguments about the extent or significance of, and solutions to, identified problems. These dynamics occur in markets and political systems, and thwart consensus and action. This process can go on indefinitely, and society continues to suffer avoidable harms because of the inability to arrive at a desirable negotiated outcome.

Foran and Poldy (2002) talk about this complexity in discussing our national 'dilemmas': aging, physical trade, material flows, greenhouse emissions, natural resource depletion and environmental quality.

> Each dilemma and the interactions between them are guided by the assumptions of the underpinning starting scenario, and the laws that constrain the physical world. Single dilemmas are mostly open to resolution within the current settings of technology and ideology. Resolving two, three or more dilemmas in parallel is more difficult because of human behavioural dynamics that lie outside this analytical capability, and generally outside the comprehension of policy development. (2002: 218).

Why is reform so slow?

Social processes can inhibit any effective reform even when problems are understood and decisions have been made. An example is the management of greenhouse emissions. In 1997, over 2500 economists from the American Economic Association, including eight Nobel Laureates in economics, called for preventative steps to be taken to deal with the risks of climate change. They stated that: *'we believe that global climate change carries with it significant environmental, economic, social and geopolitical risks, and that preventive steps are justified ... Economic studies have found that there are many potential policies to reduce green-house gas emissions for which the total benefits outweigh the total costs'.* (Decanio 1997: 2)

In spite of this much-publicised statement, relatively little has happened in the last seven years. In 2001, the US and Australia refused to sign the Kyoto Protocol, the most prominent global document committing countries to strategies of change. Both the US and Australia argued that this solution is the wrong one (while agreeing broadly that a solution is needed).

It is true that there remains disagreement about the best way of bringing about change. Many economists, including those signing the climate change document, believe that market instruments must be the central mechanism for change. Other scientists, such as Professor John Byrne and Research Associate Leigh Glover of the Center for Energy and Environment Policy at University of Delaware believe that market-based instruments should only be considered in the context of agreed commitments to sustainability and equity (Byrne and Glover 2000). This contest between possible solutions is only one part of the protracted negotiation. If there were consensus about one single approach, perhaps it would be harder for the opponents of change to maintain their position in the debate. However, as with many social issues there is a myriad of solutions that might work, but a need to agree on only one.

Such debates provide ample fuel for those whose interests would be harmed by moving towards a solution to argue for delay and more research. They provide many opportunities to encourage divisive debates and argument, even among those who believe that a solution is needed. Collectively, such dynamics cloud the issues and make political action less likely.

Social change is inherently political and cumbersome. Much of what is written about how to achieve sustainability is advocacy of particular instruments such as markets or regulation. The implicit assumption is that the 'goodness' of the solution is the important concern. Of equal importance to the sustainability strategist should be the overlay of politics, self-interest, ignorance, relationships and many other factors that will determine whether particular strategies are feasible for a given political and social context, even if the feasible solution is technically less than ideal.

Behavioural strategists who want to be effective have two sets of issues to think about. First, they must understand the social and economic context in which the issues exist, and define the problem with this in mind. Secondly, they must understand the instruments at their disposal, so that they have a range of possible solutions to choose from. Right choice is a process of matching these two sets, and effective implementation is a process of change management.

Sustainability strategies are effective when they change individual decisions that are made about natural resource use and consumption, and in turn the aggregation of changed individual decisions will change the total outcomes. The system will have to be changed, in order to change both individual and collective decisions and in a way that ensures it still delivers wealth and opportunity.

Aiming for systemic sustainability

As resources diminish, or if we do hit the disastrous limits that some commentators suggest, change to our use of natural resources will be inevitable. However, forced change is likely to be disruptive, perhaps catastrophic. The least disruptive approach is to manage change at a rate that allows society to minimise the costs and inequity that could otherwise arise, but fast enough to prevent us hitting too many physical limits to our ability to harvest what we need from the Earth.

Table 1.2: What would behavioural sustainability look like?

	Sustainable	Not sustainable
Does the pattern of wealth production reward conservation more than exploitation?	✘ Yes	☐ No
Is conservation seen to be a means to wealth and power?	✘ Yes	☐ No
Will the resource use by powerful people be limited by conservation?	✘ Yes	☐ No

What level of behavioural change would be sufficient to ensure sustainability, taking into account wealth production? We will know we have achieved enough change to ensure sustainability when 'No' is no longer the objective response to the questions asked in the table above.

Is this transition achievable, without social revolution? To a fair degree the answer is yes. The strategy we promote through this book is systemic change in small steps, and focused upon incrementally changing the patterns of incentives and signals to those who consume and conserve. If over time we can change beliefs, knowledge and understanding, then we will have achieved (or at least cleared the path for) radical change without excessive social disruption.

Are environment and economy co-dependent?

It is political currency that the key to sustainability is to have a thriving economy, so we can afford protection and restoration of our environment. One requirement, it is argued, is to have a larger productive population in Australia. In their CSIRO report *Future Dilemmas*, Foran and Poldy (2002) considered our resource availability and the needs of populations of varying sizes. They concluded that there is no simple answer to sustainable resource use, at any level of population in Australia. Resource use challenges are significant at the current level of population and will be greater at a higher population level.

The population/consumption dilemma

Foran and Poldy identified ten major issues that must be dealt with during the next generation, whatever the population:

1. Air emissions in city air sheds and traffic congestion;
2. Dependence for personal mobility on continuing supplies of oil and natural gas;
3. Loss of land in the agricultural heartlands and increasing salinity levels in river systems;

4. Dependence of physical trade exports on old economy manufactures and commodities;
5. The place of mature-aged citizens in the national workforce;
6. Greenhouse gas emissions from the fossil energy sector;
7. The per capita levels of material flow underpinning the monetary economy;
8. The energy and material content of personal consumption;
9. Incentives for large-scale investment in long term natural capital;
10. The steady transition from an old 'physical' economy to a new 'brain' economy.

They argued that it is possible to continue to grow Australia's population without calamity. But:

> Any significant progress towards sustainability in Australia's physical economy will require that population futures are managed in unison with the futures of infrastructure, lifestyle and personal consumption, energy, international trade, inbound tourism and technological innovation. (2002: 246)

The economic capacity of a larger population may be greater than that for a small population, but to expect a benign outcome without behavioural change to (in the short term) reduce the rate of the harm we are doing and (in the longer term) to begin to reverse past harm is foolish. Changes of incentives and values towards conservation are indispensable prerequisites if we are to achieve benign outcomes for future generations.

Loh explains that an increasing population contributes to what is termed the National Ecological Deficit. Loh's *Living Planet Report* (2000) calculated 'biological capacity', that is, the relationship of each individual to each hectare (area unit[7]) of biologically productive space. In 1997, Australia's population was 18,524,200 and had a biological capacity of 1.11 (area unit/person). The population now exceeds 20 million and is increasing at over 200,000 people per year. The same formula now produces a National Ecological Deficit of –0.67.

The challenges highlighted in *Future Dilemmas* are developed in the Commonwealth government's *Intergenerational Report 2002-3* (2002). This report, prepared by the Australian Treasury Department, forms a basis for government policy on responding to the ageing of the Australian population. It highlights, as shown in Figure 1.2, that Australian governments are likely to find it harder to maintain a balanced budget. Future generations will need to pay more in taxes or the government will need to

---

[7] Area unit is one hectare of biologically productive space with world-average productivity. In 1996 the biosphere had 12.6 billion hectares of biologically productive space corresponding to roughly one quarter of the planet's surface. These 12.6 billion hectares of biologically productive space include 3.2 billion hectares of ocean and 9.4 billion hectares of land. The land space is composed of 1.3 billion hectares of cropland, 4.6 billion hectares of grazing land, 3.3 billion hectares of forest land, and 0.2 billion hectares of built-up land.

spend less. The report indicates the challenges that will arise in paying for basic services like health, unless we are able to markedly improve our economic performance (or constrain these expectations). It also illustrates the naivety of expecting that a democratic government will/can resist economic growth demands in favour of safeguarding depleting resources:

> In 2001-2 the Commonwealth is spending around $1.8 billion to conserve Australia's natural capital ... The value Australians place on their natural environment is likely to rise ... However, this need not translate into more Commonwealth spending. (2002: 52)

Figure 1.2: Fiscal projections (Australian government 2002)

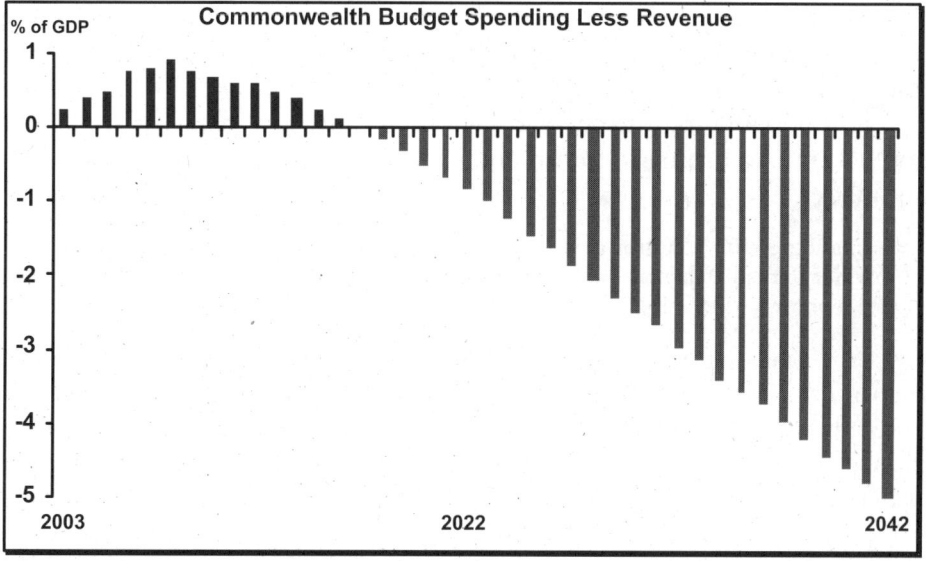

According to the Australian Treasury, State and local governments are best placed to make changes to encourage sustainability, and most changes should occur through 'integrating policy approaches to economic development to minimise environmental damage' (2002: 52). This is largely the current approach – one that has been failing to make the required gains for sustainability.

Many environmentalists, and many concerned about social equity, are alarmed at the prospect of an Australian population of 50 million as advocated by some business groups. They extrapolate current environmental and social problems and are frightened by the possibility that we will repeat our failings on a larger scale with a less resilient stock of natural capital. But those who focus on the economic capacity of the country are similarly disconcerted by the proposition of limiting Australia's population to only 20 or 25 million. They argue that this limits the nation's economic growth, prejudices our national security, and our ability and willingness to take in people displaced by environmental disaster or other causes.

Environmental impact is a function of population numbers, multiplied by impact per head. To achieve an acceptable level of environmental impact, we can either manage the impact each person has on resources or the number of people in total. The only other outcome that is possible is accelerating degradation of our natural resources, with adverse impacts on future generations.

There will be legitimate debate about the acceptable level of harm to the environment. There will be differences in predictions about the degree to which innovation will allow us to reduce the per capita impact, or replace one source of ecological services with another. But even accepting different views, if the per capita impact we are having today results in unacceptable harm, then to aim for a larger population without having reliable ways of reducing per capita impact is to ignore the tyranny of that underpinning equation.

Is it possible for Australia to be ecologically sustainable with a larger population? According to Foran and Poldy, in some ways the answer does not matter.

> Ceasing population growth will not cause the physical economy to stall, nor will it immediately make key issues of resource use and environmental quality disappear. (2002: 246).

Opinion polls show strong community support for government and industry to place a stronger emphasis on sustainability. But there is generally resistance when government and industry take the action needed to give effect to sustainability actions (through regulation, or reducing the availability of harmful alternatives, or adopting higher environmental standards which increase the costs of goods or services).

Many harmful effects can be reduced by voluntary action: walking instead of driving, using less water, reducing the consumption of highly processed foods. We could also reduce human impact on the environment by making relatively low-cost changes to how industry operates, such as by consumers placing higher priority on energy or resource conservation, or suppliers marketing products which are more environmentally friendly. But too few of us take the voluntary action that is needed to make the required impact.

To achieve this, direct political action is called for, at the level of particular environmental issues and within the democratic framework of local, State, and federal governments. Contributing to the development of new sustainable technologies, and advancing understanding through education are also necessary. However, these tools are not the subject matter of this book.

Instead, this book deals with the many management approaches that hold promise of improved outcomes. The US EPA (National Centre for Environmental Economics 2001) has outlined hundreds of practical examples of regulatory, market or voluntary schemes that are promoting environmentally sustainable behaviour. Environment Australia has published a similar study of incentive programs (James 1997). An investigation of over 1100 companies in Australia has shown that there are many products, technologies and services that languish unsupported in the marketplace even though they have the potential to help achieve sustainability goals.[8] The problem is not an insufficiency of possible solutions; it is a failure of society to change to meet even the clearly identified challenges.

---

8   Based on a database of almost 1200 Australian environmental goods and service providers. Interviews with proprietors of environmental firms suggest that regulatory requirements or the opportunity for cost savings are the most common drivers of their markets, and that the market is very price-focused.

VOICE OF EXPERIENCE: URBAN BEHAVIOUR

Peter Schmigal is a principal of Nolan ITU, a leading advisory firm in waste management and environmental issues.[9]

If you were commissioned to develop a strategy to bring urban water consumption within sustainable limits, where would you start, and what would you concentrate upon?

What we experts now do know is a lot about what fails. There is a wealth of international and local experience to show that urging people to change their behaviour by education and advertising is not an efficient strategy. It is almost definitive that increased awareness is not directly linked to changed behaviour.[10] Yet time and again governments take a top-down, single-minded approach to changing behaviour through advertising and education.

Social systems as ecosystems

The alternative way of thinking is to mirror how we think about ecosystems in the way we think about managing resource consumption. Society is a complex, resource-consuming organism. Before we try to change it, we should understand why the system operates as it does.

To change water use in cities, Peter suggests, will affect a lot of people.

We need to think about what it means to them, as people, and what tradeoffs are possible to make it worth their while. We need to think about practical details like what appliances are available to them, or the fairness of what we are asking just as much as we think about their attitudes.

Above all, we need to avoid the temptation of thinking in a linear, rigid fashion about social systems that are neither linear nor rigid. Governments, in particular, tend to think about such issues in neat categories or 'silos'. Silos don't flow, and water, money and relationships don't stay in silos.

An inclusive process

When asked to specify the process he would use to attack such a problem, Peter is definite.

The key is inclusiveness. The people who are involved have to own the process, even if they may not all want the outcomes. In a world where cynicism is prevalent, and complexity is everywhere, you have to break through disinterest and fear. You can only do that with a close relationship.

---

9 <www.nolanitu.com.au>
10 See Chapter 10 for illustrative examples.

Peter would start with a stakeholder assessment, to identify who would be affected by the decisions or could effect change. In his words:

We need to understand the organisms in this ecosystem. His recommendation is to look for the ecotome, the rich location where different ecosystems interact. Then find who lives in this place. What he is saying, he explains, is that in any social system there will be people and organisations that are at the centre of what is going on. If you can find them, and get them involved, their knowledge and experience will be far more valuable than any amount of partly informed market research or economic analysis.

Multi-faceted strategies

And what of the strategies that he thinks would be most likely to emerge as feasible?

In an ecosystem, organisms that are isolated die. Narrowly-focused change programs working in isolation also die. In thinking about what should work, you ought reflect on the interdependence and complexity of ecosystems, and assume the system you are trying to change will have these characteristics.

Peter suggests that a complex situation will require a multi-dimensional change program, incorporating information, regulation and policy, and financial and economic incentives.

And if I had to choose what will have the most effect, I would have to say the economic drivers consistently dictate what will happen.

His view of such matters is ultimately pragmatic.

Our economic paradigm is not well suited to achieving sustainability outcomes. Short of changing that paradigm, you have to harness the tools of the market, knowing that the market itself is part of the problem. That is not to say that radical change is impossible or undesirable, but that it is not likely to occur in the short term, and it is in the short term that we have to make changes.

Other comments

Most people are fundamentally good, but the situation they are in makes it hard for them to be good environmental managers. We (at Nolan ITU) see this clearly with industry. Industry is making gradual progress, driven mainly by the commitment of individuals in organisations. We are beginning to see major companies influencing their supply chains to improve their environmental performance.

Nolan ITU sees this with packaging and transport. Some managers are using sophisticated approaches, like Life Cycle Analysis, to find where environmental savings can also deliver financial benefits. Sometimes the results can run counter to conventional wisdom and be difficult to introduce.

Peter gives the example of dairy product packaging. To reduce the substantial financial and environmental costs of leaking packages, dairy suppliers may have to reduce the recyclability of their packaging. This could introduce an environmental public relations problem, even if the environmental results are improved.

Peter also makes the point:

If you don't really understand the people you are trying to convince, then you make basic mistakes.

He cites attempts to convince Korean urban residents to recycle, for environmental reasons. At that time (as was later discovered) environmental reasons were not seen as terribly relevant. However, once the strategists discovered that creating a better future for our children was a very relevant message, the campaign was restructured.

Once they got closer to the people they wanted to convince, they were able to come up with a message that made sense, in their terms. And recycling took off. You can't do this from a report. You have to get out and talk to people, get to think like them, and get to like them. Only then can you expect to influence them.

I have seen campaigns intended to help smash repair shops improve their oil disposal, where the approach was to put them in a room and lecture to them. Within about half an hour half the class was acting just the way they did when they were last in a classroom that they didn't want to be in. Throwing bits of paper, chatting, laughing and ridiculing the teacher. You only had to talk to a couple to know that school was, in their minds, about the least relevant thing in their lives.

Chapter 2

ACHIEVING BEHAVIOURAL CHANGE

Why do people act the way they do, and how can we change their behaviour? The first part of this question is at the heart of the frustration that many social activists feel, and the second preoccupies those who try to improve environmental and social equity outcomes. In this chapter we outline a model for structuring how to think about these issues. Our model uses a systems approach to integrate theories from a number of behavioural sciences disciplines. We will also explain systems thinking concepts and show how to apply them in the analysis and management of behaviour.

Common themes in understanding behaviour

There are many books, reports, conferences and workshops designed to show how to achieve sustainability. Unfortunately, often the proposed 'solutions' are contradictory. We can find convincing arguments that support property rights as the key for achieving appropriate behaviour, and equally convincing ones that disagree. Some people argue that ethical responsibility should be the core interest of sustainability strategy. Economists often propose less regulation, while others propose more effective regulation. Some believe that the only issue is the efficient production of consumption goods within a framework of (un-enlightened) self-interest. There are also those who believe that technology will solve the problems, alongside those who predict imminent doom if we rely on the potential of technical change to address sustainability.

Can one of these views be right and all other views wrong? Probably not. It is more likely that each of these views contain elements of truth, even when these truths appear to conflict. In order to find where the truths might lie we need to overcome two barriers: unstated assumptions about the basis of human behaviour and specialist jargon.

Different disciplines assume different motivations and controls for human behaviour. Economics deals with markets, costs and prices, and economic efficiency. Marketing deals with 'target segments', and elevates the effect of information and attitude in determining behaviour. Law focuses upon rules and precedent. Sociology often focuses upon power relations. Psychology considers intrinsic as well as environmental drivers of behaviour. In spite of these marked differences, there are common themes. We will use these themes within a systems approach to explaining natural resource use behaviour.

Societies, organisations and people are systems

A system is a concept; a way of thinking about something to help us understand how that thing behaves. Most people have seen a drawing of an electric circuit for a household appliance, or have seen pictures of how rain is made, or the operation of the food cycle in nature. None of us believes that what is drawn is a faithful reflection of the actual – we do not expect to open up a circuit board and have it look exactly like the wiring diagram. But the representations provide us with simplified information to understand why the household appliance works, or why rain falls, or the importance of parts of the food chain. Once we understand those basics, it may be possible for us to take the important step of intervening in the system to modify its behaviour.

We will use four systems terms in this book:

1. *Elements*: A broad term to describe the things that make up a system. Elements may be people, or ideas, plants, animals. It simply refers to some thing that has been identified as forming part of the system. At times we may use the word 'actor' if the element we are describing is a person (or organisation) who is part of the system.
2. *Stocks*: The state of things that can be observed or measured at any time. Stocks may be funds, or information, or plants or animals. They are the inputs to and the outcomes of the processes that occur within the system
3. *Flows*: The movement of elements, which create the system dynamic. It may be the flow of air, water, ideas, funds or resources.
4. *Structures*: The way in which things are located within or around the system that shape the flows within the system. For example, the presence and arrangement of rocks alters the way in which water flows in a river. We will use the word 'institution' for social structures, such as law, commerce or culture.

A fundamental concept is that systems are made up of elements that interact. In a system it is possible to trace the connection of every element to every other element, even if the pathways involve several indirect steps with intervening elements. An ecosystem, such as a pond, is made up of all elements that sustain life in the pond, including water, nutrients and energy. An organisation is also a system, with staff, information, technology, specialist individuals, funds and other resources that interact. Legal or economic systems consist of people and organisations interacting around particular types of transactions (such as developing and applying law, or buying and selling).

The outcomes of systems are determined by the elements and the dynamics of the system. A powerful demonstration of the effects of the dynamics of a system is chaos; complex systems can generate results that are unpredictable. A social systems example of unpredictable dynamics is the assassination of a minor European sovereign at the start of the 20th century. The event contributed to two world wars, a restructuring of the political landscape of Europe, Africa and most of Asia, technologies such as the rocket, and major social changes including the European Community.

Interaction, friction, and delays in feedback are some of the dynamics in systems. We will be exploring these in more detail later in the chapter. Before we do so we should explain some characteristics of the type of system we are interested in.

What system shapes human behaviour?

The relationship of man and the environment is shaped by physical action – decisions which result in the application of resources (including human or mechanical energy). Decisions are the result of the interaction of three factors:

1. Flows of information (from the senses, science, communication, literature, and media);
2. Flows of resource (money, goods and services as physical movements in the environment, and between people and organisations);
3. Internal structuring of information by the individual, the organisation or the society (decision-making).

People talk loosely of 'educating' or 'changing attitudes' or 'managing perceptions'. In reality, since we cannot reach inside another person's head to change their mind, all we can do is adjust the flows of resources (incentives and disincentives) and information to eventually impact on how people decide. This is how behaviour is changed. Decision-making is the process of blending signals which are the result of information or resource flows, with attitudes and beliefs resulting from education, information systems, corporate structure etc which in turn shapes how information and resource flows are interpreted. The relationships are circular, time lagged and incomplete. People filter out information that conflicts with their prior knowledge or beliefs, because they discount what might be counter to their interests or because it is outside their understanding, or simply because they don't know how to process or use that information.

People pursue resources (rewards) and avoid losses. In this way they operate as an open system needing to import energy (resources) to maintain themselves. Another example of an open system is a river system. It needs to import energy from sunlight, and uses nutrient and sediment runoff to grow the plants and provide the food on which animals and micro-organisms depend. Similarly, a business imports the energy of workers, the funds of investors or customers, and the resources of suppliers, to keep operating. Without constant import of resources, open systems cease functioning.

Imports and boundaries

Many behavioural science disciplines believe behaviour is determined (wholly or in part) by context (using terms like 'situation', 'environment', 'market', or 'contingencies'). 'Environment' is a boundary defining term that simply speaks of everything outside the system being studied. For example, everything outside a person (the system being studied) is their environment.

Open systems constantly react with and influence their environment, changing their shape in order to be better able to win the resources that they need. They have a capacity to learn, improving how they collect and processes information, and thereby make better decisions to secure the resources they need. In living organisms, learning and adaptation may mean physical changes.[1] In social systems it may require different power structures and institutional regimes to make the system more efficient at winning resources. Competitive behaviour is an example of adaptive behaviour, with individuals, organisations and societies constantly adjusting their activities in order to win resources. This is why competition is such a powerful driver of behaviour.

When we talk about sustainability, we are basically interested in ensuring the survival of human society and recognise that our survival is dependent upon maintaining our environment in a condition which will enable us to continue to draw from it what we need. In order to do this, we need to know how to change the pattern of our decisions and our actions, including how to learn better and how to compete differently.

The model we have developed explains how humans make their resource consumption decisions across three levels of human systems – individual decisions, decisions by organisations, and decisions of societies. We have termed it the Resource Consumption Decision Model (RCDM).

Three levels of resource-consumption decisions

Many sustainability strategies are focused on changing resource-consumption decisions – through laws, setting up market-based systems, and education programs. But those developing these strategies rarely examine or understand what comprises the consumption system and how the actors within the system interact. Without such an understanding, strategies are only partly informed.

---

1 Termed 'evolution'. Time has an important role in the operation of the system, which we will discuss later.

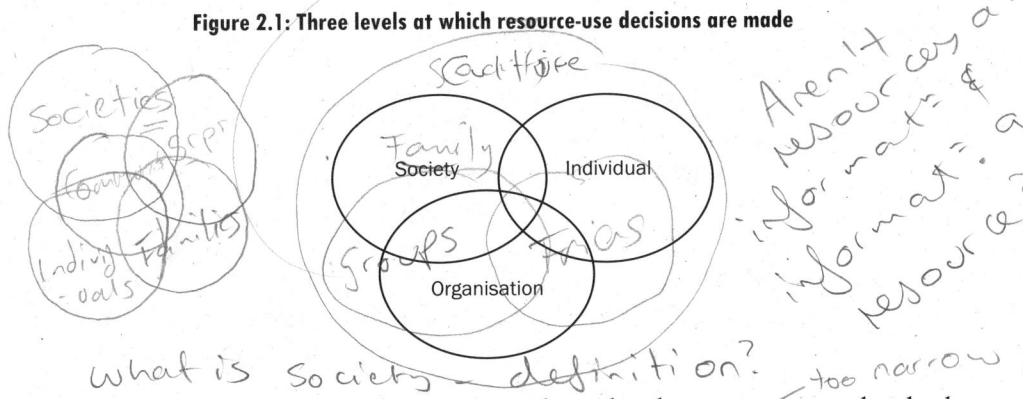

Figure 2.1: Three levels at which resource-use decisions are made

- Society
- Individual
- Organisation

People make resource use decisions at three levels in society: individual, organisational and societal. Each of these decision-making entities can be studied as systems in their own right, but they are interdependent. Society is made up of individuals and organisations; organisations are the instruments for collective action, operate within society and made up of individuals; and individuals are influenced by the society and organisations to which they belong. Together, these three subsystems provide the structure of the society.

Each of these subsystems has research disciplines devoted to it, though all disciplines cross their boundaries. Psychology, marketing and law are focused on the individual; sociology and economics concentrate most on the society, and various management disciplines consider organisational behaviour. There are many common threads in the issues with which they grapple. Unsurprisingly these threads from different disciplines are aligned with the concepts of open systems: the need for resources; the need for information; and the need for structures for interpreting information.[2]

1. Flows of resource shape behaviour in all three subsystems

We have already noted that open systems pursue resources to prosper. This is a fundamental explanation of behaviour, regardless of disciplinary perspective. For the individual these resources include food and water, shelter, and companionship. Society requires physical resources for its operation. Organisations need raw materials, finances and human inputs. Regardless of whether one is talking of individuals or groups, the flow of resources impacts decisions and the pattern of rewards in turn impacts on culture and knowledge through to adaptive learning. It is also through the allocation of resources that action is taken. Finally, the pursuit of rewards shapes the purposes of the subsystem, and consequent resource flows provide signals to the subsystem that also will influence its direction and actions.

---

2   More detailed illustration of the model operating across the three subsystems can be d from <www.profitfoundation.com.au>.

2. Flows of information enable decisions in all three subsystems

Systems also require information to make decisions, to find and process resources, and to coordinate effort. To obtain information, each subsystem has mechanisms to process data, interpreting it and forming it into useable forms for decision-making and action, which is termed 'information'. People distil information from 'signals' or 'data' from the environment but do not necessarily seek the same information. Two people walking through a patch of bush may derive very different information. One may observe that the bushland is green and there are many trees. The other person may have had training in the identification of plants and observe that the bushland is degraded with weeds. Their structuring mechanisms are different, though the available data are the same.

3. Information is structured and evaluated in all subsystems

Systems need to make sense of signals from the environment to turn it into information useful for obtaining and manipulating resources. Individuals have cognitive skills. Education and experience refines this ability and enables decision-making. Organisations have formal mechanisms, represented by team structures, analytical tools like software, formal authority and communications etc, which serve the same purpose. Society has its equivalent in legal, political, educational, religious and market institutions. Regardless of the level and complexity, the same function of information processing has to be carried out to allow the system to act.

The processing of signals is never fully objective. Decision-makers attach values to different possible outcomes, and to different inputs. For example, an individual may place a higher value on a wealth-creation outcome than a social-good outcome, and may attach more value to information from one source than another. Another person will weight signals differently.

The process of valuation is informed by beliefs. These beliefs are embedded in cultures, behavioural standards and norms, and values/ ethics. Different belief systems explain why people or groups who have the same information about actions and consequences arrive at different conclusions. For example, one person provided with information about deteriorating water quality may modify their activities to prevent pollution and even improve water quality, another person may install water purifiers in the home, and yet another may deny the problem exists. Similarly, organisations will select different goals and value different types of information in making their choices, depending on whether they regard themselves as existing for the public good, or for private profit.

Beliefs are important in assessing information. Using our earlier example, the bushwalker with the capacity to identify plants used her belief system to judge the bushland as of little value. An ornithologist recognising the weeds, however, may not assess the bushland as degraded

Figure 2.2: Information, decision and action

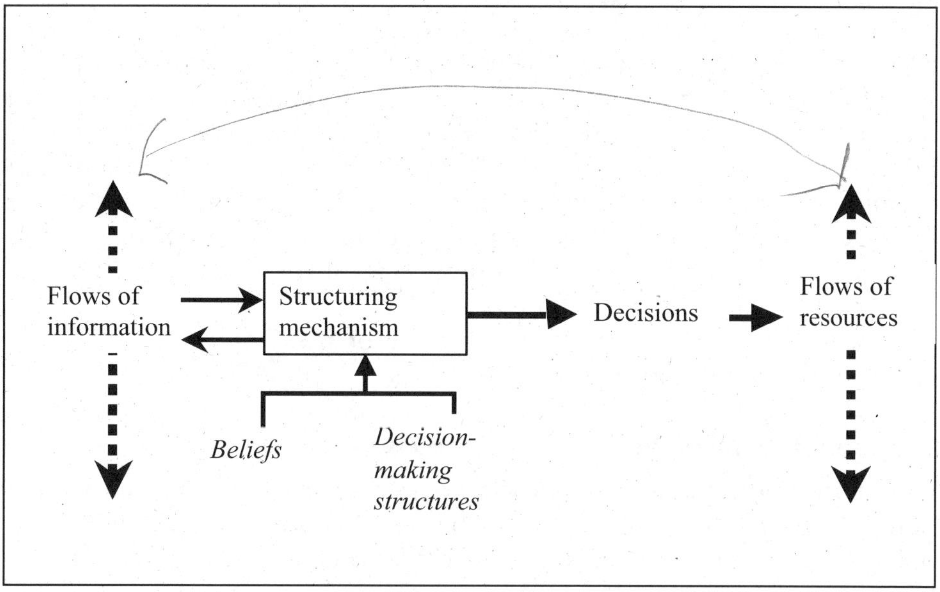

because the weeds may harbour small birds. The ornithologist's belief may be that the value of the plants is high.

The social systems thinker, Niklas Luhmann (1984) wrote on the development of beliefs. He emphasised that resources and information shape our beliefs but while resources and information flow through the system, beliefs, like knowledge, do not flow. Beliefs and knowledge are informed but internally created. Luhmann's observation is important. It highlights the only two factors that can be manipulated to change behaviour are the flows of information and the flows of resources. It is through adjusting these two flows that every kind of behavioural change instrument works – regardless of whether the instrument is market, regulatory, or educationally based.

Decision dynamics impact on system outcomes

Feedback loops and unexpected interactions make open systems complex. This is illustrated the by the apocryphal example of how the air movement caused by the flutter of butterfly wings in the Amazon leads to hurricanes in the US. But understanding decision-making dynamics can help us better understand likely outcomes. We liken these to the effect of 'friction' in a physical system: in a natural system such as weather, we know that wind will behave differently over large flat bodies such as water or desert plains than over forested hillsides. The latter will slow wind speeds. We know that friction is a major determinant of the operation of all physical systems.

In social systems analogous 'friction' exists because transactions form a vital part of the system. Individuals work with each other or interact socially; they sell their services and wares, accept goods, and give and receive information. Organisations take in and adjust information, move resources through processes and on to consumers. Negotiations and political decisions are part and parcel of social systems. It is not the least bit surprising that these transactions create their own 'noise' or friction, and that this friction in turn will impact substantially on decisions and the consequences of decisions.

Different disciplines deal with aspects of these dynamics. We have grouped these dynamics into four categories:

1. Filtration reduces the information received

Communication researchers know that people 'hear' only a small part of available information and filter out the rest. Without such filters society, organisations and individuals would be overwhelmed by information and be inefficient in making decisions, acting or adapting.

One basis for this filtration is whether the information is believable – that is, whether it aligns with established beliefs ('known' facts or values). Standards, personal values and collective culture are part of the filtration system, as are the formal processes that social subsystems put in place to filter information. Individuals may elect only to read certain newspapers, listen to certain news channels, attend certain courses, listen to certain people or be associated with certain organisations. Organisations invest in technologies and design their structures – reporting relationships, procedural manuals, etc – to manage information flow (to collect what is predetermined as relevant and to filter out the rest). Societies have specialised functions – such as courts, parliament, or the media – to process and deliver relevant information. All these are designed to select from the pool of signals or data only what is deemed relevant, filtering out the rest.

2. Transaction costs shape the dynamic

Transactions (the means through which information and resources flow) occur constantly between individuals, organisations and society, and to and from their environments. Economists in particular are aware that transactions are never cost-free. The costs result from the need to identify with whom to transact, deciding how to carry out the transaction, executing the transaction and guaranteeing the outcomes. These transaction costs 'tax' the flow of information and resources. If the costs are too high, the decision may be made not to proceed with the transaction. Transaction costs are a reality in all systems and can significantly influence the nature of outcomes.

Because of the importance of transaction costs, we devote a significant part of the discussion below to their influence, and to how their management is an important part of sustainability strategies.

3. Time is part of the dynamic

It takes time for social systems to capture, filter and transfer information. Social science (in particular social anthropology) acknowledges this through the study of the evolution of culture. Social systems adapt slowly because it takes time to recognise subtle changes in their environment, and because there is generally resistance to change. Organisations set up functions like committees, reviews and studies to try to ensure that they capture and act on environmental signals, but these processes are cumbersome in themselves. Even when individuals or organisations want to address environmental issues, it takes time to make decisions and to act on them – and then for the actions to take effect. One only needs to think of how long it takes to get a committee to agree, and then to move from agreement to resourcing, and thence to implementation, to understand the lags in system behaviour even with simple decisions. The more profound the change needs to be, the more likely it is that decision-making and action will take a long time.

4. Technology is the key to solutions

Technology is part of the dynamic of making and implementing decisions, affecting and transforming resource and information flows and our ways of structuring. Monitoring, analysis, production, distribution and decision-making all have embedded technologies, and these technologies are the hidden shapers of our decisions. Technology also plays a part in shaping belief systems.

In the past few decades technology has allowed us to access resources and process information in ways that prior generations could not envisage. There is a flimsy distinction between what we are able to do technologically, and what we ought to do ethically or practically, with morality and foresight being important constraints on what we choose to do. While advances in technology have caused many environmental problems, many people now believe that continued advances will automatically overcome current problems. This belief poses difficulties for those who are convinced of the immediate need to change resource use. Even if technologies do overcome some of the environmental problems we face, the technologies themselves will cause unpredictable problems. For example, the development of genetically-modified food species may be a significant technological advance for food production, but the consequences of that technology may harm the biodiversity on which food production, or other important environmental and social values, ultimately depends.

In the *Future Dilemmas* report, Foran and Poldy talk about the 'rebound effect':

> When technical efficiencies are introduced into a nation's energy system or its farming, fishing and mining sectors, it is often assumed that the resource requirements from the physical economy will stabilise and then fall, as the innovation penetrates the production system. In fact, resource use generally increases as production efficiencies improve. In both the physical and monetary economies this perverse outcome is termed the 'rebound effect'. (2002: 15)

Understanding how resource competition works

Limits to resources trigger behaviours in human systems, for example, innovation, conflict, and competition. The existence of wars, market competition and social inequity in times of plenty are all evidence of the centrality of resource availability in explaining behaviour.

Each subsystem in our society relies on other subsystems and on the environment for resources. Individuals rely on organisations and society, society and organisations rely on the inputs provided by individuals, and all rely on the coordination of the activities of institutions and organisations. Each must constantly find ways of 'convincing' other actors to give it resources. Companies seek the resources of shareholders, employees and suppliers. Governments seek taxes, votes and labour. Individuals seek income, security and infrastructures. The desire for resources is at the heart of transactions within society, and creates interdependence.

Interdependence also explains other social characteristics, such as cooperation, ethics, and accountability. Society – groupings of people sharing a culture – must therefore ensure that the environment continues to share its resources. Every society has developed norms for interacting with the environment to ensure resources. For example, Aboriginals had elaborate rules that guided when to harvest, what to harvest, how to prepare and dispose of materials. Social institutions direct the way we interact with the environment. Markets and government allocations control resource acquisition. Market mechanisms, regulation, penalisation or taxation can also deny resources to those deemed irresponsible.

There is a constant debate about the obligations of custodianship, and a shifting battle for the control of resources. Individuals and organisations may be able to exploit power to gain resources at the expense of others. This can lead to over-exploitation of the environment, or unfair outcomes. When social institutions distribute environmental goods equitably, there is pressure to reduce the transactions costs; when institutions significantly benefit one group at the expense of others, this can trigger radical action. Boycotts, strikes, demonstrations, public inquiries etc are manifestations of bids to gain or regain resources. These re-allocation activities can increase transactions costs and reduce pure economic efficiency (but preserve the fundamental ethical structures of society on which economies also rely).

How do decisions have an impact?

Decisions are ineffective until action is taken, and action is taken by directing resources to support the decision. For example, creation of a new instrument like a tradeable water quality credits scheme may make sense but will fail if the financial capacity of buyers or sellers is insufficient. If no one can afford to implement the quality improvements that will give them something to trade, or no one can afford to buy credits when they are offered for sale, the instrument will do nothing. Similarly, a regulatory approach may appear to make sense but if there are no funds for policing then the desired behavioural outcomes are unlikely to occur.

This suggests a test for sustainability strategies. If we are to choose between competing strategies (such as economic instruments, regulations, or information programs) we should focus on a threshold criteria: which of the alternatives will marshal the greatest level of resources to make it work? On balance, more resources suggest the greater potential to change behaviour.

There are many ways in which strategies to promote sustainability fail by violating the requirement for sufficient resource flows:

- *Regulatory instruments which wrongly assume a practical means of implementation:* An example is the requirement that noxious weeds be removed from river banks when there is no herbicide which can be used without (also illegal) contamination of the water and there is no capacity to employ hand weeding techniques safely.
- *Incentive schemes which require matching funds* when the resource manager simply does not have the funds, or lacks complementary resources such as capital equipment to be able to take advantage of the scheme.
- *Market instruments introduced with the expectation that this will allow resource use dependent communities to improve their economies* when the only resource users who can afford to speculate are wealthy corporations in distant urban areas.
- *Information and education programs which describe methods of resource protection or rehabilitation which are not feasible* within the available implementation resource.

Any strategy must consider the ability of those who are expected to implement a change to access resources, otherwise the strategy will likely fail.

What is the role of information filtration?

In living organisms, information about the environment – food and shelter, predators, competitors, or potential partners – is vital for survival. So, too, are internal signals such as pain, sexual urges, hunger, thirst, and fear. Information serves the same survival purposes in organisations and society, though the signals are, of course, different. The information gleaned from these signals makes possible the decisions in pursuit of fit[3] with other systems and the environment.

A system needs information about the functioning of both its internal elements and the external environment. We have previously noted that not all signals are turned into 'information' and that we use filters to sift and interpret information based on existing beliefs and perceptions. Different disciplines in the social sciences highlight different types of information as being critical, illustrating this point. Economists talk about market signals to explain the flow of information in an economy. Lawyers use rules of evidence to put boundaries around the signals they will accept to inform judgement about cases before them. The education systems that support economists, biologists, lawyers, psychologists, politicians, and all other disciplines have invested much time and energy to produce cognitive systems[4] and technologies[5] to enable decision-makers to pick up the required signals to make decisions. The filters that are built into these cognitive systems are necessary to ensure we capture appropriate signals.

But these filters can also make us 'blind' to changes in the environment. If we do not have the ability – for whatever reason – to interpret signals that tell us that resource flows are likely to change, we cannot act.

There are many examples where, in hindsight, we can say the signals were abundant but we did not interpret them. An individual crippled with back-pain may reflect that had he known the muscle twinges he felt would lead to his incapacitation he could have acted. A bankrupt organisation may assess that it had been monitoring the wrong financial signals. A society faced with significant environmental problems may discover that the institutions it had promoted now effectively block the necessary changes to address those problems.

Our dependency on cognitive systems and technology for information processing has implications for the development of strategies for promoting sustainability. People are more able to absorb information about the environment if it is presented in ways that are consistent with their existing thinking and knowledge. If the information is unusual, or requires them to behave in very different ways, then filtration is likely. The

---

3   We use the word 'fit' to define the state when the outputs of a system match the input requirements of other systems.
4   By cognitive systems we mean ways to think about the problem.
5   Which includes the range of things we use to help us capture information – pens, paper, maps, computers, software programs, microscopes, telescopes etc.

How can we become blind to reality?

The Norwegian economist Erling Moxnes (2000) provides elegant examples of the consequences of filters. Moxnes wanted to test whether the cause of environmental degradation was greed[6] and lack of environmental signals, or some other factor. He designed laboratory experiments in which he eliminated the need for people to compete for a resource – that is, they were in full control of the sustainability of the resource. He also ensured participants in the experiment received plenty of signals about the state of the environment.

In the first experiment, he had 82 people act as fishers in charge of a cod resource. Fifty-nine of the participants were professionals (fishers, managers or researchers). They were asked to build a fleet that would maximise sustainable harvest. They were given a range of signals about the state of the fishery consistent with the type of signals fishers receive in real time:

The median participant built a fleet 92 per cent above the fleet size that maximised the net present value given full information, and 56 per cent above a boundedly rational benchmark with imperfect information. The average fleet size was slightly higher. Only 4 per cent of the participants underinvested in their fleets ... there was limited learning even after considerable evidence of overinvestment had been received. The median participant reduced the fish stock to 15 per cent below the benchmark.

The results are to a large extent consistent with historical observations ... The observed tendency to overfish is less pronounced in the experiment than what is often seen in fisheries around the world. (2000: 328)

In a second experiment, Moxnes had participants role play as reindeer herders in an area where lichen – the food for reindeer – was overgrazed. All 48 participants were aware at the beginning of the experiment that they needed to cut back on the number of reindeer. Many participants did not cut back numbers in spite of information over consecutive years that lichen stocks were continuing to decline:

Thus, instead of rebuilding lichen from its initial level of 32 per cent, most participants contributed to its depletion, in spite of both short- and long-term economic incentives to do otherwise. (Moxnes 2000, p329)

Moxnes re-ran this experiment with professional herders and other professional managers, but the results were almost the same. He concluded that people generally find it difficult to deal with dynamic, stock resources, tending to treat them as if they were static, flow resources. Information about the dynamic nature of the resource, such as reduced fish size, depletion of catch, is interpreted as temporary aberrations in natural environmental cycles.[7] Short-term self-interest and the lack of an information structuring capability to deal with this type of problem, was sufficient to trigger filtration of vital information.

---

6 Many commentators believe that the combined effect of everyone trying to use a resource without considering the needs of others in the resource pool causes degrading of the pool. This theory is called the 'tragedy of the commons'. We will discuss this theory later in the book.
7 Recall in Chapter 1 we noted that Foran and Poldy (2002) also highlighted the difficulty society faces in dealing with a number of dynamics at the same time.

information might be most effectively presented in ways that attach it to ideas that the recipients are comfortable with. Alternatively, the strategy might be to introduce the information gradually, ensuring that each new stage builds on the technology and abilities acquired in the stage before.[8]

Unfortunately major changes are required to conserve resources. Many people have neither the abilities – including value systems and education systems that support abilities – nor the technologies to understand sustainability signals. In addition, the signals that continue to support unsustainable behaviour and support the culture of consumption are very strong with sophisticated messages that consumption is inherently good: everyday conversations gravitate around consumption themes, television shouts 'consume' out in program content as well as in advertising. Those who veer from this path, are often viewed with disdain and are labelled 'miser', 'feral', 'unfashionable loser', 'alternative'.

In 2003, Australian mainstream advertising expenditure was around $A9.3 billion. In Europe, advertising expenditure consistently tracks at around 1 per cent of GDP.

This is the tip of the iceberg. Web advertising is increasing (now estimated at about $A250m per annum) and lifestyle magazines and television programs turn consumption into entertainment. This figure does not count the consumption promotion messages in books, movies, magazines, media and word-of-mouth. This is an enormous weight of resource-use promoting messages compared to the weak conservation signals provided by environmental activists and state-sponsored conservation promotion.

In the face of mounting evidence of environmental degradation we tend to overstate the relatively few signals that science and technology will solve environmental problems. Past technological breakthroughs give us hope. Modern technology allows us to: produce more food than we can consume; live in comfort in houses built on land that would have been inaccessible for building a few decades ago; and battle against diseases that debilitated and shortened the lives of our ancestors. The mass media contains many stories of science's pursuit of solutions to sustainability challenges and the economics literature puts the case for reliance on price signals and anticipated innovation to achieve a sustainable balance. We are happy to elevate these signals beyond their worth.

In addition to employing effective information filters, many people also say that the problem is beyond our control and too distant to matter. Terry Leahy from the University of Newcastle interviewed scores of people about their views on the environment. Many of them expressed feelings of impending doom but felt powerless to change their own behaviours, or change the system that contributes to environmental problems. Their

---

[8] We saw an example of this in the interview with Peter Schmigal about reducing waste by migrant communities.

attitude was simply to live life to the fullest and pretend the future would be the same as the present (Leahy 2000b).

How institutions filter our discomforting information

Filtration is not merely personal or organisational. It is also institutional. Craig Deegan, Professor of Accounting of the University of Southern Queensland, explains the way accounting systems filter out signals that might otherwise lead to changes in the way in which enterprise could respond to the sustainability challenge:

> Traditional financial accounting is limited because it is restricted to considering stakeholders with a financial interest in the entity; adopts an 'entity assumption' which requires the organisation to be treated as an entity distinct from its owners, other organisations and other stakeholders. If a transaction or event does not directly impact the entity then it is ignored for accounting purposes; expenses are defined in such a way so as to exclude the recognition of any impacts on resources that are not controlled by the entity (such as the environment), unless fines or other cash flows result; for an item to be recorded it must be measurable with reasonable accuracy. Trying to place a value on the externalities caused by an entity often relies on various estimates and guesstimates, thereby typically precluding their recognition in the financial accounts. Similar criticisms can also be made of the manner in which actions calculate their economic performance, where success is often measured by reference to outputs such as Gross Domestic Product. Obviously a metric that focuses on output levels does not consider issues of resource efficiencies or the equities associated with resource distribution. Sustainability requires a reduced reliance upon indicators such as GDP.

Our financial mechanisms facilitate resource exploitation, and create barriers to change even when the signals of the need to do so are clear. The fisherman who pursues the declining fish stocks by buying a new high-powered boat, or the farmer who borrows to add more fertiliser to squeeze more out of the depleted soil, invest scarce capital. The struggling fisherman and the farmer typically borrow the capital and enter into a repayment schedule. Failure to repay has serious personal consequences, and so the likelihood is that the natural resource will be exploited beyond sustainable limits. Even if the resource user knows about the consequences of over-exploitation, the personal costs of not exploiting are so great that he or she continues to do so.

There is a bid to close the gap between financial and environmental signals about resources. In *Natural Capitalism*, Paul Hawken, L Hunter and Amory Lovins, stress the importance of valuing 'ecosystem services':

> The economic implication of declining ecosystem services] finally received proper attention because the scientists put a price tag on the annual value of seventeen ecosystem services: $36 trillion on average, with a high estimate of $58 trillion (1998 dollars). Given that in 1998 the Gross World Product was $39 trillion, the figures were surprising.

> Most of the ecosystem values the scientists identified had never been economically measured. They included $1.3 trillion a year for atmospheric regulation of gases, $2.3 trillion for the assimilation and processing of waste, $17 trillion for nutrient flows, and $2.8 trillion for the storage and purification of water. The greatest contribution, $28.9 trillion, was from marine systems, especially coastal environments. (1999: 154)

There are fundamental conceptual problems with placing a value on things on which we are ultimately dependent, compared to valuing things where consumption is discretionary. The value of a glass of potable water varies depending on the context (for example, whether in the middle of a rainstorm or the middle of a desert). The value of brand-label clothes may vary, but the brand remains merely discretionary. As economic signals are readily incorporated into business decision-making, valuing environmental services is an attempt to alter information to fit with decision-making structures. The fundamental weakness of the logic of valuation can be ignored in favour of is potential practical benefit.

How can beliefs shape consumption?

Beliefs play a significant part in how society, individuals and organisations interpret signals from the environment. Belief systems comprise the standards and value sets of individuals, and the culture of society and organisations. The cultures within which we live and work shape beliefs, and the beliefs of individuals in particular groups translate into the culture of society and organisations. Beliefs also reflect philosophies formed from past experiences or passed on as learning, interpretation of experiences, and knowledge about likely consequences. They substantially determine what individuals and groups will value.

The development of beliefs is self-referencing. Ideas breed new ideas, which breed new ideas on the back of the decline of the old idea. The development of artistic representation - dance, sculpture, painting and music - demonstrates this process. One new idea leads to others, and the process goes on even if there are no new stimuli (though evolution of ideas is slowed by this absence). Beliefs do not always have to be well-grounded, nor practical. Some beliefs can drive people to excesses and self-destructive behaviour. The evidence of an increasingly degrading environment does not mean that society will efficiently come to believe that there is a problem and adopt a culture of resource conservation.

We can see the application of many of the tools for changing belief systems in society today: Many schools teach children - and through their children, parents - about environmental sustainability issues; Governments and private industry conduct anti-litter campaigns. Celebrities are engaged to present environmental messages to target groups. For example, the actor Jack Thompson was engaged by Greenpeace to spread the message about the importance of old-growth forests; Pierce Brosnan endorses

Changing beliefs is difficult

Albert Bandura has spent more than five decades studying the way people absorb and react to information. His book *Social Foundations of Thought and Action: A Social Cognitive Theory* was a milestone in the understanding of why people behave the way they do, how they acquire beliefs and why they change those beliefs. He writes:

People generally overestimate the adequacy of their knowledge, especially in areas of limited familiarity. In addition to possessing incomplete, if not unreliable knowledge, they tend to use what they do know in ways that lead them to overestimate the validity of their judgement. They favour confirmatory evidence by disregarding contradictory evidence. Instances in which actions produce positive outcomes are easily remembered, whereas it is difficult to remember also all the instances when actions failed to produce the outcomes or when the outcomes occurred without the actions, and to figure out the probabilistic relationship between actions and outcomes. As a result, outcome information is more likely to be represented in memory as frequency of successes than a probability of successes. (Bandura 1986: 223)

Social cognitive theory suggests two strategies for affecting the cognitive systems that direct behaviour:[9]

1. *Information and feedback:* It is important to provide information to support desired values, and to reinforce the reliability and accuracy of that information with feedback. Not only the information, but also its delivery needs to be orchestrated. The message should be delivered by people who are credible to the target group (for example, it would probably not be optimal to have an environmentalist providing information to farmers engaged in damaging broad-scale clearing). Standards setting (such as through procedures, benchmarking and legislation), and positive and negative incentives are tools that support information and feedback flows.

2. *Build capability:* Strategists should ensure that individuals can act in sustainable ways as well as believe they should. For example, it is difficult to expect individuals to reduce consumption of packaging when all items they wish to purchase are heavily packaged; or to expect people to reduce private car use, when public transport is not available. At another level, it is impossible for individuals to use complex information well if they have not been taught how to understand it and how to use it. Any strategy to introduce change should overcome gaps in knowing how to apply new information and technology.

the importance of reuse and recycling programs;[10] Robert Redford promotes the protection of sensitive environments through a program called 'biogems'.[11] It is significant that groups who traditionally were antagonistic to the demands of sustainability are now advocating change. Examples include the Business Council of Australia, the mining industry (notably through Western Mining) and the farming lobby who combined to produce a publication called *Guide to Farm Conservation in NSW*.[12]

---

9   For a more in-dept discussion of the application of Social Cognitive Theory to promoting desired behaviour, refer to Verbeek, M (1987). *The Effects of Power on its Users* PhD thesis, UNSW.
10   See <www.greenpeace.org> and <www.planetark.com>.
11   See <www.savebiogems.org>
12   See <www.nswfarmers.org.au/nht>.

Incremental loss and slow response

Many sustainability problems arise gradually in hard-to-detect stages. The gradual dying out of a species, the erosion of a river-bank, the slow loss of habitat or the accumulating pollution of a river or an airshed, are gradual but significant.

Mike Young, a leading Australian economist and researcher on sustainability, likes to start his conference talks on aspects of sustainability by pointing out that it is useless to attribute blame to people for taking actions that in hindsight are damaging. 'Among my happiest memories,' he likes to tell his audiences, 'are those of working with my father to clear our farm land of vegetation.'

The other point he makes is that changes to the environment are cumulative, they may be non-linear, discontinuous, interactive and depletion beyond thresholds may be irreversible. This means that the time between a problem arising and it being noted for action can lead to the blossoming of a small issue into a major challenge.

These characteristics should lead society to build institutions and technologies that are sensitive to environmental changes. Instead, we have developed organisational structures that focus on short-term evaluations. However, other societies, such as Australian Aboriginals have built institutions and technologies that better reflect those of nature. Deborah Bird Rose describes how the Aboriginal people of each country depend on others for the proper management of the relationships that sustain them all, and each group depends on others for the pragmatic practices of land management. Restraint is equally part of this system. There are sanctuaries where people do not hunt or fish or gather, and places where burning is done with extra caution or not at all. There are responsibilities based on totemic relationships: the kangaroo people can forbid others to kill and eat kangaroo, for example. As a general rule, totems are linked to taboos that enforce restraint and that are managed by the appropriate people.

Differentiated and complementary responsibilities sustain regional interdependencies. There are few hard and fast boundaries, but rather strong ecological, social and spiritual links that are reproduced through the generations. (Rose 1997: 138-39)

There are few such norms guiding modern resource use. Our attitudes were born of a period when 'opening up the country' was the imperative. Our cultural heroes remain the people whose claim to fame was their capacity to rapidly exploit, and then secure wealth through that exploitation. Now, as we are developing an appreciation that sustaining the country is essential, we still have in place structures that act counter to our new understanding.

Our slow response acts to our detriment, even when we know adaptive change is vital. A 1997 study commissioned by the Commonwealth Department, Environment Australia, estimated that the total financial and environmental subsidies to the use of natural resources in Australia is in the order of $13.7-14.8 billion a year (3.2-3.5 per cent of GDP). $6 billion is in direct financial subsidies and $7 billion is in the form of environmental subsidies. These subsidies are built into the infrastructure of the economy. They include: non-recovery of public management costs, favourable tax treatment, direct contributions and lower than normal rates of return, and non-payment of environmental disruption costs by the organisations causing the disruption. (DEST 1997). There is a shift occurring away from such subsidies, but it is grudging.

Changes in beliefs occur only slowly under the weight of confirmatory signals, and resource-winning results of experiments with different behaviours. It is likely that the accumulating effect of many small shifts towards sustainability will create a climate for further behavioural change. What is far from certain is whether this shift will be sufficient to allow us to meet the sustainability challenges we face.

In summary, why are we so slow to learn?

1. The signals from nature are often not clear and direct enough for our information systems to detect. We are slow to listen to signals that are inconsistent with our traditions of resource use and consumption.
2. The technology we have has allowed us to divorce ourselves from the immediate impacts of changing resource conditions which makes us insensitive to the challenges.
3. Self-interest in resource consumption provides a strong incentive not to respond.
4. Institutional frameworks reinforce these adaptive delays.

Looking more deeply at transaction costs

We have noted earlier that transaction costs are an important part of the dynamic of resource use. As they are relevant to many strategies we will expand on them a little more. Transactions occur constantly between individuals, organisations and society, and are the means through which information and resources flow. Transactions include group decision-making, contracting and exchange, and transfers of goods or services. In natural resource management, key transactions include policing transactions, trading in rights or interests in the environment, such as carbon credits or water licenses, and natural resource transactions, such as buying or selling plants and animals.

Transactions contain uncertainties and managing these uncertainties creates costs (Alchian 1977):

- *Search costs.* The more unique the need for a good or service, the greater these costs are likely to be. Information services such as brokers and intermediaries reduce this cost.
- *Investigation of owner's rights.* It can be difficult to know whether the person with whom you are trading has the right to deal. Are they the true owner? Do they have the authority that they claim? Various forms of title registration or assurance reduce this cost.
- *Investigation of the physical attributes of the goods.* There are two elements – determination of the attributes of goods (quality, suitability) and risk sharing about these attributes (for example,

by warranties). This investigation can be sufficiently costly to prevent transactions occurring. There are many other ways of obtaining relevant information, including reliance on reputation and brand, warranties, commitments of wealth, free trials, and imposed standards.

- *Price search and price predictability.* Finding the correct price for a rarely traded or unique good can involve costly research and bargaining. The risk of price variance can be costly when transactions take place over a long time or where markets are volatile. This is important particularly where the time needed to carry out research or bargaining is valuable or limited. Price predictability is valuable in, for example, stock and share trading.
- *Contract stipulation, which involves processes of bargaining and agreement.* Costs can be reduced through mechanisms such as standard contracts. Where there are long-term mutually beneficial relationships at stake, specification may be less important because the parties know that they will be dependent on each other for a long time.
- *Contract performance, which includes monitoring and control, and subsequent adjustments.* It can be difficult and costly to ensure that the other party does what they have contracted to do. Even a relatively simple contract like an agreement to employ someone, or to build a house, can carry monitoring costs.

Transaction costs arise in markets and also exist in regulation. Wherever information and resources flow, transaction costs are present. The form of the costs may differ, for example, financial (court) costs incurred in the judiciary system, or regulatory costs which exist as legal regulation.

The extent of transaction costs is important

Transaction costs are strategically important. If the costs of securing a license to pollute are too high, the potential polluter may be discouraged from seeking the licence (though if the incentive is high enough, they may continue polluting). If the difficulties of identifying how to control effluent pollution are too great there is little incentive to stop polluting.

How a natural resource management instrument is designed impacts on the transaction costs of implementation. A system which requires extensive gathering and analysis of data (such as technical information or evidence), time-consuming or complex communication, high uncertainty, and opportunities for dispute, is likely to be costly and difficult to operate. That, of course, describes many ill-designed regulatory systems, rights markets, and incentive or subsidy programs. That such programs fail to have the desired effects is not surprising.

It is not only the extent of transaction costs that should be considered. Whoever stands to bear the transaction costs has the strongest incentive to make the strategy efficient, and whoever bears the cost of failure of the strategy has the strongest incentive to make the strategy work.

For example, in most policing systems, the costs of detecting the offence, identifying the offender, taking action and providing the prosecuting evidence and then collecting the penalty, all fall on the regulatory agency. If the policing system fails, the offenders get off free. They have no incentive to make the system work, and every incentive to maximise the policing agency's costs. Is it surprising, then, that many policing-based systems are expensive and inefficient? But this need not be the case. It is possible to shift the transaction costs of a management instrument, and to shift the default outcome, so that the incentive to make the system work is markedly changed.

The German Green Dot Program illustrates that not only is it possible, it is effective to do so. When the German government set out to ensure that industry minimised ecological impacts through recycling, it decided on a regulatory program. Industry protested vehemently. It claimed that the costs of the proposed program would be horrendous, and that the outcomes would be less than if industry initiated its own voluntary programs. Eventually the German government agreed to let industry try, but with a sting in the tail. It left the draconian regulations on the books, but deferred their commencement for so long as the voluntary program was meeting its defined (and quite stringent) targets. In this way, the highly effective German 'Green Dot' eco-labelling program – with its associated recycling and efficient manufacturing programs – was born.

By ensuring a default outcome that the costs to industry of failure would be high, the German government transferred the risk. Industry, with a powerful incentive to make the system work, found effective ways to minimise transaction costs, and make the program work.

To summarise, it is necessary to consider three aspects of transaction costs in the design of natural resource management strategies:

1. Strategy design determines the level of transaction costs;
2. The incidence of transaction costs determines the incentive to make the strategy efficient; and
3. The cost of failure determines the incentive to make the strategy work.

Why is innovation vitally important to sustainability?

Innovation is central to achieving sustainability. Innovation is the only way to bring resource use under control while maintaining the essence of our society with a larger population.

Technology plays a central role in the social system. Technological innovations build on the capacity to use resources, increase our productivity and bring us the standard of living we enjoy.

Social and technological change

Changes in technology can be socially disruptive, as well as economically important, especially where the change is in the *process* rather than the *product*, requiring adjustments at many institutional and cultural aspects of society.

Consider the interaction of technology and social change that occurred during the Industrial Revolution. The groundwork for the industrial revolution was laid in the preceding century – in the 'Enlightenment'. The scientific method was used to advance knowledge – in spite of opposition from the Church; there had been innovation in the administration of organisations, laying the foundations for control and coordination of large-scale enterprises; The notion of equality and the need to provide opportunity to all through public schooling and health care was being trialled in several countries in Europe; and the economic norms for industrial scale marketing and transaction of goods were established.

These new ways of organising gained relevance as Western Europe experienced an unprecedented growth of population (caused by the introduction of new foods such as the potato, and a lengthy period free from epidemics), which spurred societal change. Old institutional arrangements for inheritance no longer worked when a majority of descendents survived, and merchants and artisans had to innovate to become more productive to feed larger families.

Innovations, the steam engine being one, emerged under scientific inquiry. Their use – indeed ongoing innovations – required skills that could not be taught in traditional familial-based apprenticeships, encouraging the development of institutions of learning. Many innovations required new ways of organising labour, notably in factories, spawning an understanding of organisational management. With increased centralisation of production, more sophisticated means of distribution were needed. With more mobile populations drawn from rural areas into centres of employment, individuals and families could no longer rely on traditional, family-based health care, society required public health care systems. A more mobile population and a radically different method of finding employment also required equality of opportunity, challenging traditional inheritance-based allocation of employment and social standing. Social and technological change together created the new paths, and broke down the old frameworks that would have held people to the old pathways.

Our success in using technology is a significant cause of the ecological dilemmas we now face. We can now harvest fish from every part of the ocean, build residential estates on previously inaccessible sites, convert resources to goods at unprecedented rates – and as a result create waste at rates that overwhelm the environment's absorptive capacity. Air travel, computers and cars have had immense impacts on the way we live our lives. They have, in effect, enabled globalisation. However, it is not such creativity and innovation which are the problem for innovation is our path to social and technological improvement. Careful direction of this energy is essential if we are to escape the consequences that past innovations have presented us with.

Innovation effort is naturally directed toward those activities that are perceived to maximise wealth. Where the benefits of change accrue to the rich and powerful, acceptance of change is more likely. If no benefits accrue to them then they will not pursue innovation. There is a complex dynamic of competitive impacts that arise from choices to support sustainability, and this competitive element is important to determine what types of innovations are likely to be introduced. Institutional frameworks emerge as a result of and in order to promote certain technologies. But the institutions and culture of society also enable certain technologies to develop and stifle other innovations. For example, one reason for the slow adoption of recycling centres is zoning laws and public perception that classify such industrial units as waste facilities in the same category of putrescible waste centres. The transaction costs that result – extra requirements needed for development approval and negative neighbourhood sentiment that needs to be overcome – inhibit their development.

The sustainability agenda will require incorporation of environmental objectives into the development of all technologies (Norberg-Bohm 1998) and sustainability strategies must be flexible enough to assist rapid adoption. Sustainability strategies, which limit performance and incentives, curb the potential for technological innovation to support sustainability. Over-specifying solutions locks all producers into a certain method of controlling adverse effects and frees them from the responsibility of having to innovate for more sustainable means of production. The freedom (and incentive) to innovate is the argument that is often used in favour of market incentives rather than regulatory control. However it is an argument that can be over-emphasised. Among other reasons is the fact that there are relatively few technology-specific regulations in place.[13]

In spite of the dangers that regulatory instruments may discourage innovation into less than optimal paths, their role is crucial. Porter and van der Linde, staunch advocates of the free-market system, highlight the role of regulation:

---

13 Though administrative arrangements for implementation can be much more specific and often can be criticised for compromising the original intent of the regulations that they are intended to implement.

> We are now in a transitional phase of industrial history in which companies are still inexperienced in handling environmental issues creatively. Customers, too, are unaware that resource inefficiency means that they must pay for the cost of pollution ... Regulation ... is needed for six major reasons:
>
> To create pressure that motivates companies to innovate. Our broader research on competitiveness highlights the important role of outside pressure in overcoming organizational inertia and fostering creative thinking.
>
> To improve environmental quality in cases in which innovation and the resulting improvements in resource productivity do not completely offset the cost of compliance; or in which it takes time for learning effects to reduce the overall cost of innovative solutions.
>
> To alert and educate companies about likely resource inefficiencies and potential areas for technological improvement (although government cannot know better than companies how to address them).
>
> To raise the likelihood that product innovations and process innovations in general will be environmentally friendly.
>
> To create demand for environmental improvement until companies and customers are able to perceive and measure the resource inefficiencies of pollution better.
>
> To level the playing-field during the transition period to innovation-based environmental solutions, ensuring that one company cannot gain position by avoiding environmental investments. Regulation provides a buffer for innovative companies until new technologies are proven and the effects of learning can reduce technological costs. (Porter and Class van der Linde 1995: 69)

Technology has the capacity to provide more sustainable means of production and consumption, and to increase the knowledge and the means to more effectively monitor the impacts of man on the environment.

We are increasingly using technology to integrate many types of knowledge, creating a picture of the ecology that is becoming ever more layered and subtle. For example, the electron microscope enabled the discovery of bacteria, leading to the realisation of the important function that microbes play in our ecosystem. Such information is becoming the key to uncovering the richness and importance of often hidden ecosystem services.

We have proven that given the right incentives, innovation can allow us to solve apparently intractable problems, and to overcome fundamental environmental challenges. The key to a sustainable future must lie in finding ways of channelling creative energies towards new technologies and new strategies that will ensure our collective ability to prosper.

Principles for the sustainability challenge

This chapter has expanded on the system fundamentals introduced in Chapter 1. It suggests some basic principles to guide the development of sustainability strategy.

1. The pursuit of resources is the force that motivates action by individuals, organisation and society and adaptation is driven by the need to continually change the system to ensure access to resources. It is

not decision-making, but the deployment of resources as a result of decision-making, that causes decisions to have impact:

- (a) Instruments that change patterns of resource allocation are the most powerful ones for creating desirable information flows and shaping belief systems;
- (b) Sustainability strategy should therefore be concerned with changing the patterns of resource allocation towards those that support sustainable natural resource use; and
- (c) Desirable patterns of decision-making should be supported by the right array of implementation resources, and barriers to effective implementation removed.

2. Information flows must be shaped to provide better information about impacts of resource use, to promote sustainable consumption, and to improve decision-making about the environment and resource use. Filtering mechanisms will be a significant cause of inertia:

- (a) The strategic implication is that instruments that are reconcilable with current patterns of information flow will be more successful than those that seek to create new ones; and
- (b) Instruments that require acceptance of new, disbelieved information must be supported by sustained effort (including reward and penalty mechanisms) to alter both belief systems and information ordering structures.

3. Instruments should be introduced with strategies for dealing with effects of information filters, time lags, transactions costs and technology. In some cases, as we will illustrate, these factors will be more powerful in shaping the rate and direction of change, than will more obvious considerations such as attitude and direct economic or social incentives.

With these principles in mind, in Part 2 we will look at the instruments that can be used and examples of their application. In Part 3 we will look at how the principles we have outlined in this chapter can be combined with the instruments we will describe to create strategies for sustainability.

VOICE OF EXPERIENCE: CORPORATE BEHAVIOURS

There are very few living academics whose title is 'Distinguished Professor', and probably none who have earned it more than Dexter Dunphy. His is an international reputation, peppered with accolades, publications and practical work with industry at a very high level. His focus is at the intersection between business and sustainability, and his lifelong campaign is to make business a force for, not against, the environment.

The question we posed was 'if we were to ask you to tackle the challenge of having business embrace waste reduction in a particular region, where would you begin?'

I would start with the question 'who, and what businesses, are you asking me about?' I would want to know what exactly is the waste involved. I would also want to know how the businesses themselves conceptualise 'waste'.

I would want to know this because increasingly what has been seen as waste is merely inefficiency and lost opportunity. In nature there is no such thing as waste, and leading corporations I work with are coming to the same realisation.

An example is Fuji Xerox. Prior to making some major changes, they were much the same as all the other companies; when a customer's machine broke down, they would identify what had broken, and in most cases the apparently efficient step was to replace the assembly or replace the whole machine. There was no detailed diagnosis of the causes or the possibility of remanufacturing. Neither the company nor the customer had any method for looking in detail at the possibility of avoiding the waste that went with replacement. It all looked very efficient, but the waste stream generated was enormous.

Then, Fuji Zerox moved from selling the machine to providing a maintained lease service. The costs of throwing things out became something that they had to think about, because it affected their pricing and profits. This led them to innovate in reducing waste, into recycling and remanufacturing. Then they found that their carbon waste stream was in fact a revenue stream. You can see from examples like this, that waste is a product not only of production, but also of business models and ways of thinking.

It is this aspect of waste that I would begin to work on. If you look at industry waste today, you can often see the cost and profit problems of tomorrow. The chemical industry of thirty years ago is now having to pay for its waste, in legal costs or trying to dispose of accumulated chemicals. The businesses in the Nordic countries or Japan are perfect examples of what Australian businesses are going to have to do with their wastes in a few years. I would start by making businesses aware that waste disposal is not merely a cost, it is a loss of opportunity and a risk.

This would be an approach based on educating, and harnessing informed self-interest. What would you want to do to give an incentive for business to act on this knowledge?

Regulations have to be used to set a floor on the standards that are expected of all industry. The standard has to be set high enough, and has to be gradually increased, to give industry a real incentive to innovate to find solutions to waste. If industry knows that it is going to be increasingly difficult and costly to generate waste, then it will find ways of reducing it. In the process they often learn that it is a more profitable way of doing business anyway.

Coupled with this, government has to remove the many perverse incentives that encourage waste. Industry has to feel the full cost of the externalities, the cost of throwing things 'away'. There is no 'away' left to throw things to! Australia has a tiny population and a large continent, but all around the world people are learning to move towards industry that is more like nature, in which there is no waste. Everything gets used and reused. In other countries, like Germany, that realisation is creating new companies that are leading the world, where the key to their competitiveness lies in the fact that they discourage waste, and turn what was once classified as waste into a profit stream.

An example is my Miele washing machine. It is totally designed around environmental performance, and the company does everything possible to stop you throwing it away and creating waste. That is the way of the future, one of the keys to competitiveness. Some companies, like Visy, have realised this, but many have yet to. There is real financial value in innovating to reduce or recycle waste, because waste is inefficiency in business.

The only way to assist business to get into future, and out of the approach of the past, is to make sure that there is a financial reward from doing so. Tighter regulation, and less subsidy for the old ways, would help provide this.

If I were to be working to change business I would work on these incentives. I would also give them the positive examples about how the change can lead to enormous success, and give them direct financial support and information to help them make the change.

This would mean getting to see that the scenario for Australia's industrial future is already in place, in countries like Scandinavia or Japan. There, industry has been forced to take waste seriously and so companies have had to make the choice: do we make zero waste a key strategy, or do we go out of business? Once the choice of disposal to landfill is gone, creative business people do innovate and create radical improvement. This has been the key to many remarkable sources of competitive advantage.

You could accelerate the change by seeding investment in research and innovation in technology, to assist companies. I would make this a short-term approach, giving industry a message that after five or ten years the support would be gone. That would encourage them to accelerate the change.

After discussion of some of the sorts of transitions that business would be able to take, we asked Dexter what he was doing in his quest to have a positive impact. His approach illustrates the thinking of a strategist, taking an indirect route to change a system that would be less receptive to a more direct approach.

In the last year or so I presented on change and sustainability to over 2000 professionals – line and staff managers, business advisors and consultants, around the world. These people are change agents who can help bring the future into being. I have been outlining the links between environmental sustainability and corporate success. My work group has also established a sustainability network and a Change Agent Network at UTS, aimed at the same type of people – professional, skilled human resource and change managers and consultants to business.

Why have I focused on professional change agents? Because business listens to them, and because they have an interest and a need to find new directions for industry. They deal with people at the top of organisations, and they are concerned to keep their clients up to date and competitive. They understand that a company's reputation as an environmental citizen is relevant to maintaining its licence to operate and to attracting the best new staff, and that business does have to continually rethink strategy to remain competitive. They are sensitive and opportunity-seeking, and not afraid of change. They can get the ear of business leaders, and influence firms to embrace sustainability for sound business reasons.

We asked Dexter to summarise what he would do, if he were advising Australia's government on industry policies for sustainability.

My focus would be first to remove all the disincentives to sustainability, such as subsidies for resource use. This is essential if we want to create a true 'level playing field' for business to pursue efficiency. My next step would be to establish a base level for environmental impact, and enshrine this in strong regulation that is actually enforced. This would provide a specific baseline for industry to work to, I would aim to ensure that there are no 'unpriced externalities' for industry. I would encourage innovation and allow tradeoffs between companies [eg, green offsets], to further encourage innovation and competition for sustainability.

I expect that in the first instance, if necessary, the benchmark would be lower than we really need eventually, and so I would make it clear to industry that over time this standard will be raised. Political feasibility would be a concern, but not the paramount concern.

On the encouragement side, I would propose an industry policy focused upon supporting profitable, sustainable industries. Subsidies would be available for the pursuit of innovation with a sustainability goal. Again, my viewpoint is that innovation in this area of business is vital to international competitiveness, and I would see this as being as much about international competitiveness as about forcing industry to become sustainable. From a national accounts point of view, my concern would be about the future balance of payments if we are not able to get industry to make these essential changes.

Finally, I would couple this with a program to accelerate diffusion of best practice, and to make it easy for industry to learn from the successes of others.

A mixture of unambiguous performance base-lines, and support for innovation and learning, is the formula that is most likely to assist industry with competitiveness, and also assist Australia to achieve sustainability.

PART 2: THE INSTRUMENTS

Chapter 3

INSTRUMENTS AND INSTRUMENT CHOICE

So far, our discussion has concentrated on the concept of strategy, including evaluation of the issues and the context. This chapter establishes a framework within which to consider what instruments to use, and complementary strategies and resources to make them effective.

There are many management tools that can be used for sustainability. Many have existed long enough to prove themselves as viable instruments. Others are still in the experimental stages. Some promising instruments have proved to be failures. All require a certain mix of contextual factors to work.

This section introduces a variety of the tools available in shaping strategies for positive change. Concentrated sources of instrument descriptions are the analysis carried out by the Unites States' Environmental Protection Agency (US EPA) (National Centre for Environmental Economics 2001); the study conducted by James for Environment Australia (1997); and a global study carried out by Stavins in 2000 for the Washington based Resources for the Future.

Instruments are typically categorised as regulatory or market incentives, though this is not as clear a distinction as one might think. All regulations have market impacts, and all market instruments require regulatory support. Overlaid on this are program elements like tradeability, and supports such as voluntary programs, education, standards and support for innovation.[1]

Regulation

Regulation is a well understood intervention which is frequently used to protect endangered environments. Forms of regulation vary from simple blanket bans and penalties to complex rules for exemptions, penalties, fees structures and education programs. In Australia, there are over 250 State and federal regulatory instruments that have an environmental aspect to them, and many more regulations. There are also statutory plans and delegated decisions with regulatory effect. There is an antagonism in the economics literature to the inefficiencies associated with regulation. This has contributed to a proliferation of non-regulatory innovations. This proliferation needs to be considered against the background of the

---

1   The most sophisticated sustainability strategies employ a cocktail of instruments tailored to the social and institutional context, and to the problem being tackled.

demonstrable significance of regulation in protecting environmental and social values, and the fact that all interventions by governments have a regulatory component. Regulation remains the cornerstone of all government-initiated interventions for the environment.

A distinction is made in this book between public regulation, which is regulation created and enforced by government, and private regulation whereby private citizens and organisations exercise their common law or statutory rights. Legal remedies available to private citizens are discussed in Chapter 7. Instruments for improved public regulation are considered in Chapter 8.

Taxes, fees, penalties

Taxes, fees and penalties are economic instruments that create disincentives to harm the environment. They influence both the price and risk aspects of consumption decisions.

Such programs are widely used for reducing the waste stream: Switzerland has a 'pay-as-you throw' system for solid waste disposal; in San Jose, California, residents subscribe to specific cart sizes and pay fees for weekly collection of the waste. When they have too much garbage, they can put the excess in 32-gallon plastic bags with a sticker, sold for $3.50. The city also offers free curbside collection of recyclables and yard waste and collection of white goods for $18 for up to three items. This program has significantly reduced waste sent to landfills.

The Italian government addressed the problem of plastic bag waste by introducing a tax of 100 lira (about 10 cents) per bag. In doing so, the Italian government created a new signal to the market economy – the cost of plastic bags was now greater than the alternatives. From 1989 to 1992, the government collected over 250 billion lira through this tax, but the real value is in the bags that were not purchased and used.

The Quito authorities in Ecuador impose fines on mobile air pollution sources, including cars, trucks, and buses in an effort to reduce air pollution in the city's central historical district. The Swedish sulfur tax, set at twice the marginal cost of abatement, has successfully reduced emissions. In Poland, the government charged emission fees for sulfur dioxide and particulate matter and coupled these with penalty fees for emissions above regulated levels. The twist in the Polish scheme was the penalty fee. The 'normal fees' were set too low to cause significant emissions effects, but the penalty fees proved a significant deterrent.

Strategies that take into account the context and resources of the people or industries which are regulated and also those overseeing and enforcing the regulation are generally more successful than regulations that simply require compliance. The 1993 Columbian legislation requiring water charges to incorporate the cost of service and environmental damages failed in changing behaviour because it did not take the resources of the managing bureaucracy into account. Ninety per cent of Colombia's regional governments declared the law too difficult to implement (Stavins 2000: 10).

In contrast, the Australian *Ozone Protection And Synthetic Greenhouse Gas Management Act* 1989 (Cth) was effective. The government worked with industry to design a phase-out period, a structure of fees to cover administrative costs, a licensing structure to enable trading with revenues from the licenses to be allocated to information programs at need.

The German Ordinance for the Avoidance of Packaging Waste also considers the context in which it operates. Manufacturers must reuse outer merchandise packaging or pay to recycle it. Consumers are able to leave secondary packaging they do not want with retailers. Suppliers return packaging waste to the manufacturers who are required to use it or recycle it privately, outside the municipal waste stream. The law allows manufacturers to pool resources to form a large collection and recycling system. German industry responded in an innovative way to this government edict by introducing the Green Dot system that certifies the recyclability of materials.

Successful programs combine incentives with penalties and/or education strategies, and many added a further factor by enabling voluntary control, such as the German Green Dot system, or through trading of licences or credits.

Market instruments are addressed in detail in Chapters 4 and 10.

Trading and credits schemes to create opportunity

Various controls can be refined to allow the trading of credits or entitlements. Those manufacturers who can control the harm with the least cost not only make savings but also profit from trading credits with others whose compliance costs are higher. Trading also provides a mechanism for more gradual transition towards full compliance without major disruption to industry or society.

Many programs to reduce sulfur dioxide $(SO_2)^2$ emissions are based around a trading scheme. A centrepiece of the United States *Clean Air Act* 1990 is a tradeable permit system that regulates SO_2 emissions. The legislation allowed for a two-phase program with the first phase targeting the most emissions intensive generating units, and the second phase including a majority of other emitters. The US EPA allocates each emitter – on an annual basis – a specified number of allowances related to its share of heat input during a baseline period. The allowance holders can transfer their permits among one another and bank them for later use. There is also a penalty of $2,000 per ton of emissions that exceed any year's allowances. A robust market of bilateral SO_2 trading now exists. The US EPA estimates

---

2   The main cause of acid rain.

that had the legislation relied purely on fees and penalties, the program for reducing emissions would have cost $1 billion annually.

An innovative program to reduce the use of wood fires for domestic heating and cooking was introduced in Telluride region of the US. The authorities did not ban wood stoves but, rather, required owners of existing wood stoves to meet stringent performance standards within three years. To install a wood stove in a new building, the owner now must produce permits to operate two fireplaces or stoves, acquired from existing owners. A lively market in second-hand permits developed. In the mid-1990s, permit prices were approximately $US2,000.

Market-based schemes to encourage people to either change behaviour or use the resource in a more sustainable manner also apply to water distribution and water quality. In the Hunter Valley in New South Wales, salt discharged from mining operations significantly increased the salinity of the local river water. In 1995 the NSW Environment Protection Authority introduced tradeable salt discharge credits, allocated according to a merit formula. The industry has strongly supported the scheme and the result is reduced salinity levels in the river.

Credits can also be used to control cross-territory effects. In the US, the government introduced wetland mitigation banking in the Farm Bill 1996 as part of the Wetlands Reserve Program. Banks were created through a memorandum of understand (MOU) among federal and State officials and a bank administrator. Credits, which are usually denominated in terms of acres of habitat values, may only be used to mitigate development within the same part of a watershed. Most MOUs allow the bank operator to sell credits only after the bank has accomplished wetland enhancement or preservation. There are now about 100 wetland mitigation banks in at least 34 States, and more are in advanced stages of planning.

Costa Rica and the United States have a significant two-country program to consolidate and legally protect national parks and biological reserves in Costa Rica. The program is called the Initiative of Joint Implementation. The program encourages the US private sector to use its resources and innovations to reduce greenhouse emissions and promote sustainable development worldwide. The project will generate funds to purchase lands from the sale of Certifiable Tradable Offsets (CTOs) or 'carbon bonds'. Each CTO represents 1000 tons of carbon the project sequestered the previous year. An experienced commodity trade monitoring firm manages the detailed monitoring and verification of the original baseline and the carbon's sequestration. The Costa Rican government will guarantee the CTOs for 20 years.

Broadly these mechanisms are defined as 'market instruments' or 'trading instruments'. A more detailed discussion follows in Chapter 5.

Fees and levies

Many programs are focused not only on changing behaviour but also on providing the funds for infrastructure that will enable the resource to be used more sustainably.

For example, the managers of Parc National Des Volcans in Rwanda charge a fee for gorilla viewing. The $200 per day fee is a major contributor to the preservation of this region and its wildlife. In the Netherlands, a happy consequence of a levy on the emission of oxygen-demanding discharges is that companies have dramatically modified their discharges. The original intent of the levy was to raise revenue.

In Sydney, fees are levied on aircraft landing at Sydney Airport under the Commonwealth *Aircraft Noise Levy Act* 1996. This levy raises around $40 million a year. The money is used to fund works to alleviate problems caused by noise pollution – such as making surrounding homes more sound proof.

Florida's Mitigation Park Program, initiated in 1986, is the oldest fee-based wetland mitigation system in the United States. Fees paid by wetlands developers finance the purchase and management of large, biologically-defensible Mitigation Parks ranging in size from 400 to 1,500 acres. Clustering individual mitigation activities into selected areas increases the viability of the wetlands. The fact that developers have participated in fee-based schemes suggests that paying fees is more economical for them than on-site mitigation activities.

In many cases authorities collect fees for investment in technology or for encouraging positive practices. Several of the above examples include such implicit outcomes; other programs are quite explicit in this objective.

For example, in France, a widely-accepted program yielding impressive results is the levying of charges on public or private groups or individuals if the activity:

- Contributes to the deterioration of water quality;
- Alters a river basin's aquatic environment; or
- Extracts water for use from natural sources.

Hand-in-hand with these penalties, authorities provide subsidies for improving or safeguarding water quality. Authorities also introduced a system to offset the water pollution charge for people or organisations that treat waste water before discharging it.

In the United States, over 34 States impose fees on automobile tyres. The charge imposed is low relative to the price of the tyres. States use their tyre fee revenues to subsidise markets for end uses of used tyres, and for cleanup of tyre disposal sites and enforcement of laws designed to prevent illegal disposal.

The Polish National Fund for Environmental Protection and Water Management is the largest of 50 environmental funds throughout the country. The National Fund derives its revenues from pollution charges, non-compliance fines, and natural resource user fees, as well as revenues from fund investments and bilateral and multilateral assistance agencies. By 1993 the fund contributed 22 per cent of Poland's total environmental expenditures, nearly as much as all private sector resources and loans combined. Soft loans to environmental projects accounted for 77 per cent of its disbursements.

Supporting sustainability innovation

Many programs do not concentrate on raising revenue but support good environmental performers and help industries to develop appropriate sustainability standards.

The Victorian government initiated an Accredited Licensee Scheme. Good environmental performers are allowed increased flexibility to manage their environmental performance within the legislation. Benefits include lower licence fees, capability to determine their own environmental works, and no prior approval needed for certain new works. The scheme harnesses the good will of businesses, giving them rewards for performance. The US EPA has a similar strategy. They run a two-tiered reward structure to stimulate superior environmental achievement. Through a 'Performance Track' approach, firms receive a standard package of incentives such as public recognition for meeting environmental criteria. Firms that routinely do much more than meet established requirements receive recognition and incentives tailored to their individual needs.

The Victorian Environment Protection Agency (EPA Victoria) strategy is targeted at helping companies identify opportunities for cleaner production. Ford and Cadbury Schweppes have worked with the EPA Victoria and achieved demonstrable economic returns. New processes at Ford saved the company approximately $300,000 per year in reduced heating costs and disposal of caustic residues. The capital outlay for the equipment to bring about this result was $120,000, giving a payback period of less than five months. Additional benefits included cost savings of $100,000 per year, resulting from a 2 per cent to 3 per cent reduction in the reprocessing of reject items.

The Dutch government runs an Accelerated Depreciation of Environmental Investments Measure (VAMIL) program offering accelerated depreciation on environmentally-friendly operating assets for small- and medium-sized firms. The government determines a budget for the VAMIL every year, setting an upper limit for tax allowances. Apart from its favourable effects on the environment, the measure is an incentive for the supply of environmental technologies in The Netherlands. The cost to the government consists only of lost interest.

Many governments support environmentally-sustainable products through procurement programs, such as the purchase of recycled paper for documents, or setting sustainability criteria for building materials. Some environmentally conscious organisations have similar policies. Some, such as Volvo in Sweden and the homewares company Ikea, require their suppliers to have environmentally-sound management practices.

But providing economic incentives is only part of an integrated strategy. Information and standards are also tools that are widely used.

Information and standards to change behaviour

Information is the feedstock of decision-making and some instruments are focused exclusively on improving access to information. In Sweden, the County of Vasternorrland and Sweden's Association of Local Authorities have compiled documents for environmentally-adapted procurement together with criteria for different product areas. The file also contains information on national environmental targets and legislation as well as eco-labelling systems. The group has sold the file to more than 220 of Sweden's 288 municipalities. Commentators on the Vasternorrland project say that publishing policy and criteria are not enough. In order for environmentally adapted procurement rules to work, information and training is also needed.

The US EPA piloted a program called Sector Facility Indexing (SFI). The EPA integrated environmental data from five industrial sectors: petroleum refining, iron and steel, primary non-ferrous metals, pulp and paper, and automobile manufacture. Users could review data on releases from, and compliance history of, individual facilities and then compare these data with other facilities in the same industry. Early indications are that SFI is a useful tool.

The US EPA maintains a network, the Environmental Accounting Project (EAP), of over 800 members. Members share information and ideas on energy costs, capital and operating costs of equipment that control pollution, remediation efforts, salaries of environmental managers, public relations outlays, and other costs associated with the environment. On the back of this network the EPA has prepared guidebooks for implementing environmental concepts, and has developed case studies that illustrate the gains that can be achieved.

Not all standards programs are government led. Responsible Care is a 190-member industry trade association of firms in 40 nations that represent more than 85 per cent of the global chemicals industry. It provides guidance on management codes in community awareness and emergency response, pollution prevention, process safety, distribution, employee health and safety, and product stewardship.

Many of the instruments and programs considered in this book use information. Chapters 4 and 9 particularly address the use of communication and information.

Using education and rewards

Most successful programs marry information or education with other instruments to create a change strategy. These include awareness-raising programs such as environment awards, community and school workshops, State of the Environment reports, specialist reports and media coverage.

In 1990 Singapore launched an annual event called 'Green and Clean Week', held every November. Activities during Clean and Green Week include media campaigns, exhibitions, seminars and workshops, beach cleaning and the planting of trees. Green Leaf Awards, in recognition of the achievements of individuals and organisations in protecting and preserving the environment, are given out during the week.

In an attempt to create better monitoring, the New Jersey government rewards citizens who report illegal dumping. The State gives citizens 10 per cent of any civil penalty or $250; whichever amount is the larger. Information leading to criminal convictions is rewarded by 50 per cent of the collected penalty. The identity of those reporting illegal activity is protected.

Harnessing the good will in the community

Voluntary action is driving the gradual shift towards sustainability. Many people do not need to be persuaded of the benefits of behaving in a sustainable way. Rather they require the opportunity to behave in appropriate ways. Some examples of incentives are provided below. (Incentives are considered in detail in Chapter 9.)

Texas created an Adopt-a-Highway Program in 1985. The program involves agreements by organisations to clean up a stretch of roadside two to seven times a year, for one to three years. The State offers trash bags, safety vests, and other gear and also provides at least one sign to be placed on the adopted roadside with the name of the adopting organisation. By 1994, only four States in the US did not have such a program. In 1994, 121,700 groups, consisting of 1.3 million volunteers, were participating in the programs and over 200,000 miles of roadside had been adopted. This is now a widespread international innovation.

Another successful program enabled farmers to dedicate land that might otherwise be put to productive use. Under the Conservation Reserve Program (CRP), farmers in the US receive annual payments of as much as $50,000 for land in the Conservation Reserve for ten to 15 years. Applications for the program must include conservation plans. The US government pays annual rents and one-half the costs of conservation measures. Since 1992, 36.4 million acres – the maximum acreages allowed under the program – has been placed in the CRP. This is nearly 10 per cent of the total US cropland. In 1990, 33.9 million acres were enrolled with an estimated net social benefit of $4.2 to $9.0 billion over the life of the program. Conservation covenants (with a small amount of tax support) are increasing in Australia.

Also targeting farmers, the Canadian government runs a Permanent Cover Program (PCP). The government funds landholders to convert lands at risk of soil degradation by planting perennial forages, or trees for recreation or wildlife. Applicants enter into long-term contracts for 15 or 21 years.

Poland has an innovative scheme to harnesses the need of other countries. The Ecofund is an arrangement with several lender countries to channel money from the conversion of official foreign debt to environmental purposes. Its environmental objectives include: reduction of trans-boundary emissions, reduction of pollution in the Baltic Sea, and preservation of the biodiversity of Poland's natural environment. Not only does the Ecofund produce environmental gains, it could reduce Poland's debt by $US3.1 billion.

The US EPA Supplemental Environmental Projects (SEPs) program has a different angle on voluntary support for the environment. The EPA negotiates settlements with an environmental law violator in which the violator agrees to undertake an environmental project in return for an agreement to lower the penalty. More than 200 projects were approved in 1992 alone. By 1995, EPA negotiated SEPs valued at $104 million. Estimates place the cost of the SEP at one-half to one-sixth of the reduction in the fine. SEPs offer improved environmental performance, positive publicity, reductions in waste management costs, and industry preparedness for increasingly stringent regulations.

Using risk as a lever for change

Sometimes the best efforts to ensure sustainable practices cannot ensure a good outcome. A mechanism to ensure remediation of harms that do occur is required. Often the main contribution that can be made is to pool risks to ensure that money is available to cure the injury to the environment. For these circumstances, a form of insurance or bond is attractive.

For example, the US government has set up an Oil Spill Liability Trust Fund. The fund uses taxes on all petroleum products, regardless of how they are transported. The fund can be used to meet unrecovered claims from oil spills. This scheme may not have encouraged the use of safer ships or other means of transport, but at least provides funds for clean-up operations.

Bonds are widely used in the mining industry. In Queensland, a bond is used for the environmental management of mining. The security depends on the full estimated cost of rehabilitation. Performance discounts apply and the mining department carries out audits to assess performance against operation plans. The system is meeting environmental objects but is claimed to be costly, prompting a move to self-regulation.

In the US, the *Surface Mining Control and Reclamation Act* (SCMCR) of 1977 requires the purchase of performance bonds before surface coal mining and reclamation permits can be obtained. The fee depends on reclamation requirements, anticipated difficulty of reclamation, and revegetation potential. The performance bond gives companies an economic incentive to reclaim mining sites. They are backed up by a regulatory requirement specified in the permit. The reclamation requirement may have more of an incentive effect than the deposit, since a firm's ability to obtain leases in the future depends on satisfying regulatory requirements.

Observations on strategies

The first part of this chapter has provided examples of the diversity of instruments being used in pursuit of sustainability. There is, however, a difference between instrument choice and strategy. An analogy is the construction of a building. The starting point for construction should be a clear purpose, leading to a design to suit that purpose. Design ought be based on careful assessment of the needs and resources of those involved, and on the external conditions (including available materials and other resources) that might impact on the project. Once that evaluation is complete, a plan can be set, and the tools and materials assembled. The project plans follow the strategy, and the selection of tools depends on how the strategist sees the situation. Typically the architect will have a range of possibilities (like using wood or brick, or locating the house in the valley or on a hill); and will take into account the complementary resources available (like the skills of the work team) in making their instrumental decisions.

Design, project planning, and evaluation, is not a simple linear process. For example, while carrying out the design the strategist (architect) may find that materials are not available, or the craftsmen are too costly. Or he or she may find that there is a natural feature of the site that can be incorporated into the building. The process of strategy formation and implementation is, to at least some degree, reiterative. However, if construction is embarked upon with a concern only for the tools and the materials at hand, rather than the aims and the context, experience suggests that there is a substantial risk that the outcome will vary widely from the ideal.

This is the case with sustainability. Creating a plan by focusing on the tools, without a full understanding of the broader aims, context, resources and strategies is a high-risk approach. It is not uncommon, however, and the results (in terms of sustainability outcomes) reflect the poverty of investment of strategic effort in creating programs. We observe this in the regulatory failures to achieve sustainability goals, and with community education programs that simply fail to work.

Each tool has a different use, and will fail if complementary resources are not available. If, for example, there is no effective mechanism for enforcing private property, then a market instrument is not likely to work, even if the same instrument has worked elsewhere. Regulation may fail if the culture of the community is un-receptive, and an educational program will typically fail if all other pressures are counter to sustainability.

The job of the sustainability strategist is not to advocate tools. It is to construct a strategy based upon a realistic assessment of the context, and the resources available to make it work. Only then can a practical choice be made about which instruments will be right for the job.

Issues marketing failures

Doug McKensie-Mohr and William Smith (*Fostering Sustainable Behaviour* 1999) point to a litany of failures of marketing programs, going so far as to suggest that virtually no conventional programs are designed to work. They highlight that strategies are often flawed. The evidence for their comments is powerful.

They point to one instance of intensive education on domestic energy use in the US. Exit strategies showed significant increases in knowledge, and improved commitment to responsible action. This did not translate into action. *Of 40 workshop participants, only one had followed through on the recommendation to lower the hot water thermostat. Two participants had put insulating blankets around their hot water heaters, but they had done so prior to attending the workshop. In fact, the only difference between the 40 workshop participants and an equal number of non-participants was in the installation of low-flow showerheads. Eight of the 40 participants had installed them, while two of the non-participants had. However, the installation of the low-flow showerheads was not due to education alone. Each of the workshop participants had been given a free low-flow showerhead to install.*

A limited response to energy conservation information was also found in the Netherlands. School education programs are similarly limited. High school students who received a six-day workshop that focused on creating awareness of environmental issues were found in a two-month follow-up to be no more likely to have engaged in pro-environmental actions.

The authors ask the pointed question: 'If we know that such programs do not work, why do we continue to rely on them?' They highlight that improvement in attitude and knowledge is weakly correlated with behaviour. They illustrate this with examples from around the world, spanning auto emissions control, litter, recycling and energy conservation.

They do not say that education and social marketing are bound to be ineffective, but reiterate that information provision is a weak tool unless it is supported by other means to ensure internalisation, commitment and action.

When instruments fail

Deciding whether an instrument has been successful or not is a partly political act. Advocates will rarely agree with a negative assessment. The examples[3] below are some of many that seem not to have worked as planned (though they may have stimulated some improvements).

- Columbian law requires that water charges incorporate the cost of service and environmental damages. As discussed earlier 90 per cent of Columbia's regional governments declared the law too difficult to implement.
- The Sydney Water Board Special Environmental Levy (1989-1993) was intended to raise funds to upgrade Sydney sewerage treatment. It gained community acceptance till doubts were raised that money was not being spent on relevant programs. Public support evaporated.
- In Australia writing, tissue, toilet paper and paper bags were exempt from sales tax when made of recycled paper. This changed the price relativity of recycled product. The scheme was abandoned after three years because it created unforeseen market distortions.
- A coalition of government and private interests developed a trade-based instrument to reduce phosphorus releases into the Dillon Reservoir, USA. Trading was very slow. Causes include limited population growth (due to recession), and treatment plants finding cheaper means of controlling phosphorus.

Other examples are highlighted in the following chapters. Many failures show the need to embed any instrument within a broader program, and to take account of possible contexts in determining strategy. No instrument is universally successful.

How many strategies are possible?

Because of the complexity and interconnectedness within open systems, there is never only one 'right' solution to the question, 'How can I change this system?' The biologist von Bertalanffy (1968) who did much to develop systems thinking, called this characteristic 'equifinality'. A river with increased levels of nutrients can reduce its biological complexity (species die) or increase it (new species arrive which reduce nutrient load to enable continuation of ecosystem function), or by changing the mix of species. A social system may adapt to reduced resources by reducing demands (say through reduced population) or by technologies that use different resource types, or by social re-adjustments. Warfare, technical innovation, or social reforms are alternative strategies to achieve similar adaptive ends.

Consumption of oil, for example, might be equally addressed by a consumer education program in cities, or by better education in factory operations in industry, or by a subsidy to replace inefficient farm equipment. Intervening in all ways would create the greatest potential for

---

3 For details of these and other programs, a comprehensive listing including references is available from <www.profitfoundation.com.au>.

systemic change. There is never only one strategy to change an individual, an organisation or society; there are many 'equifinal' paths. The constraint is the resources to pursue them.

Because of complexity, it can be expected that any strategy may have unpredictable impacts. The interaction of two or more interventions might even operate to cancel out the effectiveness of each strategy, or cause surprising effects.

Instruments for sustainability operate at the intersection of the environment and social systems. They can act on information or resource flows within society, either directly or through changing structural relationships. They shape beliefs and decision-making. In the pursuit of sustainability, a regulatory strategy may be no better (or worse) than a market-based strategy; or an education program be no more or less effective than a peer-group-based management scheme. More often that not, the key to effectiveness is how well any selected approach is implemented, and whether it integrates well with other dynamics of the system.

Is there a 'best' instrument?

The instruments outlined in the following chapters are complementary ways of achieving the same end. Many academic arguments promote one kind of instrument over another as if they were competing. For example, the review of the operation of instruments conducted by the US National Centre for Environmental Economics (2001) concludes that economic instruments are more cost-effective for government than regulatory instruments. However, the review does concede that there are examples of education contributing to the effectiveness of both, or consider synergies between regulation and market solutions.

Each instrument is useful in different circumstances, and depends on others to be effective. Market instruments are best supported by efficient regulation and a knowledge base. Personal property, the cornerstone of the free market, is underpinned by the legal system. Without that system, and the social beliefs that support the law, property rights would be ineffective. There are examples from Eastern Europe of market instruments failing because the citizens had little confidence in legal institutions to support ownership and trading. As a result, they did not choose to trade, nor did they actively seek to defend the newly-created ownership rights.

The dependency of instruments on one another is inherent. The distinction between a 'free market' and a 'command economy' is a distinction between degrees of reliance on intervention by government as individuals order their own relations – with the greatest private market freedom when the law stands behind private transactions rather than government participating in or controlling them.

To illustrate, the regulatory requirement for environmental impact statements has an effect on the available information about the project, and about the environment. It increases the ability of those with concerns to raise them and test them. This forces proponents to identify their projects' unacceptable impacts and propose how to avoid or reduce expected problems. This will impact on the costs. Innately less harmful (or less contentious) alternatives will suffer lesser-cost impacts, and be competitive. This will mean that some activities and projects, or some technologies, become uneconomical. Technologies that reduce harm will become more desirable, because their costs will be lower (either because of the reality of greater sustainability, or because of a perception). In all instances the market will be stimulated to follow a different direction.

In a social system, intervention at any point will have effects elsewhere. The principle of equifinality means that the distinctions between different types of interventions are far more blurred in practice than on paper.

Why think about institutional capacity?

The institutions of society are analogous to the structures of a natural system. An institution shapes relationships in a social system. It influences the flows of information and resources to create the patterns of outcome from that system. Team sports provide a simple example. The allocation of roles and positions, and the role of the umpire, interacts with the team communications, learning and capabilities (as well as the physical arena and the ball), to shape the dynamics of the game.

If the institutions are not 'up to scratch' to support a particular strategy, the strategist needs to find a different strategy, reduce their expectations of the outcome, or design a strategy to reform the institutional structure. To date, institutional reform and instrument choice have rarely been attacked simultaneously.

Institutions are made up of tangible and intangible elements. For example, the institution of marriage involves laws that shape economic relations between the parties (and their dependents) alongside civil and religious frameworks and beliefs. To term something as an institution is not to define its boundaries, but to declare its function of ordering the flows of information and resources in society.

Since resource use is important in society, there are many institutions that shape resource use. Table 3.1 opposite lists some social institutions and their tangible and non-tangible elements.

Instruments are co-dependent with institutions. New instruments trigger change in the institutions that underpin them, whether changes to tangible structures (establishing a new market, or a new policing body), or intangibles (changed skill sets of those who work with the new instrument). Since beliefs and knowledge are partly responses to experience, changes eventually feed back into the character of all institutions.

Table 3.1: Some institutional arrangements

Institutional arrangements	Tangible aspects	Intangible aspects
Law	Courts Lawyers Judges Police forces	Judicial culture Concepts of justice Decision-making through precedent
Politics	Parliaments Political parties 3 levels of government Commentators Elections	Political beliefs Social philosophies Alliances and arrangements Lobbying
Economics	Markets Businesses Analysts Interest groups Production resources	Capitalist beliefs Value Economic techniques Aspiration Trust in institutions
Information	Media Educational organisations Industry associations	Professional beliefs Decision methodologies
Knowledge	Scientific organisations Engineering organisations Professions	Scientific method Knowledge diffusion processes

This is a two-way street. A change to an institution will also lead to changes in the instruments that are applied. For example, new scientific knowledge about natural resource issues will feed eventually into arrangements for managing that resource (subject to transaction costs and filtration effects).

Institutions also interact. Markets, politics, and law interact with the state of knowledge and information in shaping how resources are used and protected. Change in one institution eventually leads to change in another.

Sustainability strategists should take account of the institutions in place, and their capacity to implement instrumental choices. As we will see in the next few chapters, the failure of market or regulatory instruments can be often traced to the lack of a sound institutional basis for their implementation.

Many barriers to implementation of sustainability strategies are the adverse secondary effects of beneficial institutions like the market economy and political democracy. Concepts of ownership and freedom to exploit, or the right to advocate for self-interest, are part of democracy and capitalism. Owners of resources, provided they do not interfere with other resource owners, have been free to exploit their holding. Religious and political institutions have supported these interests, with modification to address social equity. It would be naïve to expect that these expectations of what is acceptable will be suspended or change rapidly to meet the challenges of sustainability. History has given ample illustration that change in institutions always lags changes in social context.

Views about institutional capacity

Australians pride themselves on their social institutions. Nonetheless, when it comes to sustainability Australia suffers from institutional weaknesses. In a series of workshops, 200 stakeholders were asked about institutional preparedness.[4] The issues raised were a reminder that Australian institutions evolved when the need to efficiently conserve, as well as effectively use, resources was less pronounced.

Resource allocation approaches inhibit the pursuit of sustainability: User pays and privatisation are shifting resource control to those who control capital. Competition for funds is driving implementation priorities of agencies. The 'squeaky wheel' syndrome, rather than strategy, often dominates decisions. Politicisation and a failure to adhere to policy reduce the effectiveness of natural resource management. Processes over-reward administrative and political skills, and under-reward outcome delivery. There are difficulties (and a lack of principles) in determining what is fair. Overall the resources are insufficient to implement sustainability. Resourcing is often too short term to deliver real results.

Over-accommodation and negotiability, rather than principled implementation, undermines policies: Agencies are often responding to expectations of 'rights', even if these go beyond legal principles. A pattern is emerging that 'all is negotiable', even implementation of law and policy. Courts undermine policy-based action, creating uncertainty that is exploited. Responsibility at the agency level is avoided. A culture that 'all problems belong to someone else' is a result. There is a problem of conflicting accountabilities and mixed incentives, particularly when environment protection agencies also make their money through its exploitation. There is a failure to reward those who make the effort to protect the environment.

Information flows are not sufficient: Management decisions are not well informed by science and data. One reason is the failure to collect measurements. Administrative structures are adding to confusion. There are too many policies, strategies plans, rules and organisations, and too little energy and resources. Organisational barriers to coordination erode effectiveness. There is over-reliance on 'soft' marketing rather than effective communication backed by accountability. There is disinformation and politicisation of information. Government policies are insufficiently clear and not supported by implementation programs. Poorly designed consultative processes fail to reflect policy priorities, leading to decisions that weaken implementation. Responsibilities are rarely sheeted home as accountabilities.

There are many policy gaps: For example, management of coasts and estuaries is weak compared to on-land issues. Population and consumption policies are lacking as are natural environment emergency risk management plans (like invasive species,

---

4 Southern Catchment Management Board, detailed in Part 3.

sea level rise or climate change response plans). Silo-based decision-making within government reduces accountability.

There is not a clear quality framework for policy formulation and implementation: We lack universal standards for environmental decision-making and implementation, equivalent to those for financial accountability. Community participation often results in plans that do not reflect formal policy, and allow 'shopping' to select outcomes that are politically palatable in the short term. Plans are often not based on predictive thinking, but on back casting what has happened. This partly reflects a lack of predictive indicators.

Regulation is used too often and too poorly: Regulation is over-relied upon, and its effectiveness is limited by conflicts with ownership freedoms. Much environmental regulation is not implemented with vigour.

Not all institutional problems are so deeply rooted. Some reflect transitional confusion with any major realignment of resource use. Jurisdictional conflicts, poor alignment of administration with policy and the like are not surprising given the depth of the changes needed. This transitional state is reflected in:

- The proliferation of participants in transactions;
- A welter of policies; and
- An explosion of legislation.

The more pervasive the changes, the more one can anticipate complexity in adjustment. The more new ideas fly in the face of established power structures, the greater the degree of resistance expected and the greater the transitional disturbance. The Industrial Revolution, democratic choice with the French revolution, or the introduction of technology like the automobile, were all characterised by chaotic and sometimes violent change.

There are many sustainability initiatives around Australia. These include:

- Catchment Management Authorities to set the natural resource management agenda for governments;
- Local government groupings like Regional Organisations of Councils as vehicles for coordination and shared strategies by local government;
- Specialist committees to address vegetation management, water and other pervasive natural resource challenges, and to improve community engagement;
- Attempts to better integrate administration.

These are reforms within the existing paradigm. Unfortunately, they do not always reduce the complexity of the system. The search costs involved in identifying responsibility, and the costs of managing the details of the many programs and instruments that are used, make the transaction costs

74 SUSTAINABILITY STRATEGY

The proliferation of participants

The following illustrates the number and range of participants in resource management decision-making in a region in NSW. This daunting picture does not create confidence in the capacity of the system to effectively manage and deliver natural resource outcomes. Actions are poorly coordinated and create waves of confusion.

Figure 3.1 Many participants in resource decisions

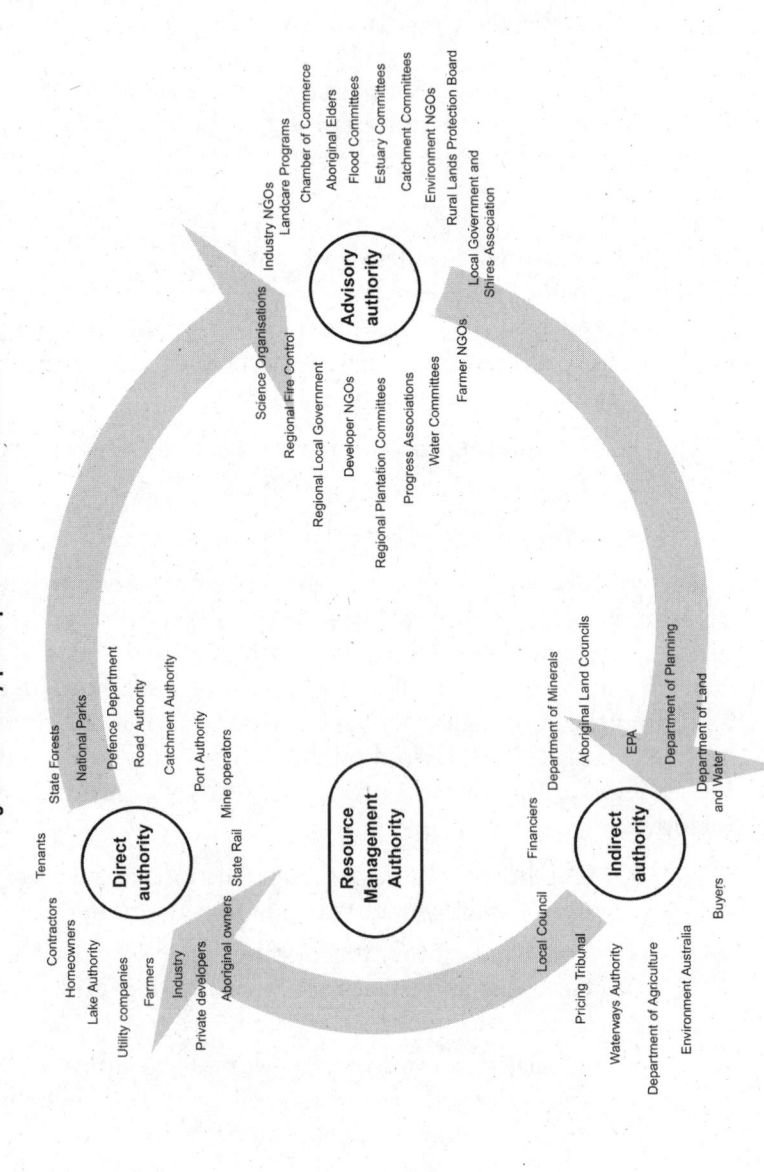

Direct authority: Tenants, Contractors, Homeowners, Lake Authority, Utility companies, Farmers, Industry, Private developers, Aboriginal owners, State Rail, Mine operators, Port Authority, Catchment Authority, Road Authority, Defence Department, National Parks, State Forests

Advisory authority: Science Organisations, Regional Fire Control, Regional Local Government, Developer NGOs, Regional Plantation Committees, Progress Associations, Water Committees, Farmer NGOs, Industry NGOs, Landcare Programs, Chamber of Commerce, Aboriginal Elders, Flood Committees, Estuary Committees, Catchment Committees, Environment NGOs, Rural Lands Protection Board, Local Government and Shires Association

Indirect authority: Local Council, Pricing Tribunal, Waterways Authority, Department of Agriculture, Environment Australia, Buyers, Financiers, Department of Minerals, Aboriginal Land Councils, EPA, Department of Planning, Department of Land and Water

Resource Management Authority

of this managerial structure high. These costs are overlaid by many difficulties: in building relationships between the public and agencies, and even between the agencies, because of competition for power and resources; coordinating activities; and assigning accountability.

There is no doubt that achieving sustainability will be difficult, in part because of the embedded advantages of exploitation over conservation. While it is not possible to calculate how much of the scarce resource for conservation is consumed in transaction costs, it is easy to believe that it is a substantial drain. Nowhere is this more telling than with regulation.

The explosion of regulation

In 2000 more than 250 State and Commonwealth laws intended to achieve sustainability objectives were identified (Martin and Verbeek 2000). This review did not take into account:

- International conventions;
- Implementation regulations;
- Local government regulations;
- Administrative rulings, policies, strategies and programs.

This problem of excessive and poorly-coordinated regulation is not new, nor impossible to solve. By the early 1960s, a national Companies Code was created (later supplemented by National Competition Policy) greatly simplifying the structure of regulation for companies. A similar reform structure for environmental law has been proposed elsewhere by the authors of this book.[5]

Can we reframe sustainability as a markets problem?

Many new approaches to sustainability are informed by economic concepts. The economy does not always comprise buyers and sellers using money for exchange. The concept of the market expands to take into account non-monetary exchange, encompassing any form of goods or services where demand has the potential to be greater than the (perpetually) available supply. Seen in this light, sustainability is about a market balance.[6]

Restated in economic terms, the sustainability problem is: If (immediate) consumption demands on natural resources are greater than the (immediate) capacity of those natural capital resources to replenish, then there will be a sustainability problem. That our current rate of natural resource use is greater than its rate of replenishment has been established.

---

5 Martin, P and Verbeek, M, *Cartography for Environmental Law: Finding new paths to effective resource use regulation*. Report: Methodology for MRN Law in Context Studies. Project No TPF 1, June 2000.
6 Such intellectual sleights of hand are not limited to economics. Redefinition is one way of bringing complex issues into the purview of established disciplines.

In economic terms, we are heading to 'insolvency' unless we can find enough capital, or means of resource renewal to head off permanent loss.

In nature, over-expenditure and collapse is well known. When a species threatens to overwhelm resources, the numbers of predators explode. Adam Smith's 'invisible hand'[7] is acted out, though with a different dynamic, in nature. Predators run out of food and their numbers, in turn, diminish till equilibrium is established. The system is typically self-regulating before irreversible harm is done to the environment.[8] In economic terms, a 'price' mechanism is working to constrain demand and preserve the capital – brutal but effective rationing of scarce resources.

In nature, most time lags between excessive demand and adjustment are relatively short, and there are few ways for the consumers to avoid the price of over-consumption.

For humans, the lag between harmful action and recognition of the cost can be far greater. Society can innovate to find alternative resources by for example, using technology to increase the yield of resources and to widen the net of exploitation, with the result that the resilience of the total system is reduced by the time that the range of exploitative strategies has been completed (as with the Northern Cod Fishery in Europe).

The language of economics helps to clearly frame the problem of sustainability. The sustainability problem has three aspects:

1. Over-demand for the services of the environment – natural resources;
2. Under-supply of these services; and
3. Capital (natural resources) depletion feeding back into reduced capacity to continue to supply services.

Different instruments work on various aspects of this problem, seeking to bring the system back into balance by acting on either supply increase or demand reduction. They will seek to:

1. Constrain demand either by:
    (a) Restricting access to the resources; or
    (b) Restricting the means of exploitation to make this less efficient.

---

7   In 1776 Adam Smith wrote *An Inquiry into the Nature and Causes of the Wealth of Nations*. In it he said:
    Every individual necessarily labours to render the annual revenue of the society as great as he can. ... He intends only his own gain, and he is in this, as in many other cases, led by an invisible hand to promote an end which was no part of his intention ... By pursuing his own interest he frequently promotes that of the society more effectually than when he really intends to promote it.
8   Of course the system post-adjustment may be less valuable to man, or less hospitable to species that previously thrived. For example, where a life form invades an area where it is not usually found – cane toads, lantana, melaleucas in the Florida everglades, etc. These can overrun endemic species and radically change the nature of the environment.

2. Increase supply by:
   (a) Increasing the capacity of the resource to meet the demand, for example, by creating new ways of delivering the desired service; or
   (b) Finding new resources to meet the same demand, for example, switching from non-renewable to renewable resources; or
   (c) Increasing the rate of regeneration of the capital (and therefore its ability to supply at a future time), by works designed to support that regeneration or to remediate past harms.

Innovation has to be a focus of sustainability

Innovation is central to sustainability. Innovation can reduce the amount of resource needed to deliver a service, or change the incidence of demand. It can provide ways to restrict and supervise use, or to find new resources. It can help to rebuild the resilience of the environments.

Changing how people win' wealth, transform resources through production, achieve consumer benefits, and manage the undesirable consequences of all these essential activities are critical if we wish to maintain economic growth and reduce impact on finite natural resources. Foran and Poldy, wrote in *Future Dilemmas*:

> The national goals espoused by most modern democracies generally include continuing moderate levels of economic growth, reasonably full employment levels, progress towards reasonable levels of social and economic equity and a transition towards sustainability. These goals present a number of difficult trade-offs that could remain insoluble without the introduction of revolutionary changes.
> ... (material flows, greenhouse emissions, resource depletion and environmental quality) are intimately linked through the structure of the economy, the industries which function in it and the technologies and procedures of management used. (Foran and Poldy 2002: 244)

In 2000, Kenneth Simons had arrived at a similar conclusion. His concern was how to achieve worldwide industrial output growth of 2% and remain sustainable with a global population of about 10 billion people by 2100 (the United Nations prediction). He suggested this scenario would only be possible if technological changes allowed us to:

- Achieve improvements in erosion controls, fertility maintenance, yields, and pollutant emission, such as:
  - 0.5 per cent annual increase in crop yield without increasing soil erosion; plus
  - 0.5 per cent annual reduction in pollutant emissions per unit of industrial output:
  - improved attention to maintaining the fertility of agricultural land.

- Reduce resource consumption for key materials and perhaps energy sources at about 1 to 3 per cent per annum.

Technology is the mix of ways we transform resources. It includes social arrangements, management, algorithms and mechanical processes which create and deliver services from nature and deal with the adverse impacts it causes. Social and industrial technology can maintain these services within the limits of the environment.

New technologies are the outcome of innovation. Research on innovative organisations shows that three variables stimulate innovation (Robbins, Bergman et al 1997):

1. Structures that are flexible, adaptable and allow cross-fertilisation. It helps if organisations have abundant resources to turn creative ideas into products, services or methods.
2. Cultures that encourage experimentation, rewarding both successes and failures. Innovative cultures accept ambiguity; tolerate the impractical; have minimal rules, regulations, and policies; tolerate risk; focus on ends rather than means; and have an open systems focus – monitoring the environment constantly.
3. Investment in education to maintain the currency of knowledge.

This suggests that the quality of our social capital is an important element in our ability to innovate and adapt. Innovation is a social process stimulated by patterns of incentives – both social and economic. The direction of innovation is shaped by what is systematically encouraged and punished. Social structures set the framework for innovation direction. The application of resources to some endeavours and not others shapes the incentives to innovate, and the direction of future innovation.

These observations suggest that key criteria for instrument selection must be the ability of instruments to:

- Create freedom to innovate;
- Generate patterns of rewards and punishments that direct innovation into positive paths.[9]

Any successful sustainability strategy has to garner enough support from the community, including resources, to be successfully implemented. Achieving the necessary politics of adoption and resourcing is also vital.

Should we worry about fairness?

Sustainability itself is not a process (it is a state of balance in resource use), but achieving it requires social change – a process – from one type of

---

9   Innovation will follow socially perverse paths when the incentives are perverse. For example, in the 1960s, the High Court's 'black letter law' restrictive interpretation of tax rules encouraged the blossoming of the tax avoidance industry.

behaviour to another. Social changes are political: they vary established patterns of winning and losing in society. As we noted above, the quality of social capital is a consideration in determining our ability to change and adapt.

Market and regulatory approaches depend on legal restriction of access to resources (or to reduce harm-doing to resources). Inherent in this is the risk of harm to the less privileged. Property interests (using markets) and regulation of access protect scarce resources, but also reduce free or cheap resources for those who cannot afford ownership. For example, Aboriginal people have highlighted that the creation of National Parks has deprived them of access to ceremonial lands, and estuary protection policies have often deprived them of the right to freely fish or access traditional resources. Inequity is not an accidental by-product, for access reduction is the purpose of ownership and regulated use. What may be an accidental (but often inevitable) consequence are the inequities. Economists frequently refer to such 'distributional effects' as outside the realm of conventional economics, but within the realm of politics where values-driven choices are best made.

The need to consider social equity was recognised in the Bruntland Commission in the 1980s and given renewed impetus following the United Nations Conference on Environment and Development (UNCED) in 1992 and the adoption of Agenda 21. Justice and fairness are fundamental to a cohesive society. There are functional (as well as moral) reasons why fairness is important to sustainability. Where ethics are ignored, conflict and lack of cooperation increase, increasing transaction costs and reducing other forms of social capital. It takes only a little reflection to realise that our society has evolved rules and processes (like democracy) to control over-reaching by those with wealth and power, with a functional purpose of ensuring cohesiveness and efficiency.

For these reasons, in the pursuit of sustainability strategists also need to deliver justice and fairness. Developing mechanisms for this is as important as developing technologies for using resources in more sustainable ways. The discussion of instruments in subsequent chapters will take account of the equity principle by considering the impact of instruments on different stakeholders in society.

VOICE OF EXPERIENCE: VOLUNTARY BEHAVIOUR

Les Robinson[10] is a leading consultant on public communication and social change, with more than ten years creating and implementing social marketing and education programs for government agencies, councils, business and community organisations. Les has led the development of influential studies, campaigns and communication products in this field.

Where would you start if a local council asked you to help design a strategy to look after an estuary?

I would have to start with understanding the biophysical evidence of what was happening, but this would rapidly lead to thinking about causes, which will inevitably be human. Most environmental issues have a social cause. I would look for whether the main causes are institutional (like a failure to enforce laws), or infrastructures (such as a failure of sewerage systems), or are the problems due to voluntary choices about how the environment is used (for example, power boating in a seabird nesting area), or because of market forces (such as businesses carrying out particular activities that impact on the area). We would have to tease out the causes, till we really understand the social system causes of causes and environmental effects.

The next step would be to prioritise these, on the basis of how 'attackable' they are by the local body, given its resources. You have to take on challenges that are realistic given the capacity of your organisation, though, of course, capacity is not a fixed limit. The process of analysis and prioritisation is not something that should be done by experts in isolation. It has to be participative to work. There are plenty of examples to show that unless you involve the people who know the area and the issues, and the community, you are taking a real risk that the approach you develop will not work.

Assuming that you have done this, and you have found (for example) that an important issue is how people elect to use the estuary. What would you then suggest?

Voluntary choices are frequently central to sustainability. You often need a program to influence voluntary choice, and this is where you begin to strike some of the limits of incentives or policing. These approaches continue to work only for so long as the incentive or control is seen as attractive or powerful. But if you want sustained change then you are in the arena of culture, of voluntary choices. You have to develop your approach with a deep understanding of social causes, including local values and norms.

---

10   For more detail, and access to many valuable resources, (including Robinson, L and Glanzing, A, *Enabling EcoAction* Humane Society International, WWF Australia and World Conservation Union, 2003) see <http://media.socialchange.net.au/people/les>.

Because there are so many possibilities about how you can approach this problem, you have to be rational about where you intend to focus your limited resources. It may, for example, be that a council with $40,000 to spend decides to spend it all on lobbying for a stronger regulatory approach, or they decide to invest in the local community. You need to do enough research to be sure this is a rational decision, with 'bang for buck'.

If you are decide to focus on community change, you have to start with a participatory process.

[Les outlined some processes that lead groups to proposing voluntary change.[11]] Why do you concentrate on participative processes?

If the approach to program design is participative, then it is already starting to empower change within the community – even while you are just developing the solutions. Culture change is really about psychology, not engineering. The first lesson, the one that we have to always remind ourselves of, is that people change for their own reasons, not the agency's. They do not change because of an ephemeral policy or a marketing campaign. Change is rooted in deep issues in people's lives, and if we think we can sit back in our offices and guess what these are, we will get it wrong.

What are the implications of this for the design of instruments and strategies to achieve that change?

My experience is that 70 to 90 per cent of voluntary change begins with some strong inner dissatisfaction with something in people's lives. There is a gap between what they want to be, and what they see themselves as being. If you can find this, you can find a way of creating change. You begin with understanding this, and accepting that because everyone is different, you will not get the maximum impact by rolling out one approach for everyone. It is often hard for people who design programs to realise that their program will have to adapt to the audience, not the other way around. For instance, assume you want to change farming practice in a particular valley. You might be able to start with promoting permaculture, and that might be relevant to two or three farmers in that valley. So then you might have to move on to supporting organic farming, because that is relevant to a lot more, and because there is a market for the produce. Even that will not be relevant to everyone, so maybe you have to promote biological farming for the bulk of people there who are not ready to take the risk of investing in a 'greener' approach. If you stick to one idea, you will only get a small part of the people involved, and you will not get the maximum effect. Thinking this way, about evolving your ideas and approach, is much more powerful than having one idea and trying to make the world change around you.

So where do you start this process, for our estuary?

I would begin by asking people about what they find dissatisfying about, for instance, the experience of boating in the estuary. I would phrase the questions very carefully – in essence I would ask them to highlight what they would like to change, and why. Then by probing deeper I would begin to understand more and more about aspirations and interests at stake in the boating experience, about knowledge or skills 'gaps' I would need to fill, and about influential role models that could lower the perceived risk of changing their boating and fishing habits.

---

11 Ibid.

Importantly, change depends on people talking to each other, not on marketing or media. My job is to create the space for boaters to discuss environmental issues with each other. Once we have people talking we can mobilise positive role models, we can respond to counter-productive rationalizations, and we can build people's confidence to act. You can do this using field days, walks, barbecues – there is a myriad of ways.

The central idea, though, is that you have to understand that this is not about downloading information to people to make them change. Change does not happen that way. It is about discussion and learning, from both sides, based on shared aspirations, not just the aspirations of the agency.

How can this small-scale, face-to-face approach be leveraged up to achieve major change across a lot of people?

To understand this, you should think about the idea of a tipping point[12] in a society, where an idea takes off under its own dynamic, once it has been accepted by a sufficient number in the community. That number does not have to be large. However, in implementing social change, you should never expect to do anything in just one year. In the first year, you may get a small group to participate in designing the change program. In the second year, you would launch and may get to interact face-to-face with a few hundred people. These are the early adopters, and if some become credible and influential role models, then the ideas will begin to take off. They would also be your teachers, telling you how to adapt your program to make it relevant for larger audiences.

However, you do have to be prepared to change your ideas as the community comes to grip with them. You cannot have a dialogue if only one party is prepared to think about things and change their position.

Change is a social process. It is a negotiated process, and flexibility and trust, and good relationships, are the most powerful tools for achieving it.

---

12   Malcolm Gladwell, *The Tipping Point*, Little, Brown & Company, New York, 2000.

Chapter 4

MARKET FORCES AND CONSUMPTION

This chapter and Chapter 5 examine two aspects of the role of markets in the pursuit of sustainability. This chapter deals with 'real' markets in which goods and services are bought and sold, and the next chapter deals with 'rights' markets, where the rights to real things are bought and sold. This chapter considers approaches such as increasing the price of natural resources to reduce demand, or assisting the growth of environmentally benign industries.

How markets work

Market instruments are often advocated as a more cost-effective method than regulation for promoting sustainable outcomes. Market instruments rely on supply and demand, and pricing and trading to provide incentives for sustainable behaviour

The Council of Australian Governments' (COAG) Water Reform Framework principles[1] illustrate a common perception about the relationship between pricing, markets and sustainability. The principles for the use of market instruments to allocate water require:

- Establishing a comprehensive system of water allocations and entitlements backed by the separation of water property rights from land title and clear specification of entitlements in terms of ownership, volume, reliability and, if appropriate, quality (cl 4(a)), and
- Trading in entitlements so that water maximises its contribution to national income (cl 5) – this requires clear definition of property rights, the benefits promised by the water right and the rights holder's ability to realise those benefits.

This is a typical example of the emphasis that is placed on harnessing markets to achieve sustainability and social goals. However, simply creating ownership, and tradeability, does not ensure that the market will operate in a benign manner.

---

1 See <www.ea.gov.au>.

The relationship between markets and property

A market exists when there are buyers and sellers of material goods, services and also rights– where there is more demand for such things than freely available supply. For example, the market for water could include water, services of water supply, the right to a share in some volume of water, or the right to contaminate water. Property need not be tangible. Ideas, for example, are protected through intellectual property laws, and are tradeable in a market.

Whether or not an ownership right exists depends on choices by society to allow some members to have access to resources to the exclusion of others. When others are excluded from the benefits of resources enjoyed by some, those resources are owned. They become property and can generally (subject to the recognised rules of ownership) be traded in the market where ownership is transferred. The market is the mechanism for controlling who has the right to enjoy that scarce resource. Beneficiaries of ownership can be individuals (private property) or groups (common property).

How do cost and price adjust consumption?

There are three components of a market – supply, demand and transactions. For a transaction to take place, parties must be able to communicate (information flows), agree (valuation[2] and decision-making), and there must be a flow of benefits between the parties (resources flow). This reflects the structure of the RCDM model.

The cost of goods and services provides the signals and resource constraints that shape behaviour. The cost of buying includes all costs of acquiring (transaction costs), as well as the price paid to the seller. It includes time and trouble involved, and the value that may have been achieved by alternative uses of that same amount of funds, resources and effort (opportunity cost). If demand increases faster than supply, then the price rises. Costs may also increase over and above the price, for example, search costs or taxes. With increased cost, demand falls and supply may be stimulated to increase. When the cost increases, markets may respond in three ways: reduce consumption (limit demand); innovate to increase production or to more efficiently use the good or service; or switch to alternatives. This mirrors the discussion in Chapter 4 about the range of strategies available to pursue sustainability.

The pivot for market behaviour is the price mechanism (though transaction costs are also important). Price reflects a society's belief systems and resource allocation priorities. For example, in one society the price of healthcare may be minimal, while in another it is inflated. Similarly,

---

2   Largely dependent upon beliefs.

the price of natural resources reflects social priorities as well as the state of nature.

Price is also subjective and contextual. An example of the subjectivity in prices is the price of furniture. There is a hazy line between a piece of old furniture being considered worthless or being worthy of being restored, and classified as antique. This subjective, contextual nature of price helps explain why resources once un-priced now have a price tag. For example, a right to fish was once free, as was the right to discharge waste. Now, by collective action through government, the free supply has been reduced, and a price becomes payable for the natural service. As the opportunities reduce, and as beliefs change, price becomes behaviourally meaningful.

Price and value are not the same. How can a price be put on something on which we utterly depend? What is the *real* value of air, water, the fish in the sea, or the microbes that break down waste products and preserve our environment? At first blush, the value must be infinite, but in a world generous in the supply of our fundamental environmental services, the historical price has been minimal – except where supply has been less than our demand at a particular time, such as water during drought.

Revaluing eco-systems

Underpricing encourages over-use. This is a fundamental of the relationship between humans and their environment, and the challenge of sustainability. Traditional pricing of resources is based in the expectation of inexhaustible supply, or at least inexhaustible supply of feasible substitutes – either produced by nature or by technological innovation. The perception of unlimited supply has made the price for most natural resources almost meaningless, apart from the cost of extraction. This is changing as more information becomes available about the integrated nature of the environment and its finiteness, as governments implement programs to create scarcity value or to tax consumption.

One of the concepts arising from a better knowledge of the environment is 'ecosystem services'. The concept acknowledges that a healthy environment provides a service to individuals, businesses and society in general. It relies on the understanding that this service needs to be paid for – has a price tag – if the resource is to be sustained. Many environmental organisations, and researchers in universities and research institutes such as the CSIRO, are working to set meaningful price tags on environmental services. The 1991 calculations by the Australian Conservation Foundation (ACF) for the price tag which could be set for Melbourne's water supply is an example of how researchers price ecosystem services.

> Currently it costs around $700 to supply Melbourne with one megalitre of water. But regrowth forests are much less efficient producers of clean water

than mature forests and it has been calculated that if logging were banned from these forests (in Melbourne's water catchment) the annual savings in terms of increased water yield (up to 75,000 megalitres) would be of the order of $50 million pre annum. (Mercer 2000: 153)

Debates about the 'true' price of natural resources are interesting, but it may be more useful to reframe the problem into one of deciding what price will lead to changes in consumption patterns.[3] There is no true price for fundamental natural services, so the concern is behavioural rather than about measurement. The more important task is to better understand the elasticity (price responsiveness) of demand for different natural services given different levels of price, and to set a price with regard to behavioural aims, and to develop strategies that use this lever to aid sustainable management.

Is privatisation a solution?

The foregoing discussion provides a framework for examining how private ownership might contribute to sustainability. Markets work through self-interest. Entrepreneurs 'read' the environment, seeking situations where their gain is larger than their effort. Arbitrage (buying cheap, selling high), investment (obtaining an interest in something that will increase disproportionately in value), and innovation (finding more profitable ways of winning or using resources) are all ways of making profit.

Market strategies harness the energy of wealth-seeking entrepreneurs, fostering the application of their energies, intellect and resources to find innovative ways of bettering their position. Government administration (regulatory strategy), on the other hand, has the necessary disadvantage that personal gain is limited, the number of participants in the system is limited, and the rules are constraining.[4]

Markets are amoral – although individuals within them may have strong moral principles. The incentive to innovate will be determined by the potential for personal gain. The pattern of innovation will be determined by the underlying pattern of resource allocation, which creates the opportunity for gain.

These observations about private self-interest and system amorality are fundamental to understanding how markets can be harnessed to support sustainability, and why at present they largely do not. The RCDM model indicates that to achieve a desired particular pattern of decision-making, the strategist needs to:

---

3   Since the value of most environmental resources has no upper limit (they are essential) but the market price is zero apart from processing cost, it is hard to see how the conventions of the pricing/valuation approach can meaningfully apply.
4   When governance institutions are weak, personal entrepreneurship can flourish within government but the direction is typically towards corruption rather than creativity in service of the public.

- Consistently reward that behaviour that is desired from the system;
- Support that incentive with information flows that make the opportunity tangible and accessible; and
- Provide decision-making structures that support the desired behaviour.

Once these contingencies are in place, the beliefs in that society, over time, align with the desired outcome, and the established pathway will be the preferred one. This will occur because beliefs will eventually be shaped by the pattern of rewarded behaviour. Through this means the (amoral) outcomes of the market gradually acquire cultural importance and moral authority. In other words, until there is a clear pattern of reward for the desired behaviour, the preferred outcomes will not eventuate. This points to a key lesson, that if we can change economic reward patterns, over time we also change the decision system behind resource use.

It is important to note that this systemic change does not come from generating ownership. Ownership is not a solution in itself. The behavioural change comes from a shift in the pattern of incentives, supported by ownership. Privatisation of common assets is only part of a strategy, and if the incentives remain aligned only with consumption rather than rewarding conservation, privatisation is not likely to deliver the environmental benefits that some advocates would claim.

Can we choose not to use market instruments?

Given the dominance of markets and the behavioural centrality of reward, there is little choice but to harness private markets to promote sustainability. That is not the same as saying that the market can be trusted to deliver sustainability merely through the granting of property rights. Earlier examples and experience demonstrate that so doing is no guarantee of improved outcomes unless the fundamental patterns of rewards for the use of private resources also support sustainability. This issue is developed in Chapter 6.

Rather, with the careful structuring of the pattern of incentives and information flows, coupled with appropriate private rights granting, the market can be used as a tool in a suite of approaches. This is the context for the discussion of market instruments in this and the following chapter.

Can ownership create incentives to conserve?

To achieve a change to the reward system, the community must adopt different beliefs – and then change patterns of rewards and penalties – or the context must change so that rewards are no longer available except through the desired behaviour. Both these shifts are beginning to occur in natural resource use – but slowly. In the consumption-based market economy, wealth and power are rewards predominantly from resource exploitation, and are often enjoyed through further resource consumption (particularly conspicuous consumption). Calls for resource conservation are easily characterised as a bothersome overlay on this fundamental structure, and may be seen by the successful as a form of envy by economic 'losers'.

Those who advocate conservation in our market economy often experience a lower quality of life than those who are happy to pursue its rewards. There are relatively few 'greenies' who are rich through environmental activities. There are, of course, ethically-motivated people who spend wealth to improve or protect the environment, and many forego wealth to live out their moral commitments. Although self-sacrifice is laudable, it is not a reliable basis for social change. It will not bring about the shift to sustainability. The most effective transition would be for sustainability to become a path to wealth and power, not a path that is resisted by the wealthy and powerful. This is not a statement born of cynicism, it is a goal based on fundamentals of decision-making.

Similar observations relate to the choice to conserve. The pragmatic choice of the private resource owner is to exploit today, or to hold for the future. Only if that owner can be reasonably confident that they, or those whom they care for, will be able to enjoy the benefits of conservation and these will be greater than the benefits of consuming today, will conservation consistently occur. Insecurity about the future, including the future right to exploit the conserved resource, can trigger early exploitation. People who control or own resources have always made conserving choices, in the expectation that they will secure the long-term benefit. The choices may have been political (like the ownership right of the king to forests or herds of deer), or reflect resource use strategies (such as the oak forests planted in Elizabethan times for the construction of ships), or as part of the normal cycles of capitalism (such as protection of wood lots or private rivers). If a person does not think that they will be able to enjoy something in the future, then their tendency will be to consume that thing in the present. This behavioural response to uncertainty is the main argument for secure property rights over natural resources.

Private markets can act on information availability to encourage sustainability. Unibanco is Brazil's fourth biggest private bank. Unibanco's initiative to provide environmental information to investors is an example of private sector innovation. It provides equity research that covers social and environmental practices of Brazilian companies ranging from steelmakers to meat packers to supermarkets. The reaction of US investors to the Unibanco initiative has been positive. Timothy Smith, Senior Vice president of Walden Asset Management, the Socially Responsible Investment (SRI) division of US Trust Company, commented: *'What Unibanco is doing is very important, because gathering information, whether in Spain or Brazil, is difficult'* (Deni Greene Consulting Services, 2001: 24).

Innovation, market and atmosphere

Markets can lead to innovation, driven by self-interest. The pattern of returns from innovation will shape its direction. Negotiations over how to control greenhouse gases are an example of innovations in the making, with international treaties and local regulations creating the essential 'scarcity value' for a market to emerge, and the market then stimulating innovation.

'*The atmosphere is being transformed from a commons, where it is available for all in perpetuity, to a commodity whose usefulness for storing waste is to be allocated and traded among nations*', observe John Byrne and Leigh Glover from the University of Delaware (2000). The ecological service being traded is the risks of climate change. The innovations that are emerging include new air-quality technologies, coupled with markets for various types of offsets. The tangible outcomes include large-scale forest plantings, as well as changes to industrial activities.

Crop insurance, storm damage, loss of profits, even personal injury and death policies, all depend to some degree upon weather conditions, particularly the hazards of extreme weather. Traditionally risks were spread by underwriting and sub-underwriting policies that contain a bundle of risks including weather risks. Now insurers are becoming more convinced that weather is increasingly uncertain and potentially disastrous. They are looking for ways to separate out this class of risk, and to find ways of underwriting it.

The result is the formation of a group of underwriters who underwrite the risks of extreme weather as tradeable 'bets'[5] about the future state of the weather. This is little different to trading in share futures, where the speculator takes a bet about what the price of that share will be in the future. In this instance, the speculator is betting on the state of climate outcomes, and undertakes to pay some agreed amount if this condition is met.

Adjusting demand

Intervention in demand in real markets can be achieved by adjusting the cost of resource use, making the use of alternative resources more attractive, or providing information that encourages different use patterns. There is a number of proven tools for these kinds of interventions.

Fiscal instruments

Fiscal instruments use government taxing and spending power to increase prices to reflect environmental or social costs. The inverse strategies, such as lowering costs for activities that reduce harmful effects or reducing subsidies on activities that cause harm, are also fiscal instruments.

Generally, governments use fiscal instruments to create a cost for the adverse public effects of private use of natural resources ('externalities').

---

[5] With apologies to the industry participants who may find this language simplistic.

Externalities can be mundane, like the harm generated by uncontrolled pets to native species, or the loss of quality of environment for others by their barking or meowing. They are an everyday part of interdependent and environmentally-dependent society. For example, there used to be little accountability for industrial processes, motorised transport, burning off, and other activities that leak pollutants to the air and damage the atmosphere. Similarly, traditional pricing of agricultural produce reflected short-term productivity of land, rather than its longer-term, on-going and necessary value as the foundation for production. As a result, many uses of water and land increased salinity, reducing the productivity of the land and rivers. Now that the impacts are better understood, the market is beginning to price them in through requiring remediation, or simply by buyers expressing a preference (through purchasing prices) for properties that are less damaged.

Pigouvian taxes

Using taxes to change prices and therefore resource use is now conventional.

- Australia introduced a tax on leaded fuel in 1995 to create a differential in price of leaded and unleaded. Simultaneously, government ran education campaigns and took other steps to accelerate the switch.
- Sweden has taxed sulphur emissions at twice the marginal cost of abatement since 1996. Sweden met its national sulphur emissions targets well ahead of schedule through fuel-switching and emission reductions.
- Poland charges fees for emissions of pollutants. They include a 'normal fee' levied on emissions below the regulatory standard, and a penalty fee for emissions thereafter. While 'normal fees' have been set too low to expect significant emissions effects, penalty fees appear to have reduced emissions, at least for sulphur dioxide and particulate matter.
- China assesses levies on 29 pollutants in water, 13 industrial waste gases, and various forms of industrial solid and radioactive waste. These Pigouvian taxes have helped reduce water pollution intensity and are a major source of revenue for environmental projects.
- In 1966 France passed legislation that enabled charges to be levied on public or private groups or individuals if they: contribute to the deterioration of water quality; alter a river basin's aquatic environment; extract water for use from natural sources; or extract water for use from natural sources. Subsidies for improving or safeguarding water quality may also be granted. Compensation was introduced to offset the water pollution charge for those persons or bodies who treat waste-water before discharging it into rivers and lakes. The program enjoys both wide acceptance and impressive results.

In 1920, Nicholas Pigou suggested that governments introduce taxes to control externalities. Many governments now use green or environmental taxes. The South Australian government levies a charge for discharges to any South Australian tidal waters. The charge is levied according to the impact level, computed by means of a formula: *impact level = flow x salinity factor x pollutant class factor x impact area factor*. Many councils set lower fees for ownership of a pet that has an electronic identifier implant and is desexed. In Sweden, the government has imposed a sulphur tax on coal, peat and oil at a rate of 3,500 tonnes of sulphur. Similarly, Denmark imposes a charge on waste.[6]

Some people argue that such taxes and fees lower productivity, reduce economic output, cause greater costs to be passed on to the consumer, lower real income and slow economic growth. But several researchers deny this is the case. The European Foundation for the Improvement of Living and Working Conditions conclude in their report that '*... there is increased scope for the use of taxes and charges*' (Clinch, Convery et al 1999: 11). The successful US entrepreneur and environmental campaigner Paul Hawken agrees: '*Integrating cost with price does not 'raise' the over-all expenditures of the consumers of the society, but rather places them where they belong, so that the consumer and producer can respond intelligently*'.

Nevertheless, in practice there is greater community resistance to government raising prices than there is to private markets doing the same. This difference comes from the belief that public policy decisions are more debatable than private pricing. This often makes resource tax decisions politically unpalatable, though they are equivalent to a private owner deciding to increase prices to the market, to conserve for future use. Rather than using taxes, governments can penalise acts that harm the environment.

For example, authorities penalise the killing of threatened species, just as parking inspectors fine cars parked in the wrong area. The risk of being caught and fined is a 'contingent price' that adds to the cost of activities and guides the choices we make.

Taxes and penalties have the advantage of raising money from resource users (or abusers), which can be directed into restoration. The effectiveness of a contingent price depends largely on how high the price is – both the penalty and the likelihood of being penalised –compared to the perceived benefits from its breach, and on the transaction cost of making the regulation work.

Adjusting the cost of consumption

Taxes are not the only way of adjusting the cost of consumption. More complex arrangements can often achieve multiple aims.

---

6   We provided many examples of tax-based initiatives in Chapter 2 of this book.

Fees are imposed on automobile tyres in at least 34 US States. Most fees were instituted as part of a scrap tyre program, which included restrictions or bans on the disposal of used tyres in landfills. The system encourages proper disposal of tires. States use their tyre fee revenues to subsidise the development of markets for end uses of used tyres, and for cleanup of tyre disposal sites and enforcement of laws designed to prevent illegal disposal.

Switzerland has instituted a pay-as-you-throw system for solid waste disposal, in which ratepayers pay per bag. The system finances waste disposal and seeks to encourage lower volume. The evidence indicates that the volume of municipal solid waste has decreased as a result of the program, but increased illegal disposal may be part of the explanation.

Are all subsidies bad?

Subsidies, unlike taxes or fees, do not raise money. Governments introduce subsidies to facilitate or encourage particular activities. Typically, the aim is to assist the replacement of the undesirable activity by reducing the cost of the more desirable one. The subsidy may be financial, for example, where the price paid for a good or service is offset by a contribution from someone other than the purchaser (generally by government). Direct subsidies can include relief from taxes (such as a fuel rebate) or a cash payment (such as a payment to retain native vegetation).

A second form of financial subsidy is where the consumer does not absorb the capital cost of consumption. Examples include publicly-funded roads, or infrastructures like boat ramps or dredging, or management infrastructures such as publicly-funded research and development bodies. It is hard to overestimate just how much these capital subsidies change natural resource use, since many of our collective uses would have impossibly high entry costs if a capital subsidy were not provided.

Subsidies can be positive for sustainability, but many subsidies, born in a time when scarcity of natural resources was not as apparent, encourage exploitation. In 1996, the National Institute of Economic and Industry Research reported on subsidies in Australia. With regard to subsidies for the exploitation of natural resources, the report concluded:

> In this study it is estimated that government payments and revenue foregone through financial subsidies to the use of natural resources, totalled at least $5.7 billion in 1993-94, equal to 4.4 per cent of the total revenue of Australian governments. Environmental subsidies, for those areas covered by the study, and where quantified estimates were possible, amounted to at least $8 billion, equal to a further 6 per cent of total government revenue. (National Institute of Economic and Industry Research (NIEIR) 1996)

The World Wildlife Fund[7] estimates that worldwide levels of direct perverse subsidies could amount to over $US2 trillion per annum. Such accounting does not fully take into calculation the impacts of capital subsidy.

The consensus among Australian governments, through COAG agreements, is that the price of natural resources should reflect the full costs (including environmental harm) of supply. But there are many examples of subsidies that mitigate full pricing. In many States, urban water pricing reflects a brief to minimise the cost of water for city consumers. This is coupled with (tax-subsidised) partial reimbursement of capital costs for investments that increase water consumption, for example, reticulated sewerage systems. The combined effect is to reduce the incentive to conserve, dampen the price signals and eliminate opportunities for water-catchment landowners to pass on the full costs of their forced water export.

Subsidies for fuel, fertiliser, water, etc, while arguably justifiable for non-environmental purposes, mask the cost of consumption and do not send conservation price signals to consumers. Attempts to remove subsidies invariably cause political debate because of likely social and economic upheavals.

The debate in 2000 about petrol taxes demonstrates the problem. Those in favour of reducing the tax for the rural sector argued that, because of distance and the type of vehicles they drove, Australian rural communities were penalised. This argument was bolstered by observations that many rural communities are economically marginal and high fuel price reduces their viability further. But by reducing fuel tax to rural Australia the government would be providing a subsidy then reflected in reduced prices for goods produced by rural communities, which may contribute to degradation in areas where production, if fully costed, would not occur.[8] The decision to remove such a subsidy is readily justified in environmental terms, but extraordinarily difficult in social (and perhaps economic) terms.

Removal of perverse effects may not require that the subsidy be removed altogether. Subsidies for sustainability are discussed further in Chapter 9. If sustainability is to be seriously addressed, all subsidies should be independently evaluated for their environmental outcomes. This would create a sustainability competition in government policy, and would be a powerful force for improvement.

---

7   See <www.worldwildlife.org>.
8   This subsidy also has other unanticipated effects, by reducing available taxation revenue for other desirable purposes. Approximately 30 per cent of the anticipated shortfall in Commonwealth government revenues noted in the 2000 Intergenerational Report could be replaced by reversing the removal of indexation of fuel taxes. Arguably the costs of subsidisation of fuel use are falling on the health and social security system (Allen Consulting Group personal communication).

Benign subsidisation

Subsidies can be sophisticated:

➢ In 1984, the UK introduced subsidy payments to farmers in designated areas of special biological, landscape or historical interest. Farmers voluntarily agreed to farm less intensively or undertake prescribed conservation practices, in exchange for a fixed annual per hectare payment. The scheme was written into UK legislation in 1985 and subsequently modified in 1991 and 1993.

➢ In the US, Louisiana's environmental scorecard program links tax exemptions for companies to their environmental performance. The scoring system determines that companies receive a base exemption of 50 per cent and then rates their environmental behaviour to determine how much of the remaining 50 per cent they could obtain. Since the system was built into an existing exemption, administrative costs were reasonably low. Data suggest that this program had a significant incentive effect. Final scores during the 15-month program averaged 94.9, which was significantly higher than preliminary scores. It gave the State the opportunity to use the exemption 'carrot' to promote not only economic but also environmental health. Industry's opposition, however, saw the program terminated after only 18 months.

While it may be politically difficult to remove a direct subsidy, even more difficult can be the removal of hidden subsidies. For example, the harvesting of timber and the extraction of mineral resources are subsidised through institutional mechanisms for research, training, education and marketing of the products, transportation mechanisms and routes, etc. Many of these supports are justified on economic or other bases, such as maintaining employment in marginally viable sectors, or building the strength of an emerging industry. The countervailing drain on our natural capital is rarely counted alongside the benefits. This is an institutional barrier to achieving a more rapid shift towards sustainability.

Can we change the dynamics of competition?

The discipline of the market is that the products that best meet the needs of consumers will be in the greatest demand, and the most imitated. Innovation, lower prices and greater efficiency in creating products with the desired characteristics should follow.

As highlighted earlier, there are thousands of businesses which offer products and services which, either cause less harm to the environment or which can reduce or rectify harms. Instruments that build demand provide a selling advantage to environmentally superior suppliers (and products). In itself this is a good reason for policy makers attending to the demand side of the economic equation, but there are more subtle reasons.

The most cost-effective way of achieving sustainability is for individuals and organisations to self-regulate for sustainable practices. If everyone consistently selects products and services on the basis of their environmental performance, the market will generate intense competition around this characteristic. Environmental performance will become a 'value driver' for business, with enterprises innovating to demonstrate how their product delivers better than others.

Much of the information we receive and social rewards we gain centre around consumption. Marketers exercise their innovating powers to influence us to believe we need to have ever-wider ranges of products and services to be happy and healthy. Even when regulations attempt to control the most threatening consumer demand, demand continues. For example, there is still a market for the hides of endangered species of cats, or the body parts of gorillas, even though there are severe penalties and well-publicised bans on their trade. However, Sustainability awareness is growing, and market-stimulation can accelerate it. Deni Greene, reporting for Environment Australia and Standards Australia on attitudes of Australians to the environment wrote:

> Australians consider the environment to be a very important issue. An international poll by Environics[9] in November 2000 found that 90 per cent of the people surveyed in Australia expressed concern about the environment.
> The Australian Bureau of Statistics (ABS) determined in March 1999 that 68 per cent of households were concerned about environmental problems. To a large extent, people believe that industry in Australia is responsible for most environmental problems, and is not working hard enough to ensure a clean environment.
> - Air pollution was ranked as the most important environmental issue, with water pollution second, in both the international poll in 2000 and the ABS survey in 1999. The ABS survey found that concerns about ocean/sea pollution, destruction of trees and ecosystems, and garbage/rubbish disposal were the issues that ranked next behind air and water pollution. Opinions about the most important issues varied somewhat in different states ...
> - Responding to the Millennium Poll,[10] 50% of Australians said that during the previous year they had punished a company seen as not socially responsible.
> - A recent NSW Chamber of commerce report cited Australian studies showing that 60% of all consumer decisions are made with an awareness of environmental impacts. The studies also found that 73% of people stated that if the quality was the same, they would prefer to buy a product associated with a good cause, and 49% said they would switch brands if necessary. (Deni Greene Consulting Services 2001:6, 7)

---

9   Environics is a Canadian-based international research organisation. The Australian sample size used for this study was a 1000 people.
10   Another Evironics research project carried out in 1999.

Environmentally-aware consumers are part of the process of changing beliefs and will influence the purchasing habits of others. It is strategically important to build the emerging 'green' consumer segment.

Sufficient numbers of consumers can cause environmental considerations to switch from being a cost issue for industry (compliance orientation) to a source of economic value (market opportunity). The direction of innovation and investment by corporations will shift in response. This in turn will alter the profitability of enterprises that supply sustainability services, with impacts on the appeal of such enterprises for equity investment.

To foster this environmentally aware market segment, we should understand the barriers green purchasers face in finding the products and services they want to consume.[11]

Why are green purchasers at a disadvantage?

Information about the environmental attributes of the product and its production, or about the sustainability performance of the supplier is not readily available unless there is a sufficient consumer interest to justify its provision. The search cost for environmental information is borne by the green consumer.

Purchasing niche[12] products requires more complex consumer behaviour. The consumer has to search for what they want, visit more shops, spend more time, and often spend more money than their less concerned fellow citizens.

From first principles it can be anticipated that smaller-scale niche suppliers will be typically more expensive than the mainstream producers. They will be unable to tap into the economies of purchasing and capital and market presence that come with being large, and they will carry the inefficiencies of limited learning opportunities. This does not deny the ability of an individual firm, through innovation and good management, to be both the environmental and cost leader, but this is a difficult challenge. This makes price-competitiveness a problem for 'green' producers. To this must be added the further associated costs and the additional information required by 'green' consumers.

These factors suggest that environmentally conscious buyers are prepared to invest more time and money in their purchases than unconcerned purchasers. Consumer information programs, green purchasing preferences, environmental standards and systems and extended producer responsibility are all strategies that can ease the burden of environmental

---

11 A previous study by Profit Foundation identified transaction barriers to green purchasing and outlined possible approaches to reducing these. It highlighted the many websites and information resources that assist those seeking environmentally positive products and suppliers. See <www.profitfoundation.com.au> to obtain a copy of the paper *Being Heard Above the Crowd – A Showcasing Strategy for the Australian Environmental Industry*.

12 Environment products are a specialised category – a niche – of products.

purchasing. Such strategies are important mechanisms for fostering a market demand for sustainability supporting products and suppliers.

Resistance to providing information

Consumer information programs require the seller to disclose information on environmental performance, easing the information-gathering task of consumers. These programs have effects over and above supporting consumers in making the choices that they want to make

Commodity markets strip out all information about products apart from price and availability. The keys to success become scale and operating efficiency. Non-priced issues like the impact on the environment (or the social costs of production, location of producers or other social concerns) disappear because there is no information on which the consumer can compare. Broadening the signals to the consumer allows them to make choices on broader criteria creating pressure on suppliers to satisfy environmental criteria. It is for this reason that consumer information can be a radical attack on some fundamental causes of natural resource degradation. This may also be why industry sometimes seems to make a disproportionate objection to consumer information, for it can go to the heart of the ability of large-scale producers to secure the competitive advantages of commodity supply (like the ability to switch between suppliers, and to oblige them to compete only on price and technical quality). An information-rich market is more complex for suppliers, and it erodes some mechanisms of market power.

Any requirement to provide environmental information affects the processing and decision-making structures of suppliers, introducing environmental performance into the mix of competitive considerations. Making such information public allows organisations to evaluate themselves against competitors and increases the pressure to refine the environmental performance of products. As environment issues are elevated in awareness within the organisation, this has systemic effects on information systems, capabilities, and eventually on culture. The more that the market rewards environmental performance, the faster and more powerful will be these changes in response to information.

Since information on environmental performance lowers the transaction costs for green consumers and signals the relevance of environmental information to less committed consumers, it does have an impact on the likelihood of market rewards to green suppliers reinforcing the organisational changes noted above.

Eco-labelling is such an information program. The energy star-rating scheme on electrical appliances is an Australian example. Eco-labelling is a relatively low-cost way of educating consumers and industry and is used around the world. Generally, however, corporations in Australia have resisted eco-labelling, because of the discomfort (economic or cultural) that changing of their operations will require.

Corporate environmental disclosures require that management consider environmental credentials as part of corporate governance, and as an element in shareholder value creation. Since directors' reputations are closely linked to disclosure, there is a powerful incentive to improve performance. These pressures add to the incentives for consistent environmental reporting by corporations.

But more could be done. Price Waterhouse Coopers comments:

> Our findings indicate that in many respects the interface between the finance sector, industry, government and advocacy groups in Australia in relation to sustainable development mirrors the trends in the international arena.
>
> There are (sic) a number of barriers and challenges unique to Australia which explain why the finance sector may not be as advanced as its North American and European counterparts in responding to sustainable development. These include:
> - Legislation – the enforcement of environmental legislation and the disclosure requirements for companies and superannuation trustees in relation to environmental and social issues is less onerous than North American and European systems.
> - Market size – the supply of financial products that incorporate sustainable development principles, such as SRI[13] is restricted by small market size.
> - Awareness – despite a high level of concern about environmental and social issues in the community, this has not been translated into a significant investment in 'green' products or active campaigning to promote sustainable corporate practices.
> - Public disclosure – the voluntary disclosure of environmental and social information is less developed than in North America and Europe. The only mandatory disclosure requirement, namely s 299(1)(f) of the Corporations Law is under review and may be repealed. (Price Waterhouse Coopers 2001: ii-iii)

Strengthening the preference for 'green' products

Purchasing preferences mean that the buyer will give priority to those goods or services (or their suppliers) that meet certain conditions. The buyer may, for example, purchase only from a list of preferred suppliers or products. The preference requirements might be environmental ('environmentally-friendly product' or 'accredited supplier'), social ('union-approved') or economic ('locally made'). Such programs help preferred suppliers become competitive by providing the stability to establish desirable products. It can assist them to build scale by increasing sales, and strengthen their ability to exercise bargaining power in purchasing; or to develop operational efficiencies though repeat production.

---

[13] Socially Responsible Investment (SRI)

Environmental information programs

In Australia, a number of regulations require environmental reporting:

> The *National Pollutant Inventory* requires facilities to report certain chemical pollutants emitted to the air, land or water. These reports are public.

> The *Corporations Code* requires an environmental statement within the Annual Directors' Report for public companies as well as private companies satisfying two of the following three tests: gross revenue in excess $10 million, gross assets more than $5 million, or more than 50 employees.

> The *Greenhouse Challenge* requires information on greenhouse gas emissions for signatories to the Greenhouse Challenge Program.

> The *Environment Protection and Biodiversity Conservation Act* 1999 requires Commonwealth government agencies to report annually on Ecologically Sustainable Development outcomes.

A number of corporations in Australia voluntarily provide environmental information. For example the Plastics and Chemical Industries Association has adopted a *Community Right To Know* program. The Australian Minerals Council has adopted a *Code of Environmental Management*; and the Electricity Suppliers Association of Australia (ESAA) has a *Code of Environmental Practice*.

A variation on environmental reporting is 'triple bottom line' reporting. Adopted by the World Business Council for Sustainable Development, this requires that corporations report on three bases – economic performance, environmental performance and social performance.

The growing ethical investment sector also provides an incentive for organisations to provide environmental information about themselves. In reviewing the role of Australian financial institutions in the sustainability sector, Price Waterhouse Coopers, concluded that there is a significant push for banks and financial institutions to take into account environmental performance in evaluating borrowers (Price Waterhouse Coopers 2001).

Both public and private sector organisations use such schemes, though some care is needed for major government schemes that could violate free trade obligations, as non-tariff trade barriers.

The preference may be an absolute where only firms with proven credentials are able to tender; partial where credentialed firms get a price advantage (say 5 per cent allowance above the price of non-credentialed competitors), or non-credentialed firms may have to meet additional tendering hurdles; or a soft preference where, all other things being equal, the credentialed firm will win the contract.

Purchase preference programs

The Minnesota (US) State Government operates a partial preference program. The State Government has a list of 97 State contracts for 'Environmentally Responsible Products and Services', a majority of which are part of the State's successful effort to buy recycled-content and refurbished products. The list includes alternatively fuelled vehicles; low-toxicity cleaning supplies; energy-efficient computer equipment and mercury-free batteries. The purchasing principles include a list of ten activities for elected city officials and staff to implement. Included on the list (along with related directives to ensure environmental quality, such as use resources efficiently, and prevent additional pollution) is a mandate to purchase products based on long-term environmental and operating costs, and find ways to include environmental and social costs in short-term prices, and to purchase products that are durable, reusable, made of recycled materials, and non-toxic. (EPA 2000)

In Australia a number of 'green preferences' approaches are being used, ranging from 'green teams' of purchasers, vendor fairs with pre-qualification for suppliers to participate, purchasing staff training and incentive programs, and vendor information approaches.

How performance standards change markets

The existence of authoritative standards assists those wishing to adopt green purchasing. Government agencies, in particular, are likely to provide a purchasing preference for suppliers who meet defined standards. These help to reduce the transaction costs by limiting the amount of investigation that is needed to qualify a supplier, sometimes down to the level of simply checking an accreditation.

It is possible to accelerate improvement based on standards. A first step is to determine that a voluntary code or standard is desirable (often as an alternative to regulation), and adopt collective self-regulation. Typically membership is voluntary, the main cost being compliance with the scheme (which can be a major commitment, involving substantial organisational change and disruption).

A second step is to help with information. A collective approach may provide education and training or develop ways of making information accessible. Benchmarking networks are an example, where businesses agree to provide detailed information to a trusted third party, who then collates and analyses the information and provides performance improvement advice to all members of that network.

There are competitive and environmental advantages possible for Australian industry using product life cycle (LCA) information (Martin and Verbeek, 1998). These include improved access to international markets, as well as better financial and environmental cost management for industry. LCA information is expensive for small enterprise to produce, as it has a substantial fixed-cost component. Only wealthy corporations and

ISO standards

The International Standards Association develops international standards on many products and services.[14] The ISO 14000 series of standards are particularly targeted to environmental performance. Part of the series, ISO 14040, sets the standards for the adoption of independently-verified Life Cycle Assessment (LCA) of the environmental impacts of products and processes. Although there are still many questions about the application of LCA, a growing number of government and private sector organisations are using it in their preferred purchasing arrangements.[15] The World Trade Organisation (WTO) allows it as a basis for permissible trade barriers.

As a result of the development of ISO 14000, a number of other initiatives have emerged. Leading edge companies such as Volvo, Ikea and Ford are giving preferred purchasing status to those companies who voluntarily establish Environmental Management Systems (EMS) (an integral part of ISO 14000) and use these as bases for improved environmental performance. Many companies, especially small and medium-sized firms (SMEs) do not have the resources or capabilities to make the fundamental structural changes required to comply with the ISO. Some larger corporations wanting to employ sound environmental practices have come to the aid of these supplier companies by providing guidance in initial stages of change.

Once multinationals raise the sustainability bar for their suppliers, the effects can be pervasive. Suppliers pay attention to even subtle signals from major purchasers, and will respond to these signals because of competition. In the process of competition, suppliers provide not only information about their own environmental performance, but will often assess their competitors' performance. They will try to show that while their credentials are sound, those of their competitors are ill founded. Conflict in the market place puts increasing pressure on all to put their house in order, and to highlight the weaknesses of their competitors. Over time, knowledge about environmental performance and the reliability of information on which to base selection improves.

---

research organisations have the resources to produce the information, and once produced it is typically confidential. The Australian economy would significantly benefit from the adoption of a national approach to LCA, to overcome these scale barriers and to reposition our companies at the forefront of environmental performance. This is the type of information that is effective when shared.

A third step is to put pressure on corporations to comply. That pressure may be from regulators or from industry, from environmental groups or through international trade negotiations. It can also come by virtue of economic advantages conferred with accreditation, such as preferred purchasing. Or it may be that the participants see that unless all members in

---

14 The overall approach of the International Standards Association is explained at <www.iso.ch>.
15 Other standards exist such as MIPS and Flux analysis, which deal with the embedded materials and energy in products. We do not intend this discussion to be an exhaustive one of available standards. For an outline of such issues and the systemic impacts of ISO 14000, see *National Materials Accounting Strategy: A path to competitive advantage for Australian industry* by Paul Martin and Miriam Verbeek, available as a download from <www.profitfoundation.com.au>.

an industry participate, they will suffer cost disadvantages. The Australian government's 'Pathways to EMS' program has prompted industry bodies like Horticulture Australia, the Victorian Farmers' Federation and the Winemakers' Federation of Australia, among many others, to actively promote ISO 14000 EMS adoption across their retrospective memberships. The action of the multinationals in insisting on environmental performance standards for purchased goods and services, then assisting their supplier SMEs to meet these standards, is an industry-led example.

A standards-based approach can trigger a competitive dynamic that ought eventually better align institutions to sustainability. Some of the action will take place as legal disputes challenging the legitimacy of accreditation, or the meaning of accreditation. Claims about the right to be accredited, or the potential to be struck off, will arise. Common law claims, such as negligence, will use 'best management practice' as the standard to be applied. Legislatures will begin to appropriate the standard to ensure reliable benchmarks. Society will eventually internalise these standards as the baseline for environmental performance.

Liability as a market development tool

One approach to environmental accountability is to make those who buy inputs or supply finished products responsible for the harm potential in what they do. The effect is to encourage them to select business partners (suppliers) who reliably produce low-impact products or services. This creates a competitive advantage for environmentally responsible suppliers. The market is effectively harnessed to support sustainability.

There are different forms of this approach. One is strengthening legal liability. The more proactive approach is Extended Product Responsibility (EPR). Under EPR programs, the purchaser or manufacturer of a product is accountable for its eventual safe disposal – the costs of disposal are sheeted home to those with the most power to reduce them.

EPR is not conceptually new. Under common law, a person is liable for the foreseeable harm caused by their activity, including injury caused by the escape of dangerous possessions from their land. Legislation to ensure accountability for disposal, pricing to encourage reuse and recycling, and other programs to encourage similar behaviour, are all well established. EPR is the logical next step.

EPR can take many forms. It can mean that producers have responsibility for taking back products once they have reached the end of their useful lives; providing the systems through which recycling and reuse can occur; using materials that are safe to dispose; labelling to aid recycling and safe disposal; or a combination of such actions.

EPR programs can be compulsory or voluntary. One early form was container deposits to encourage consumers to return containers either for reuse or safe disposal.

Many factors influence the effectiveness of EPR programs:

- *Cost effectiveness*: The cost of collecting and reusing, recycling or disposing of the product must not impose such a burden that it effects production and distribution. It helps, therefore, if the costs of recycling, and the value of materials recovered, are higher than EPR system costs. For example, if the dumping cost of heavy metals (such as in batteries) is very high, and the price paid for them is also high, then the potential for recycling is good.

- *Transaction efficiency*: If the costs of communication (for example, trying to find a recycler, or negotiating a disposal arrangement), logistics (collecting the materials and taking them to recycling), labelling (for example, where there are dangerous or incompatible materials involve) and documentation, are high, the system has a reduced chance of success. The total cost (including inconvenience) should ideally be a fraction of the value of the materials recovered. Karen Palmer and Margaret Walls from the US 'Resources for the Future' concluded that transaction costs will often make EPR less attractive than a mixture of a tax on manufacturer inputs (such as the weight of metal or plastic) and the use of proceeds to support recycling enterprises (1999). For this reason, a simple consumption tax can be more effective than EPR.

- *Strategic benefit*: If participation in an EPR program gives a strategic benefit, such as improved market image, inclusion in preferred purchasing schemes, or the opportunity to be supplier for firms with high environmental standards, the system is likely to receive support. Effective EPR programs should be part of a mix of incentives and controls.

- *Ethical support*: If there is an underlying ethic of concern for the environment, and consumers reflect this in their purchasing, EPR is likely to gain more support from industry.

- *Equitable cost burden*: Some forms of EPR, such as deposit/refund schemes can distort competition. If there is a deposit/refund scheme in one State, and not in the adjoining State, entrepreneurs may obtain waste from one State and sell it in the other. This effectively taxes the EPR scheme, and imposes competitive problems for the producers in the EPR scheme State.

In Australia there has been considerable resistance to EPR schemes, particularly container deposit legislation (CDL). One of the reasons is the problem of cross-border exploitation. That resistance has managed to stifle calls from environment and consumer groups for such legislation, in all States but South Australia. But the pressure continues to mount.

EPR programs

Extended Producer Responsibility can span many aspects of harm to the environment

- ➤ The South Australian *Beverage Container Act* 1975, then *Environment Protection Act* 1993 prohibited the sale of certain beverage containers unless marked with the refundable amount on the container. Refunds may be obtained from retailers or depots. This scheme creates favourable conditions for reuse of containers or materials from which they are made. Under the German Ordinance for the Avoidance of Packaging Waste, manufacturers must reuse outer merchandise packaging or pay to recycle it. The program divides packaging into transport use (pallets, crates), secondary packaging (outer boxes and cellophane wrapping) and primary packaging (bags, boxes, tubs, tubes). Consumers are able to leave with retailers any packaging they do not want. Retailers must pay for the removal and recycling of the discarded materials. The suppliers return the packaging to the manufacturers, who are required to use it or recycle it. The law also allows manufacturers to pool resources to form a large collection and recycling system. German industry has established a program by which materials are certified for recyclability by being given a Green Dot.

- ➤ As a way of reducing lead entering unsecured landfills and other potentially sensitive sites, several US States have enacted deposit-refund programs for lead acid motor vehicle batteries. Under these systems, a deposit is collected, and returned when depositors return their used batteries to redemption centres; these redemption centre, in turn, redeem their deposits from battery manufactures. The programs are largely self-enforcing, since participants have incentives to collect deposits on new batteries and obtain refunds on used ones, but a potential problem inherent in the approach is an increase in incentives for battery theft.

- ➤ The Minnesota Contaminated Property Tax is levied on the 'contamination value' of property, that is, the difference in the value of the property before and after contamination. Owners of contaminated property who do not have approved cleanup plans pay this fee at the full property tax rate. The contamination tax is halved for owners who have filed an approved cleanup plan. Owners who purchase contaminated land without being notified by the seller of the contamination pay 25 per cent of the full property tax rate until they file a cleanup plan, after which the tax rate decreases to 12.5 per cent. According to a local tax official, the tax gives property owners 'a strong impetus to clean up.'

The National Packaging Covenant

In response to political pressure and to the recycling challenge, the Australian Packaging Association put forward an innovative self-regulation program to increase EPR. The Scheme is called the *National Packaging Covenant*.[16] It is promoted by the Association to the packaging industry as an alternative to having far more costly programs imposed (such as container deposit schemes). The federal government has been supportive by agreeing to underwrite the Covenant with an enforcement regime.

---

16   See <www.packcoun.com.au> for more information.

In its fourth year of operation, a review by the Association showed that the Covenant had a significant effect in a few companies, but adoption by the larger population of companies was slow. The threat of CDL continues to be the biggest motivator to the acceptance of the Covenant by the private sector. This pattern is not unusual, but it need not be the case. Slow adoption probably signals that the industry has not yet seen enough incentive to embrace the voluntary code. Either the threats of regulation are too remote or the opportunities to enhance their competitive position are so small as to outweigh the perceived costs of adoption of the program. Combining EPR with other initiatives to increase the consumer 'pull' of best practice environmental performance would seem to be one path forward.

Should we replace capital goods with services?

It is the services component in goods that gives them the major part of their economic 'value'. This is true even in products as basic as foodstuffs; fancy food preparations are not more nutritious than basic foods such as bread, milk, potatoes and greens, but they are typically more expensive. The service value includes the intellectual and cultural values that are delivered with the physical product.

In Europe, the *Factor 10* movement aims to achieve a tenfold increase in the services productivity of physical materials. Put another way, it aims to reduce by 90 per cent the amount of materials embedded in each unit of service delivered. In the US, Ernst von Weizaker, Amory Lovins and L Hunter Lovins promote less ambitious *Factor 4* improvements (von Weizacker, Lovins et al, 1997).

Whether targeting an improvement by factor 4 or 10, enterprises that use the concept address three questions:

1. Precisely what is the service (physical and meta-physical) that the consumer seeks in buying the product?
2. Is there a way in which this benefit can be delivered using a business service rather than a product model?
3. Can there be improved efficiencies (and therefore profit) from delivering this business service?

If services can be delivered with reduced material inputs, then it is likely that both the environmental cost and the financial costs of these can be reduced. Both commerce and the environment can win! Remanufacturing and recycling are part of this shift from a capital-intensive economy to one with a greater potential to employ people to replace the use of virgin materials. It is also possible to couple this shift with the logic of outsourcing to specialist providers of services as an alternative to ownership and operation of business activities.

Using a services model to support sustainability

The traditional way of buying floor covering is for the homeowner to purchase the covering. Under a service arrangement, the homeowner enters into an agreement with a specialist to provide a floor covering service. The homeowner does not own the carpet, but derives the benefit of its use. The owner of the carpet is paid a rental and is obliged to replace it and remove it according to the service contract.

Another example comes from the US electricity industry. Faced with the capital costs of expanding production, and a backlash over emissions or the risks of nuclear accident, some electrical utilities have realised that energy saving is an alternative to energy production. The consumer only wants the services that electricity provides – light, heating or cooling, cooking, and the benefits of different kinds of electrical equipment. If these services can be delivered using less energy, the consumer is no worse off, and the electricity provider may be able to make more profit on the watts it sells. It may be able to profit from managing services, and defer capital expenditure while having optimal use of its infrastructures. As a result some in the electricity industry have initiated service businesses that guarantee a level of service for a fee, and use their purchasing power and savings (such as by installing reduced energy lighting, or energy management systems, or more efficient motors) to achieve a profitable outcome at lower cost to the client and to the environment.

The industry also provides energy management advisors, selling 'negawatts' (saved watts) at lower cost than the price of new electricity, either as advisors or on a savings share basis. Selling 'coolth' (the inverse of warmth) on a service contract rather than selling electricity to power air conditions, is a version of this approach.

Can we create markets where none exist?

Reshaping existing markets through the information and resource flows is taking place. But the changes are slow to stimulate the degree of innovation needed to move us to sustainable consumption. There are many reasons why. Some have to do with institutional barriers. Others are embedded in our social system, and maintained by political and economic interests and the inertia that delays social change.

We are not, however, limited to affecting the market for 'real' products and services. Whenever it is possible to create conditions under which the demand for a good is greater than supply, it is possible to create a market. Apart from intervening to make physical markets for goods and services more sustainable, it is possible to create markets in the rights to access vulnerable natural resources. What is needed to create a market is the ability to control access, and then create some right (usually tradeable) for some share of that restricted access resource.

Creating and using such a rights instrument is the subject of the next chapter.

VOICE OF EXPERIENCE: MARKETS

Bob Marks is a well-respected academic economist, who is often called on to advise government and business on complex policy issues. He has researched, advised and taught about the ways in which economic strategy can influence behaviour, including changing drug-use behaviour, and the management of environmental issues for over 30 years.

How would you respond if you were asked to advise on better use of pricing to advance sustainability?

Implicit in the question is the idea that people respond to prices, and that if the prices for resources do not reflect the full social costs of their use, then such resources will be used more than if the full costs were reflected in the price. The aim of most economic strategies for sustainability is to try to align the prices we face in the market to the full social costs, so that certain social goals, such as sustainability, are achieved. I would first distinguish between situations where there is already trade occurring, so that there is a market price that can be determined for what we are trying to manage, and those where there is no trade and therefore no price. Our strategies differ depending on this distinction.

Of course, if something is traded and there is a market price, that price may not fully reflect the social costs and the social benefits involved. If a market already exists, then the approach should be to estimate what the price would be if these costs were reflected in it, and to find ways of bringing the price up to the level of this 'shadow price'. This may be done by taxes, subsidies, or by reducing supply. Conceptually this is not difficult, although in political terms it can be very contentious.

In the second instance, we either directly intervene to set a price, or we create a market so that we can set and manage a price. Markets are created by society creating some forms of property right that can be traded.

So what does it take to make markets work for, rather than against, the environment?

To be effective, the property rights need to be sufficiently secure and tradeable that value exists from trading. We need to remember that all property rights are a social artefact, and society can create them whenever it has the ability to control access. The possibilities are enormous. A society might decide to limit access to the use of the atmosphere as a sink, by limiting who can emit into it. Or it might restrict some other resource, thereby creating a market. Once the market exists, then we are in the position where we can take action to bring market prices up to the level of the shadow price, and thence affect behaviour. We see this with SO_2 emissions markets in Europe and North America.

Once we understand the basic concepts, there is an enormous range of possibilities. But in practice we must be realistic about the behaviours we are dealing with, and the strategy must be sound given these behaviours. For example, we are told that we can make a meaningful contribution to reducing greenhouse gases if we turn off computers at night. How many people do this? Not many, and the behaviour is such that it would take a lot to have people change it. If we use pricing, we may have to put up the price to such a degree that it would be unrealistic, to have an impact on this simple behaviour.

If pricing alone is not going to work, what sorts of other strategies can work?

That is why pricing is not the only approach that needs to be considered. We can use command and control mechanisms (such as regulations and policing), or use social approaches such as education and social sanctions, either alone or in conjunction with pricing and other economic tools. The best example of the impact of education and social sanctions is the way in which smoking has been controlled. When you and I were young, a good host would even have provided cigarettes for their guests, and smoking was normal. A combination of increased pricing, tighter regulation of the sale and use of tobacco, education, and, in particular, social pressure, has markedly changed that behaviour.

Can you illustrate how we might better use markets in Australia?

Public and private transport is an area where it seems to me that careful inquiry would show that we under-price private transport, if we were to factor in all of the social costs. Raising the price of petrol to levels similar to those in Europe would have an impact, making public transport relatively more attractive. We could couple this with the sort of 'gas guzzler' labelling that they use in the USA, which identifies the most inefficient vehicles and attempts to use social pressure to back up pricing, to change preferences. That is an illustration of intervention where a market already exists. An example where a market does not exist is litter control. We know from our own experience in Australia, in South Australia, that a refundable deposit on containers creates an incentive to return them, and also an incentive for other people to collect and sell them. It is more efficient than mere regulation, but it can also be used along with regulation. With plastic bags, the problem is different, but the type of pricing scheme used in Ireland since 2002, coupled with regulation and education, could make a real difference. One of the interesting aspects of many pricing approaches is that they generate substantial additional revenue. Whilst it is not essential for the success of the approach, the benefits of a pricing strategy on today's behaviour can be harnessed with the use of these funds, to rectify some of the problems of past behaviour. An example might be to place a high tax on boat anchoring in vulnerable seagrass beds, and use all of the tax income for education and for restoration of these areas.

So in summary, where does pricing have advantages as a policy?

Economic approaches have some basic advantages, such as the generation of funds for restoration. They are far more likely to lead to efficient protection of the environment, because they create the scope and the opportunity for people to trade and to innovate towards solutions. I haven't previously mentioned the dynamic incentives to innovate through time, but they are very important, and should not be overlooked. Some people worry that using pricing, or market instruments such as tradeable licenses, is the same as giving the wealthier people a right to pollute. But the alternative approaches such as regulatory prohibitions have the disadvantage that they impose costs on the community both in taxes, and in the reduced efficiency that arises. Pricing is an absolutely essential strategy that will lead to sustainability.

Chapter 5

RIGHTS MARKETS

Chapter 4 considered ways to reshape 'real' markets to control consumption pressure. It reviewed how changing information flows, the relative price of less harmful products or services, adjusting the decision-making criteria of purchasers, and facilitating beneficial transactions can promote sustainability. Such mechanisms change the existing market structure. An alternative approach involves the 'artificial' creation of markets – the right to access natural resources.

An instrument (generally some form of license) gives its owner the right to extract specific services from the environment, and excludes all those who do not have this formal right from doing so. Provided that the exclusion is real and significant, the instrument becomes valuable for those who might want to use the resource. Creation of a market implies a restriction on the supply of rights (generally through government licensing) and usually a freedom to trade these rights. However, some instruments merely license use and do not permit trading.

Rights mechanisms allow entrepreneurs to use their creative ability to improve resource-use efficiency as they pursue profit. A user who can satisfy their needs with less resources than their entitlement allows can obtain additional profit by trading their unused entitlement to others (who are not as efficient). As the right creates both a benefit for relative efficiency (opportunity for trading profit) and a cost for relative inefficiency (the need to purchase more entitlement), there is an incentive for profitable uses that increase the productivity of natural resource use. The incentive to innovate is further leveraged as supply becomes more constrained and the price increases. This constraint can be the result of changes to the underlying condition of the asset, or via policy action to tighten up on consumption. Staged reduction in supply will result in a staged increase in price and trigger increasingly intense competition to innovate for productivity. Provided that the supply constraint stay ahead of declines in the underlying natural resource, it is possible for pricing to increase, innovation to increase, and the pressure on the resource to be thereby limited.

Rights instruments

The breadth of the potential applications of tradeable rights is demonstrated in the following examples.

Canada's Pilot Emissions Reduction Trading (PERT) and Greenhouse Gas Emission Reduction Trading (GERT) projects were pilot credit programs. Since 1996, PERT has facilitated the voluntary registry of emission reduction credits in Ontario for industrial emissions reduction below that required by regulations or voluntary commitments. Ownership of registered credits can be contractually transferred between parties. GERT's program administrators review projects and evaluate trades. Through 1997, PERT registered 14,000 tons of NOx, 6000 tons of SO_2, and more than 1 million tons of CO_2 credits.

Land reforms efforts of the Mexican Revolution culminated in the formation of *ejidos*. An ejido is an expanse of land with its title held in common. The word ejido refers to both the land and the community holding title. All forest lands of an ejido are owned and managed communally. Decisions regarding forest use are made collectively through oversight and approval plans formulated by the Mexican government forestry technicians. Management and forest use however are carried out by the ejidos themselves. Profits from timber sales are distributed to ejido members and also used for ejido infrastructure. In this way all ejido members both influence and benefit from forest activities.

Individual Transferable Quotas (ITQs) in the South East Fishery of Australia are transferable permits for total allowable catches from trawl fishing. Fines and levies are collected on permits, which include an application fee, an issue fee, a general boat levy, and a research and development levy. Each fisher is allocated a given number of quota units for each species, determined in accordance with a formula taking into account the number of boat units as well as recorded historical catches from 1985 to 1989. The units are transferable, subject to approval by the management authority. The economic efficiency of the industry appears to be improving. Although total allowable catches/ITQs are relatively successful, the multi-species nature of the fishery makes it difficult to expand the system on a species basis.

The efficiency of market instruments

Rights markets replace government taxing and administrative allocation with market rationing through price set by supply and demand, and by private trades. (Frequently the price set through the private market will be greater than the price that might be set through politics, because government price setting is politically contestable). The greater the cost of resource use, the stronger will be the profit incentive to increase productivity.

Governments also benefit from reliance on the market. They can avoid reallocation of funds from other public expenditures, or increases in taxes. That is not to say that those who are denied what they consider to be their use rights will not call on the public purse to compensate them for changes to their entitlements, for they often do.

Prices perform two other important functions in rights markets. They are the mechanism to allocate resources to users who most value the resource. Generally this will be the most productive use as a result of either the value of the output being high or innovation leading to greater output efficiency for a given unit of the costly inputs. Second, price can compensate for volume changes, due to either reduction in available resource or policy-initiated 'clawback'. Since price increases with reduced supply, reduction in supply give a price advantage to rights holders which can wholly or partially compensate for reducing the amount of available resource without having to draw on public funds to do so.

The operation of markets enables more options to maximise resource productivity while controlling environmental injury. Many farming and industrial resource-use decisions are attempts to manage business risk by transferring this to the environment. For example, the decision to pump water from a drought-affected river is also a decision to try to protect the value of a crop or livestock. By creating a market value for the river, the farmer needs to consider the diminishing of that asset with the value of other wealth-producing assets. Finance mechanisms like insurance, futures, options or other derived instruments become more attractive means of protecting the asset.

Does creating a market reduce accountability?

There is a fear among many environmental advocates that moving towards the use of markets always means reduced control over the outcomes of that market. This is not necessarily so. There is sufficient flexibility in market instruments to link the right to a resource with user responsibility to protect the natural resource. Just as it is possible for a bank to say that it will only lend to companies that meet accounting standards, or an investor to only invest in firms that meet certain social performance criteria, it is possible that a natural resource entitlement will only be maintained for so long as the resource user meets resource protection criteria. This opens up a role for governments to impose penalties (such as loss of rights) for misuse of the resource. This power to create pre-conditions for access has not been widely used in Australian rights markets, but it will become more important as community expectations of environmental accountability increase.

Creating a rights market does not remove the power of government to control abuse (otherwise the financial markets would be more chaotic than they are today). Peer groups with a shared interest in the responsible use of a resource may also establish ways of policing its sustainable use. Many fisheries operate on this basis. This is analogous to the financial rights markets. Stock exchanges are typically privately owned, but they impose strict governance requirements on all those firms that wish to take advantage of the shared benefits of the reputation of the market. Further examples are provided later in this chapter.

Social costs of markets

As discussed earlier, although market instruments offer many benefits, the fact that to work they must restrict open access potentially increases social inequities, reducing the opportunities of those who do not have sufficient wealth and power to participate. This is not a problem that is fundamentally caused by the choice of market instruments over regulation. Declining resource availability, coupled with growing demands, means that the amount of resources available at no or little cost will diminish. When this is further reduced by the (necessary) 'locking up' of resources to allow for protection or replenishment of natural capital, the result will always be increased wealth for the successful and diminished opportunities for the less powerful. Privatisation is not the cause of this serious problem, but it is an instrument of it. Doctrinaire opponents of market mechanisms tend to mistakenly place the cause of declining access to resources at the feet of the market, instead of seeing the more fundamental cause in the decline of the resources themselves.

They are right, however, in pointing out that social inequity is a companion of free markets. Markets operate to reallocate resources to those who are best able to maximise profitability, and virtually by definition this will be the successful. Advocates of free markets tend to see this social equity problem as a distinct category of policy problems, or believe that the market will always provide a more effective social solution than intervention. There are few reasons to believe this to be the case. Any market mechanism will reallocate resources and therefore have secondary impacts (positive and negative) elsewhere within the social, economic and natural system. One of these effects is exclusion – locking in resource access rights at a point in time for one party and excluding others. For example, the creation of a European property rights regime in Australia had obvious social justice consequences for Aboriginal people.

Another problem is that it is difficult to predict how entrepreneurs will use their rights. Entrepreneurs seek opportunity and exploit it. Whatever the framework, they test its limits. If a market is created, we can expect that the incentive embedded in that market will be taken to the extreme over time, and that the outcomes will outstrip any imagining of its designers. This will almost always result in undesirable outcomes alongside the desired ones.

Undesirable environmental outcomes may arise even when markets are operating effectively by increasing the value of a resource that is declining in availability. This circumstance provides some with the incentive to bypass the controls. If wealth can be achieved by exploitation of a resource that has been made more valuable through restrictions, then this will occur. There are more than enough examples of poaching, illegal dumping and smuggling to demonstrate this.

Further undesirable outcomes may arise when rights are traded away from traditional users. People who used to have access rights will lose them, but may still want to have them (as with the sale of any desirable asset). Those with tradeable rights will try to maximise their interest – achieve the best price. This encourages resource productivity, but it may not necessarily achieve resource conservation or social justice and equity. What if all the farmers, or all the fishers, or all the small factories in a community sell their resource use rights? The effects on employment or on the surrounding communities are part of the cost of that 'efficient' use of resources.

This discussion of the disadvantages of market instruments suggests that it is a naïve notion that market instruments can solve the social justice issues inherent in achieving sustainability. Market instruments have an important role to play, but their limitations should be kept in mind.

Forms of rights markets

There are many variations in how market rights instruments define interests, limit or facilitate trading, reduce or increase permissible environmental use, and manage the security and interests of rights owners.

To create markets, all that is needed is to control access to some valued resource, and create a right (usually tradeable) for a share of that restricted access resource. Broadly, there are three ways restrictions are imposed:

1. The creation of a 'cap and trade' instrument. The limit of total exploitation is set, and shares in that capped exploitation are issued. Anyone wishing to increase their use beyond their share must purchase another's right to do so. An example is water rights on regulated rivers.

2. The creation of a tradeable credits scheme, under which those engaging in resource depletion or use are limited to the issued value of their 'rights to use' credits, unless they purchase use right credits from some other person. For example, the imposition of emissions limits on electricity generators or on mine discharge within a tradeable credits program.

3. The 'natural' development of a market as a result of restriction on access to resources. For example, the markets for sand, clay or soil were once open access but are now constrained by environmental protection rules and licenses.

Capping consumption

'Capping' a resource prescribes that only a limited amount of it may be harvested or otherwise utilised. For example a cap may determine how much water can be drawn from a river (harvesting cap). A cap may also determine the level of pollutants allowable into the environment (discharge cap). A cap places a limit on supply, or environmental capacity (in term of receiving pollutants) and in doing so creates a potential market for the rights to access.

All capping mechanisms have two initial requirements to enable them to operate:

1. The ability to define the natural resource; and
2. A monitoring and control mechanism to ensure the cap is not exceeded.

These requirements mean that both technology and regulations play important roles in the success of capping programs. Technology is important for defining the natural resource and its capacity, measuring the overall use and metering the right-holder use, and monitoring the total program. Regulations set the standards for the operation of the system and ensure that the cap is respected.

Using a market structure to implement the cap means that a group of people, apart from the regulator, has a strong incentive to make the control work. If a share of the capped exploitation is owned and can be traded, all who are sellers of exploitation rights have a reason to ensure that the cap is credible as this is fundamental to them maximising the value of their interest. As the available supply diminishes, the value of their interest increases. This increases the likelihood of private enforcement of controls on unlicensed access, aligning the interests of at least some of the more powerful in the community with the interests of the government.

An ancient cap instrument

Capping instruments are far from a modern invention. The CATO institute, a non-profit research foundation provides a wonderful example of an ancient capping system:

> *Muang faai* is a 1000-year-old community river water regulation system, which still operates in many areas of Thailand. River communities negotiate rules governing who receives how much water and when, and they implement those rules through adjustable weirs made of bamboo and teak poles. By adding or removing poles, by raising or lowering the weir's height, by scouring the river and irrigation beds they ration water to all users. Upkeep of the system is proportional to landholding. Taxes to maintain the system are paid in the form of labour.
>
> The system is frequently conflict-ridden, and constantly adapting through trial and error and discussion. The system recognises that each community living along the river needs the river to irrigate its crops, water its animals, and provide for its members' personal needs. The system also enshrines the reality that land-use practices along the river are everybody's business because land-use affects rates of erosion, and thus contamination of the river and irrigation systems. In places where *Muang faai* operates, upland forests, vital to bringing the rains each season and controlling runoff, cannot be cut without permission.
>
> *Muang faai* has proven to be the basis of a sustainable agricultural system in Thai river catchments for more than a thousand years. It is successful because people who are directly affected by degradation of that environment make decisions about the environment.
>
> <http://www.cato.org/pubs/policy_report/prop-pr.html>

Does an interest have to be tradeable to be valued?

The *Muang faai* is an example of a non-tradeable interest in a capped resource. It is the simplest form of capping and basically imposes a limit on harvesting. This imposition is the same as if there is a physical limit on the resource. It is the regulator rather than the physical environment that creates the restriction.

Non-tradeable interests are useful but there is less incentive to conserve or to innovate to use less than the allowable cap, because no additional benefit is achieved through this conservation. However, non-tradeable interests do allow government to retain more direct control, and can be a safeguard against some of the possible negative impacts of a fully free market, as noted above.

The drawback to a non-tradeable interest is that the incentive by all stakeholders to cooperate depends upon the degree to which they feel secure that they will benefit from conserving. There are basically two ways that conservation can provide a benefit – either the unused interest can be traded, or it can be saved for future years. In the case of a share of river flow, saving the flow is not physically feasible,[1] but in some other instances it is possible, such as deferring a right to remove vegetation or to harvest a permanent population of some species. Where it is possible to defer use of the right, this is known as 'banking' that right. Regardless of whether the means to obtain the value from conserving is through trading or banking, to be fully effective a market instrument should provide an appropriate degree of resource security to ensure that the conserver is confident that they will be able to reap the benefit. This is why property rights are so often the catch-cry of those who propose market instruments (though as we shall later see this cry is often poorly informed).

Absolute volume or share of resource?

The *Muang faai* is an example of an interest based on a share of a resource. If the season is bad, all entitlement holders get a smaller volume, even if they maintain the same percentage of what is available. Where the individual, or group, obtains a share of the total resource, the dynamics of use are different to those where the interest is in a fixed volume of the resource. Self-interest resides in maximising the size of the 'pie' – of growing the collective resource, to reduce waste, or to 'win' in repeated rounds of bargaining among interdependent resource owners. Game theory suggests that bargaining is likely to lead to winners emerging mostly through collaboration rather than cheating each other. Just as in the *Muang faai* system, mechanisms or rules of communication and negotiation will emerge among the shareholders.

---

1 Though virtual banking is available in some tradable right systems.

Fixed volume allocations reduce flexibility

To overcome some of the uncertainty of access to a natural resource, it is possible to allocate a volume (rather than a percentage) of the resource. This reflects an understandable desire of users for certainty. The behavioural effect is different to a percentage share allocation. Entitlement to fixed volume masks interdependence. The extractor has a legal right, regardless of other users or of natural capacity. Entitlement to volume effectively invites full exploitation of each person's allocation regardless of the effect on the total resource. Since natural systems are rarely sufficiently reliable to ensure that under all conditions, all entitlements will be able to be met, entitlement to a volume creates four possibilities:

1. Conflict when the total available resource is less than the sum of entitlements; or
2. Over-exploitation if the total available resource is less than the entitlements.
3. Compensation demands if the available volume is less than the allocation. This transfers risk of resource fluctuation to whoever is obliged to compensate; or
4. An incentive to under-allocate for whoever is obliged to compensate or maintain the cap, with the under-allocation as a buffer against fluctuations.

Stepped allocation methods

One method to overcome the behavioural disadvantages of volume-based sharing is to use 'stepped' allocations. This has some of the character of a volume entitlement, but partly takes into account fluctuating availability of resources. In this approach, specified environmental conditions modify the rights holder's absolute entitlement (in terms of volume, or the timing of access, or special conditions). For example, a water user may be prohibited from pumping water once the flow in the river falls below a critical level, or fishers may lose their right to fully harvest if the fish population falls below a threshold. An alternative configuration is to make the allocation contingent on certain positive conditions being met (such as lobster harvest being contingent on some measured population of adult lobsters being present). Under some regimes, compensation arrangements come into play when use prohibitions occur.

While these approaches reduce the potential for harm from a fixed entitlement, they create an artificial sense that access is constrained by rules rather than by ecological limits. The behavioural consequence can be legal and political re-bargaining, delaying adaptation to the ecological context. Rights holders become involved in 'gaming' rules and getting around limits believing they are outwitting bureaucracy rather depleting the resource. In this setting, rights holders' innovative capacity may be directed at winning access rather than increasing the sustainability of the resource.

Where the entitlement is based on a share of a resource, it is relatively simple to further protect that resource by reducing the volume that may be extracted. This increases the value of each entitlement through the automatic operation of supply and demand. Where the instrument is a fixed-volume entitlement, this volume/price adjustment is not as easy, for it involves a number of separate negotiations. To accommodate increased protection there is generally a need for some volume entitlements to be either purchased or surrendered (with or without compensation). It is far less accommodating of changes in environmental conditions.

Variations on the entitlements theme

There are many possible variations on entitlement structures. A simple, permanent entitlement, like a property right, is the form that is often recommended but contingent arrangements for entitlement can provide additional leverage.

➢ In Australia, under the Murray-Darling Basin Salinity and Drainage Strategy, trades are permitted in terms of concentration, measured in standard units. Investing in capital works to manage salt entering the river system and enhance river flow can generate these 'salt credits'. Trades are exchanged between government. Salinity has been reduced in the lower reaches of the Murray (SA) and there are plans to extend the trading rights.

➢ The Fox River (US) program allows trading between point sources with permits to discharge wastes that increase biochemical oxygen demand (BOD). Trading of rights is allowed only if the buyer is a new facility, is increasing production, or is unable to meet required discharge limits despite optimal operation of its treatment facilities.

   ➢ In December 1992, the US EPA issued final rules for the early reduction of hazardous air pollutants. If a facility qualifies for inclusion in the program by reducing hazardous air pollutants – by 90-95 per cent in the case of hazardous particulate emissions – prior to EPA proposing maximum available control technology (MACT) regulations on the source category, the facility may defer compliance with the new MACT for as long as six years. By mid-1993, over 60 chemical plants had asked to participate in the program, so they could avoid the synthetic organic chemical MACT standard for six years. Other types of facilities also had applied to join the program.

A variation of volume entitlement that overcomes some of these issues is to use time-limited rights (for example, an annual license) coupled with periodic auctions of entitlements. The level of available entitlements is adjusted to suit policy or environmental needs. Under some arrangements, every rights holder must surrender a predetermined percentage of their allocation each year, and this surrendered share may either be reallocated (perhaps by auction) or held back. The more restricted the supply, the greater will be the price of auctioned entitlements. This allows a stepped adjustment to changed environmental conditions, and does provide a high degree of legal certainty.

Where some clawback of entitlement is needed, a refinement is to link adjustments to the demonstration of behaviour that is desired. To maximise the push towards sustainability it would be possible to have a system under which rights owners who fail to achieve certain performance benchmarks will have to surrender a greater percentage of their interest than those who meet them. Those rights-holders who have been most effective in protecting the resource would retain their rights, and those who have been less efficient must surrender their interest. This can be done with or without compensation. The compensation can be in the form of a share of any auction price of whatever entitlement is available after adjustment for the needs of the environment. Given the dynamic of competition, and the economic returns from efficient use of a resource that is scarce, such an approach should be a powerful impetus for conservation.

The most important aspect of this is that with the creation of legal entitlements to a share of a natural resource and the exclusion of those who do not have that entitlement, there is immediately potential to create a dazzling array of behaviour management tools. One has only to look at the variety of derivative instruments in finance markets (insurances, swaps, options, futures and the like) to understand the opportunities for creativity once a natural resource interest becomes a financial instrument. This potential lies within every cap system that has the possibility for trading of interests. This type of approach is considered in further detail in the following discussion.

What happens where there is a cap and trading?

Cap and trade involves an allocation of a tradable interest in a resource to an owner, with the total of all allocations being kept below the target level of exploitation. Such systems are particularly useful when a natural system is potentially approaching the limits of exploitation, and when there are many exploiters causing incremental harm. Cap and trade allows direct management of the outcome – protection of the sustainability of the resource – without inhibiting the operation of the market to adjust use to the highest-value opportunities, or to stimulate innovation to reduce resource demands.

Like all cap systems, there is the opportunity to adjust the cap to meet environmental challenges or changes in policy – an important factor when there is uncertainty about the level of exploitation that the resource can sustain or when the condition of the resource varies across time periods. The more restricted the cap, the more valuable the share. The market acts to compensate (to at least some degree) the 'clawback' of available volume by an increase in the value of what remains – reducing the call for compensation that is sometimes a feature of non-tradeable caps.

In some programs there is a pre-defined cap reduction. For example, an initial level of allowable emissions to the air may be subject to a planned 5 per cent per annum reduction over a defined period. Alternatively, it may be prescribed that some set level of licences will be bought back by the issuing agency over a defined period. This was discussed above.

Tradeable entitlements

The ability of a rights-owner to trade any part of their entitlement adds another dimension to shareholder behaviour in cap markets, strengthening their incentive to conserve and innovate. The incentive exists regardless of whether the entitlement is a share or a volume, though the behavioural differences between these two approaches are relevant even with trading.

A rights owner who cannot achieve a satisfactory return from the use of the resource can trade it to another who is able to make a better economic use of that resource. Resources tend to flow to the most valued and therefore typically the most economically productive use. There is now an incentive to conserve and therefore innovate in conserving natural resources. An innovator who can improve the efficiency of their use of the resource can profit, by reducing their needs and selling the excess, or by purchasing more of that resource on which they are able to make a higher return than other resource users.

Some approaches to tradeability

Transferable Quotas in the Southern Bluefin Tuna Fishery reflect international agreements introduced in 1982, which limit catches. Quotas may be used in joint venture arrangements between operators from Australia and those from other countries. Also in Australia, the Great Barrier Reef Marine Park Authority applies an Environmental Management charge to all commercial operations in the marine park, including tourism, mariculture and commercial construction. A permit system also applies to users of the park. Some of these permits are long-term and can be transferred.

A coalition of government and private interests developed a plan to reduce phosphorus releases into the Dillon Reservoir supplying Denver in the US. Discharges from new non-point sources are restricted through regulations that require developers to show a 50 per cent reduction of phosphorus from pre-1984 norms. New non-point sources must offset all of their discharges by using a trading ratio of 1:1 with existing non-point sources. For point sources, the plan established a trading ratio of 2:1, whereby point sources that are above their allocation must obtain credits from point or non-point sources for twice the amount of the excess from sources that are below their allocation. The system would be monitored through existing national Pollution Discharge Elimination System permits for point sources.

The government of Chile grants the water right provided that a) the new water right does not impair existing rights and b) the ecological requirement of minimum flow has not yet been reached by previous right allocations. Water use rights are granted free of charge and recorded in a national register. The granting authority reserves the right to restrict water consumption in times of water shortage. Water rights are freely tradeable and the market for water rights is quite active. Water users receive price signal indicating the highest value of water on the market, thereby creating incentives to sell the water rights to the individual who places the highest value on it. Seasonal water rentals are particularly frequent within the agricultural sector. Farmers also sell or lease water rights to water supply utilities who often find such purchases less costly than the development of new sources of supply for urban or industrial use. Individual negotiations determine the price of each transaction.

A second effect is to automatically allocate resources to allow the least-cost resource-conserving alternatives to be exploited. Resource users have different abilities to reduce the environmental costs of their consumption. For example, in a new factory pollution control may cost little to establish, whereas in an older facility it will have a much higher cost. Under a trading system there is an incentive to exploit low-cost opportunities, while the higher-cost producers can purchase entitlements to allow them to stay in operation –with the higher cost of inputs to penalise them for natural resource inefficiency. This is an impetus for those who create environmental damage to innovate to reduce the total resource cost, and optimise the economic value of the resources that are consumed. Moreover, higher-cost producers may cut back production (and so resource exploitation), or cease production if their costs – including the cost of rights to exploit – exceed their revenues. This may happen when new, lower-cost entrants have bid down the price of the industry's outputs.

Writing for the *New York Times Magazine*, John Tierney provides a good example of the effectiveness of the cap and trade system:

> Because tuna were decimated by the old open system, in the 1980s the US government imposed limits on the annual catch. Now each fisherman owns what is called an individual transferable quota – the right to catch a certain percentage of the yearly haul. These quotas, which can be bought or sold like stock shares, are not cheap, so fishermen have changed their strategy. No longer able to slaughter fish at will, they have looked for ways to make the most of each fish. The result has been the world's premier tuna ranches. (Tierney 2000)

An important effect of tradability is to reduce the incentive to cheat. Instead, the strongest incentive for many is to preserve the value of entitlements. Everyone who owns an interest has a reason for making sure that everyone else stays within the rules. If anyone is able to circumvent the rules, it reduces their need to purchase entitlements, that is, reduces demand, and therefore reduces the market value of entitlements.

'Pooling' and 'bubbles'

Similar in effect to simple tradeability is a system under which a rights owner who has many activities or sites, or a group of rights owners in an area, may pool their interest. For example, a corporation may have a licence to discharge fumes for each of its factories across a region. It may be able to innovate to reduce discharges for one of its factories, but be unable to satisfy the limit for some other factory without cutting production. Under a 'bubble' approach, the corporation will be allowed to group its discharges and licences. Provided that the total of licenses exceeds the total of discharges, it will be free to operate without penalty. A similar concept would be for a community to operate a bubble for all of the factories in its area, or all of its industrial water users.

The advantage of a bubble over a trading system lies in the reduction of transaction costs, and the ability to negotiate a transition plan towards sustainability. A bubble is often part of a strategy for an industry or a region aimed at reducing the total resource-use load over an agreed period. The bubble provides a low-cost way for better scheduling and managing the transition.

Bubbles can influence behaviour in several advantageous ways. An emissions or resource-use bubble creates a shared interest in the resource, and can encourage collaboration. That collaboration can be as simple as trading, but where there are other commonalities of interest, such as similar technology or production processes, a bubble can trigger the sharing of research costs or of technical support. In the Hunter Valley, a discharge bubble scheme is in operation under which coal miners collaborate closely to optimise the discharge of contaminated mine water.

Bubbles can also be used to mitigate some social costs of market instruments. In some communities, the underlying problem is that financial returns from the use of a resource are low. The adoption of a trading instrument can result in transfer of economic opportunity outside that community. Indeed, it is possible that some market instruments introduced into some rural communities in Australia could hasten their own demise – unless they can manage the risk of resource transfers. An example of how these costs could be mitigated would be to establish a boundary for trading of water or effluent disposal rights, ensuring that no trader could export that right. This would reduce the amount of employment-generating activity that would be lost to that region.

Third, bubbles can be used to limit transferability of impact over time or space. For example, an air quality problem may be greater in an industrial area than a country area, or a pollutant problem may be more significant in low-flow rather than flood conditions. Unconstrained trading can result in emission rights moving where the impact of emissions will be greater, resulting in further high-risk concentrations. Unconstrained trading might result in one area having all of the smelters or piggeries or some other environmentally harmful (but economically important) activity concentrated in its boundaries, leading to an accumulation that could not be readily managed. A bubble might limit the ability of firms from elsewhere to trade impacts into this area.

In effect, bubbles set a boundary around a market to constrain the behaviours or the effects of competition to achieve non-economic policy goals. While this arguably reduces the economic efficiency advantage of markets, it allows social or environmental costs of this advantage to be controlled.

Can we establish a bank for environmental impacts?

Banking of funds allows borrowing and lending across time, and between individuals. Rights banking does much the same. Natural resources such as clean air, water, or wildlife stocks, change their nature and availability over time. Traditionally, we have managed natural variation by engineering, such as building structures to store resources, or to retain contaminants. However, when we start trading rights to natural resources, rather than the resources themselves, we are able to use banking (or other financial) approaches. We can borrow or lend rights, issue options over them, and otherwise treat them as if they were financial instruments.

By banking environmental entitlements, a resource user can conserve in one year to exploit in the future. For example, a factory may have the right to use 100 units of resource in any one year. If it is able to reduce its demand for that year to 50 units, under a banking arrangement it would be able to carry the saved 50 units to the following year, increasing its entitlement to 150 units. Banking systems can bring forward conservation measures by providing security in the ability to benefit from doing so.

Banking approaches can be managed in many ways. For example, it is possible for banked rights to appreciate (the next year it is allowed to emit 160 units) or depreciate (the next year it is only possible to emit 140 units) or be made conditional (it is only possible to use the banked entitlement if the total of all other entitlements is less than 500 units). The arrangements can accommodate changes to timing and magnitude of environmental adjustments, and smooth out fluctuations.

How might tradeable credits limit consumption?

Capped allocations are useful to control an accumulation of diffuse harms, where the harm is approaching a definable critical point. Some resource issues are not like that. For example, a strategic goal might be to encourage improvements in environmental performance but it is not possible to establish a credible cap level, perhaps because of unreliable data or limits to the available knowledge. Or perhaps there are political barriers to establishing a cap, such as an industry group that will continue to oppose any realistic cap. Under a credit scheme, each potential harm-doer is issued a right for a level of harm – a quota to emit or extract. Where the aim is to stimulate improvement in environmental performance, that credit is set in line with best-practice use of the environment. To illustrate, best practice might mean an emission of 1 tonne of contaminant for every 10 tonnes of production. In an industry with 10,000 tonnes production, it would be possible to issue a total of 1,000 tonnes worth of credits, allocated on the basis of historical production figures. Provided credit holders stay within quota, they continue their activity unhindered. If they want to go beyond that level, they incur a penalty, or buy credits from rights-holders who stay below their quota by either operating efficiency or lower production. In some instances, the control on exceeding the quota is not a fine, but loss of access to the resource; for example, automatic loss of license to emit or to extract once they exceed the available credits in their quota.

Credits programs ensure that the harm to the environment remains below that which would apply if every user went beyond the acceptable harm. To set this level one would multiply the individual-use quotas by the total number of users and verify that this is below the acceptable level of environmental harm or resource demand. Those users who are able to do better than the benchmark level can sell credits to those who cannot reach the standards. They profit from their better management, and have an incentive to innovate to further reduce harm. Depending on the price of the credits, users of resources who might cause greater harm than their credit allows have a strong incentive to reduce the harm because otherwise they will have to buy credits, or incur the penalty.

The program depends on the regulator ensuring that the credit-allocation approach has integrity: The benchmark should be scientifically credible, and result in an acceptable net load on the environment; the system to ensure that the allocations are recorded and enforced must be accurate to maintain the confidence of buyers and sellers; and the regulator must set a sufficiently high price for exceeding the allocation to ensure an incentive to reduce the impacts or purchase credits at a high enough price to create a market for impact reduction.

It is not necessary for a regulator to operate the market. If the underlying constraint is credible and tight enough to create an economic reason to trade, a market should evolve. However, that does not preclude the government – or other regulator – from facilitating the market by setting up a trading mechanism or by providing incentives to improve resource management.

It may be possible, for example, to use a system of credits to control pollution into a water-supply catchment. A traditional regulatory approach would ban activities that could reduce water quality, or impose contamination prevention requirements, which restricts commercial activities of all landowners. Proposals for high impact activities – such as a feedlot, an abattoir, or a polluting factory – would probably be prohibited. But under a credits scheme, these uses can be balanced. If the proponents of the high-impact activity can show savings in contamination elsewhere (and there is a sufficient profit to justify the purchase of the required credits), they would be able to proceed. The result is relatively low-value environmental harms replaced by relatively high-value environmental harms, but within the limits of the total available credits.

'Green' offsets

A variation of the credits arrangement is to allow a resource user to compensate by an equivalent or better 'saving' of the same type of harm elsewhere. For example, if a developer under an offsets program wanted to destroy a wetland to put in place housing, then the developer would have to find a roughly equivalent area of degraded wetland elsewhere to restore or protect as an offset.

Offset arrangements in practice

In some designs, the offsetting obligation can involve long-term management, which can provide a financial basis for work elsewhere to protect or rehabilitate. This can provide an economic incentive for other resource owners to (for a fee) manage for conservation the offset resource. For example, in the US, farmers contract with developers to establish or manage wetlands on their property for conservation, as an offset to wetlands that will be removed by developers on their land.

Offsets have also been used to require electrical generators to offset air pollution by (for example) buying back old polluting motorcars. This is not only a cost-effective way of reducing pollution without adverse impacts on energy production; it also has other benefits, enabling greater recycling and discouraging dumping of old vehicles.

The advantage of offset schemes is that they generally attempt to replace like with like.[2] If it is native vegetation or air quality that is harmed, then native vegetation or air quality will be the form of replacement.

The disadvantage of offset schemes is that they do not lend themselves to the same kinds of market flexibility as other market instruments. Consequently, they do not offer the same benefits of innovation and compensation. It is important for the regulator to design the scheme to ensure that the responsibility for ongoing achievement of the desired outcome stays with the harm-doer, and not the regulator. The default cost

---

2 There is a scheme in Germany that allows offsets to be made across different classes of environmental harm, but this seems to be an exception.

of failure should remain with the private beneficiary of the offset. For example, the regulator could require that harm-doers identify the offset, guarantee the outcomes over time, and report on the performance.

Another issue regulators consider before deciding on an offsets program is that of equivalence. Ecosystems are not alike. One wetland will not be the same as another; old growth forests are not the same as new growth forests. This is a drawback when the private beneficiary seeks to replace a complex natural system (like a wetland or an old-growth habitat) with an artificial substitute. The new is not a complete equivalent to the old. To promote a system that treats all ecosystems as if they were the same would contribute to the incremental degradation of the environment. Offsets, therefore, operate better when the physical characteristics of the environment being 'traded' can be precisely specified and adequately replaced.

Some more advanced designs require that the offset be leveraged by a larger amount of conservation than the amount of harm. It is possible to require that the loss of one acre of pristine wetland be compensated with 5 acres of regenerated wetland, or 10 acres of artificial wetland, if that greater volume is necessary to ensure some ecosystem equivalence. Leverage can also provide a strong disincentive from developers treating the higher quality resource in a cavalier fashion. The greater the cost of the offset, the greater incentive there will be to protect the original ecosystem.

Regulation of market rights

Both cap and trade and credits regimes work on the basis that the harm prevented is due to accumulation from a range of sources. If the harm done is of such a critical nature that it absolutely cannot be permitted (such as release of toxins into a drinking catchment) then prohibition becomes the tool of choice.

Prohibitions have some basic processes: rules are set; an inspection system is established; a breach of rules is detected; and a penalty is imposed. Usually we implement this process through an agency of government, but it can also be provided through the market – as long as the parties are identifiable – by using contracts. Generally contracts describe behaviours that will result in a termination of the contract or a financial penalty. For example, it is common for apartment buildings to have leases (contracts) that prohibit pets. In the case of market instruments, as with any type of contract, it is possible for the parties to define and proscribe (or penalise) virtually any behaviour that they consider objectionable. It would be possible to create requirements that parties to a trade all be certified under some collective standard of natural resource management, or that purchasers of an interest use it only under certain conditions (thereby further restricting the formal legal entitlement). It is not the case that once a market instrument is created, the ability to regulate is bypassed. In many ways the potential for regulation is increased by the addition of the possibility of private regulation on top of public regulation.

Civil courts have a long history of upholding contracts. The language of contracts is somewhat different from that of regulations – penalties are damages rather than fines – and so are community attitudes. Generally we seem to more readily accept penalties or pricing attached to contracts than license fees attached to regulations. The potential for private regulation by contract replacing public regulation through legislation exists along with any creation of private market instruments. This potential contains many possibilities for stronger natural resource conservation within a private markets context, and this is discussed further in Chapter 7.

The effects of transaction costs

Transactions can make a potential market unworkable if they are too costly or difficult. They can change the dynamic of that market so that it either penalises or rewards pro-sustainability action. Any instrument design should directly address how the market will operate and how the transaction costs will be used (along with price) to secure the desired outcome.

Transaction costs occur in five aspects of the buy-and-sell process:

1. *Specification*: Where there is room for dispute about what has been bought or sold, then parties invest in specification, or the party who is acquiring will bear the risk that they have not got what they paid for.
2. *Ensuring security*: If it is possible for some other party or the State to dislodge the owner, then the owner will factor in that risk in the price they are prepared to pay, or take on some other expense – such as insurance or some other transaction to accommodate the risk.
3. *Finding transacting parties*: If it is easy to find counter-parties to participate in the transaction, then competition can work well. If counter-parties are difficult to find, the value of the transaction will have to be great to justify the efforts and delay involved, and competition will be weak in the market.
4. *Term setting*: If bargaining of terms is involved, transacting costs increase. Standard terms reduce the costs, provided they do not introduce other transaction costs such as uncertainty, or reduction of the value of the interest that is being sold. Standard terms are often a by-product of the creation of tradeable rights through legislation.
5. *Efficient logistics*: the logistics costs of some transactions – for example, transport – can be disproportionate. This is particularly the case when the transactions are intermittent; the parties are far apart,

where the documentation is complex, and where physical handling is cumbersome. A logistics system – such as a specialised transport system backed by automated processes – can have a marked effect on the economics of transaction. Innovations in logistics are important to recycling initiatives such as extended producer responsibility for batteries or oil, or recycling of printer cartridges.

Market programs that do not appropriately factor in transactions costs can be doomed to failure. If transactions costs outweigh the potential for gain, then the net effect will be that no one will use the market.

Transaction costs can be a tool

Manipulating transactions costs can be useful to promote certain activities and discourage others in a market. It is possible to decrease transaction costs for beneficial transactions; increase transaction costs for harmful transactions; and ensure that transaction costs are allocated to discourage transactions that will be harmful.

For example, if a resource such as a wetland has the potential to be exploited for mineral content but the ownership tenure is insecure, then it is less likely that a buyer will be found to take up the mining opportunity.[3] The transaction cost will limit exploitation. However, security can also have the effect of bringing forward consumption, with harmful effects on the environment. If a person anticipates that the opportunity to exploit a particular resource may be taken away, there is an incentive to harvest the maximum value today, perhaps to extinction or exhaustion. This dynamic reportedly arose with broad-acre clearing in NSW and Queensland as a result of fear of regulations to prevent that clearing.

Another strategy may be to make interests more contestable on the basis of the environmental performance of the rights holder (increasing uncertainty for those who are unprepared to meet the requirements of best environmental management practice). It is increasingly normal for government land leases to include environmental management criteria for renewal thereby increasing the risk for those failing to manage sustainably. The aim is to ensure that those who wish to exploit resources are forced to compete not only on price but also on reduction of risk to the environment. To some degree this is what is done with the requirements for Environmental Impact Statements (EIS) for major developments. A person wishing to carry out a transaction with potential environmental impact is provided with a strong incentive to put forward the least harmful means they can find to exploit the opportunity in their EIS even before they begin any development. The community is able to debate this and the resource owner's ability to secure the opportunity depends upon the

---

[3] Or the price for that resource will be discounted. This reduces the incentive to sell, but also provides a profit potential for a risk-taking buyer to purchase and overcome the barrier to their profit.

outcome. From the point of view of the intending developer this entire process is a transaction cost, but it is one that creates pressure at the design stage to build in environmental safeguards. This is a trigger for the exercise of private sector initiative to protect the environment, and for rapid uptake of best design practices as these emerge.

Allocating interests

In his seminal 1960 article in the *Journal of Law and Economics*, 'The Problem of Social Cost', Ronald Coase argued that over time (assuming low transaction costs) rights will come to be allocated in ways that will optimise use of the resource. But this is true only if initial allocations have been properly considered. Initial allocations shape power in the market, and also have consequences for fairness.

If policy makers are attempting to gain short-term efficiency, there is a strong case to make allocations along more or less pre-existing patterns of use of the resource. Existing users will have the capital and knowledge needed to productively use the resource, and there will be limited dislocation. If policy makers are attempting to rapidly achieve a shift from less to more productive uses of the resource, then there is an argument that they should use auctions or some other bid process, through which those who value the resource most will pay the most for their interest. If the aim is to achieve an environmental outcome, we should leave a sufficient margin for the environment and ensure that competition for the resource is focused around efficiency of resource conservation rather than profit alone. Or if the aim is to achieve social equity – such as recognition of Aboriginal people's interest in natural resources – then we should build in those aims in the allocation approach we use.

The eventual choice of a particular market tool is political as well as economic. Arguably, since the resource is likely to end up being controlled by the most productive users in the long run, conservatism is probably a waste of opportunity to use allocations to further other social and environmental objectives through the operation of markets. Allocating entitlements to the less advantaged is a more radical opportunity to achieve social goals as well as environmental aims.

VOICE OF EXPERIENCE: TRADING

Mike Young is arguably Australia's most experienced developer and implementer of market based instruments for sustainability. He is an advisor to governments at all levels, and has been the progenitor of many market instrument programs. We asked him to consider the case of a catchment authority trying to find a way of protecting some remaining biodiversity.

What would Mike ask them to think about in creating such a strategy?

I would ask 'Why is the remaining bushland still there?' It may not be necessary to do anything to protect the bush – At least, not until the current manager sells his property. Once you understand why the bush is still there, you are in a better position to understand what could lead to loss, and therefore to be clear about what actions may be required.

My second question would be 'How urgent is it to act?' I would like to be clear about the nature of the triggers that could alter how things are now, and lead to loss. I would then begin to consider a series of approaches, depending on the situation.

What sort of approaches would you consider?

Where the resource is slowly eroding, I would want to deal first with protecting what remains. For example, if biodiversity is threatened because it now only remains in isolated pockets, I would begin by asking what sort of incentive will it take for landowners to replant and create corridors. The incentives would be quite specifically targeted to the action and the behaviour that is needed.

I would also ask myself 'is there a way of implementing this that will not impact on our budget?' It may be possible to use tradeoffs, offsets or even other existing programs to create the incentive without draining the catchment board's budget. Tender schemes might enable you to get a greater return for the available budget.

I am aware that you have made a point of using conventional institutional structures in the design of market instruments. How might this be relevant to the design of a strategy?

I would be very concerned to ensure that the structure will last for a very long time. If you are dealing with biodiversity, then the time frames are measured in tens and hundreds of years. Property ownership turns over around every ten years. The mechanism has to continue to be effective even with many different owners. That is why I am attracted to instruments that attach to land titles, such as conservation covenants. You have to protect the value of past work, as well as creating new work, if you want to deliver value.

Covenants provide long-term legal protection and can be underpinned by an agreement to supply financial assistance.

We asked Mike about where and how transaction costs might play a part in design.

From the perspective of a catchment authority, there are two types of transaction cost. The first type relate to the costs of collecting the information needed to implement a scheme. The second type of transaction cost are those associated with negotiating and implementing agreements.

There can be a serious problem with the costs of information collection. If you do not design your information and monitoring processes carefully, it is easy to spend hundreds of thousands of dollars on monitoring and mapping, and have no resource left to protect. I would suggest that the authority consider a risk-based approach rather than a data intensive approach. They might decide to use detailed monitoring only in selected, very vulnerable instances, and rely upon broader decision criteria for the rest of the landscape.

I have seen instances where the pursuit of the ideal database has resulted in lots of reports and study but no change on the ground. This is not an effective approach. The authority should also think about how information can be cost-effectively shared, so that maximum value is achieved.

The second type of transaction cost involves two parties. The authority and the landholder as they negotiate an agreement. The authority has a manpower budget, but so too does the landowner or manager. If the process takes too long it may fail. If deciding upon and reaching agreement means that decisions have to go up the line, and back and forth, then the approach is not well designed. It should be possible for the person sitting across the table to finalise an agreement. If there are long delays you will lose many landowners and the program will get a bad reputation.

It is preferable if a manager on the ground has the power to negotiate quickly, reach agreement, and sign off on that agreement. They have to have authority to deal. Too many checks simply mean that the design has not been carefully thought through, and people will walk away from the program.

Are there other transaction issues that an authority needs to think about?

Measurement of performance is a vexing question. While it is theoretically desirable to pay or control on the basis of outcomes (like species counts), this is very costly to everyone. It can also lead to some abuses, like a landowner starting an 'accidental' fire to explain the reason for species loss so that they are not penalised for loses more correctly attributed to poor grazing practice.

Input measures, like management practices, are far easier to supervise, and less costly to enforce. They are not perfect but, in many cases, may be more practical. They can be enforced at lower costs.

What sort of payment principles would you suggest?

I have a concern about schemes that pay people for things that they would have done any way. Incentive payments should be based on the marginal cost of doing extra work, not as compensation for work already done. Similarly, one needs to consider how much is paid for work that would have been done whether or not the incentive was offered. One also needs to think very carefully about the amount of work that an incentive program stops. Without a program, people may be prepared to act. As soon, as a program is put in place, these same people may decide not to act.

There is a need to think carefully about how to obtain the maximum leverage in the design of a program. I have already mentioned offsets, or using existing grant schemes.

With close cooperation with local government (for example) it may be possible to allow a landowner who protects one area, to increase use in another. Provided that these tradeoffs are embedded in permanent legal structures like covenants, there can be great value at low cost.

What about combining instruments? Or using instruments and other approaches together?

I always look for a suite of instruments. It is a mistake to believe that everyone is the same and that they will respond to the same signals and incentives. Unless you have an unlimited budget, you need to be able to target what you offer, using a mixture of rebates, tax benefits, offsets and the like.

You can make use of a competitive tender approach, to get the maximum value from limited funds for problems that are widespread. You also need to make sure you retain some of your funding for targeted hot spots. In general, I tend to advocate a mixed approach that relies upon access to a powerful toolkit full of a wide array of instruments, and to be flexible in how you go about hitting your targets.

Mike places economic interventions within a context of other social approaches designed to ensure that community values support the market instruments, and provide an additional buffer against harming special places and environmental assets.

There are other actions I would want the authority to consider. It is important to have a strategy to ensure that the community values the asset, and is aware that they have something special to protect. This can create social pressure to ensure responsible management. You might, for example, make a serious effort to publicly promote and reward the work of those who are actively protecting the remaining biodiversity. Prizes and awards can play a very important part of an effective strategy. Making a positive example of the best managers and celebrating what they are doing and why, can be powerful in ensuring that the community will back biodiversity protection. If the community does not understand or value biodiversity, then they will not understand why protection is important.

As well as prizes and awards, you may involve local societies and groups in a field day that celebrates the area and the good work of those trying to restore or protect it. You want to make sure that people are aware, and value what they have.

Similarly you may work with local government, to have them recognise the value of what you are trying to protect, perhaps with the use of rebates or some forms of development offset.

What would be your overall advice in designing and implementing a program?

Don't try to get it 100 per cent right. Aim to get it (Say) 70 per cent right, but to get it implemented. Make progress and then revise in the light of experience. The scientists and maybe the bureaucrats will see the risks, and will push for higher degrees of perfection, but this can result in you being five years later in getting something into the field. If you can trial and design on the run, then this may be better than trying to get an abstract design perfect.

Biodiversity conservation is not a precise science. Mostly it is about people, and about winning their cooperation. Focus on that.

Chapter 6

PROPERTY RIGHTS

The discussion of markets and rights instruments in the preceding two chapters brings with it a spectre that is disconcerting for many environmentalists. This is the spectre of increased privatisation and an over-reliance on the market, named 'property rights'. Like Banquo's ghost, this needs to be acknowledged and addressed if we are to move towards solutions. This chapter aims to dismiss some of the myths and to consider the issues associated with property rights.

Property rights are the essential ingredient of capitalism. The excesses of capitalism are the root causes of environmental destruction and it is hard to imagine that the same destructive private capital tools can be used to modify the harm that has been caused. By the same token, capitalism (coupled with science) has shown itself more than capable of delivering radical innovation and spectacular efficiency improvement. The problem is that the direction of these energies has been towards ever-increased consumption and not towards responsible custodianship of the earth.

The term 'property rights' describes a range of legal interests in things (tangible or intangible) through which rights holders can exclude others and expect society to back up that exclusion. Property rights commonly refer to full ownership with complete rights of exclusion, transfer and use. However, a right to use but not transfer, or a right to share use with others, is still a property right even though it is less than full ownership. In political usage the concept is overlaid by the expectation that property rights should be or are un-attenuated (complete and beyond direct political interference) with expectations of compensation should the rights be reduced. This concept is a legal myth but politically potent. The reality is that the legal extent of property rights can vary widely. Property is always a matter of degree.

In a strict sense, property rights are community, individual, or organisational interests in goods and services that the law (society) will protect. All ownership is a construct of society, constrained through government. The same political structure that defines and protects property also constrains it. A property interest is limited at least to the degree of not overlapping the interests of other property owners. Property responds to social changes with rights being created and changed over time. Examples of recently created property include moral rights for artists (the right to have the integrity of a creative work respected even after it is sold), intellectual property in plants; and (in some societies) ownership of one's genetic information.

Property rights are powerful because of the beliefs that support them. It is normal for people to respect ownership and other's rights to property. It is rare for people to consciously violate these interests, and when this occurs the police or the courts restrain the abuse, but intervention is relatively rare. The beliefs, rather than the law, make day-to-day use of property efficient and relatively harmonious.

The nature of property rights

Beliefs about property do not always align with legal definitions. Legally, property rights are defined by whatever legal instruments create and govern that right. Typically this will be a mixture of contracts and statutes. In the case of land the property-owner's interest is defined by their purchase, coupled with any use regulations and zonings that exist from time to time. The property rights cover the natural attributes of the land, transferred through contract and specified through the Crown. As society's regulations change, the property owner's right automatically shifts. Real property in many jurisdictions does not transfer the right to the sub-surface minerals, which remain with the Crown, nor does a right to the water flowing across land go with title to the land. These things have over time been removed from the property owners' interests as society has seen the need to do so. This is analogous to a property boundary being defined by a river – as the river shifts its banks the property boundary also shifts – the extent of the ownership but not its existence is affected.

Jurisprudence reflects a history of growth of transaction types and tradeable interests, which has accompanied fragmentation of bundles of rights into distinct interests. Entitlements such as riparian rights attached unwritten qualifications to the freeholder's title. Subsidiary interests such as leases and options emerged, subordinate to freehold but with similar structures and obligations. Rights to other forms of property, such as cultural rights, followed a different path, being largely the creature of treaties and common law.

The current property rights system is made up of rights created by contract and the Crown, by common law and by international treaty. It continues to evolve and the overlap of interests and rights and competing legal system requirements is a source of complexity and conflict.

Governments create new types of property by legislation, and create constraints on access or use of valued resources. The argument is sometimes made that government should not interfere with property. Government will always change the boundaries of property, creating and removing interests. Indeed if this did not occur then it would be almost impossible to create new transaction types for environmental, social or economic purposes. The changing boundaries of property are not an insurmountable problem in markets, provided that there are sufficient perceived gains from trading to overcome any political uncertainty. If property right uncertainty were a barrier to markets then it is hard to explain the way in which markets have evolved over the centuries in the face of uncertainty caused by the rights of the Crown, or by the exercise of power by the strong. If unconstrained rights were a precondition to the trading of property, then buying and selling of land would never have emerged during the periods when all land was held at the will of the king.

Nevertheless, since the value that the rights holder has depends on the extent of their interest and is greater in the absence of uncertainty, there is always pressure to extend the boundaries of that interest, and to remove uncertainty about rights to exploit. This is best understood as an issue of pragmatics rather than high principle, regardless of the high-blown language that is sometimes used.

Protection of property rights

The market incentive for private conservation of resources, and the pursuit of innovation to reduce demands on resources, lies in the expectation of future profit. The greater that expected profit, and the greater the likelihood of it being secured, the greater is that incentive. This is an argument for strong private rights to resources.

Rights holders have an interest in strong mechanisms to protect or extend their rights, to control resource access by those who do not have formal rights, and to limit other people's entitlement (thereby increasing the value of their rights). In effect, their interest is to 'freeze' one set of interests (theirs) as paramount to all others (the rest of the community). That interest is at the heart of the argument for property rights and its extension, and leads to a number of misconceptions about property rights and the environment.

The following discussion addresses two of these misconceptions: the supremacy of private property over common property in controlling degradation of the environment; and the need for unattenuated property rights to provide incentives for innovation and resource conservation.

Must common property lead to tragedy?

The total loss of trees on Easter Island, and the extinction of large land birds on New Zealand with the coming of the Maori and then European settlers highlight the danger of sharing a resource without effective rules to limit harvesting, as technological improvement and population pressure improve harvesting capacity and demand. The behavioural effect, unless other structures are in place, is increased competition to consume rather than conserve – a dynamic referred to as the 'tragedy of the commons'.

Garrett Hardin published an article on the tragedy of the commons in 1968 in the journal *Science* that has had a significant influence on the discussion and study of property. He explained the tragedy of the commons as the situation where each person has an incentive to exploit the resource more rapidly than any other, to obtain the maximum of what is available before it runs out.[1] His arguments have lead to a myth that common property regimes must lead to degradation of the commons because those using the commons will maximise their gains without regard to the needs of others including future users. This myth confuses common property with an open-access regime.

Bromley provides a useful distinction of the different types of property regimes. Note that each type of property regime has rights attached, but the rights attach to different groups or individuals within society:

- **State property:** Individuals have a duty to observe use/access rules determined by controlling/managing agency. Agencies have the right to determine use/access rules.
- **Private property:** Individuals have the right to undertake socially acceptable uses, and have a duty to refrain from socially unacceptable uses. Others (called 'non-owners') have a duty to refrain from preventing socially acceptable uses, and have a right to expect that only socially acceptable uses will occur.
- **Common property:** The management group (the 'owners') have a right to exclude non-members, and non-members have a duty to abide by the exclusion. Individual members of the management group (the 'co-owners') have both rights and duties with respect to use rates and maintenance of the thing owned.
- **Non property:** No defined group of users or 'owners' and benefit stream is available to anyone. Individuals have both privilege and no right with respect to use rates and maintenance of the asset. The asset is an 'open access resource'. (Bromley 1991: 31)

Common property is demonstrably effective in some societies, including our own. The corporation is a common property structure that effectively manages resources and wealth production. One key to its success is the quality of the internal rules that govern how the common property is managed. Unlike open-access regimes, good common property arrangements define:

- Who the members of the group are; the rules of agreement (unanimity, consensus or majority);
- The basis of right over time (annual or seasonal rights);
- Transmission of rights between generations;
- The unit of control (community board, village, district elders, households, or other entity);

---

1 While widely accepted, there are strong critiques of Hardin's observations of the Tragedy of the Commons, both in terms of historical validity (Berkes 1989) and practical implications (Ojwang 1996).

- Means for maintaining compliance with agreed rules and conventions;
- How departures from rules are to be correction and sanctions imposed; and
- How disputes are settled.

There are many ways in which societies have organised rights of access to common property, including ethical codes or religious practice which limit exploitation or require resource sharing by those who exploit; rules and sanctions against over-exploitation or inequitable allocation; and specialised functions where the role carries the capacity to control exploitation, coupled with custodianship skills and beliefs.

In a Western capitalist society, many of these elements are embodied in private property. Our belief system includes respect for property and sanctions for breach of that respect. Property ownership incorporates the exclusion of others to allow the owner long-term use of property. It is not that common property is an unworkable system, but rather that society has evolved such a commitment to private ownership that systems based on the sharing of interests seem 'strange' or confusing.

> **Effective common property regimes**
>
> In 1989, Gibbs and Bromley pointed out that a well-functioning common property regime is distinguished by:
>
> ➤ *Efficiency* – A minimum (or absence) of disputes and limited effort to maintain compliance – the regime will be efficient;
>
> ➤ *Stability* – A capacity to cope with changes through adaptation, such as the arrival of new production techniques;
>
> ➤ *Resilience* – A capacity to accommodate shocks; and
>
> ➤ *Equity* – A shared perception of fairness with respect to inputs and outcomes. (Gibbs and Bromley 1989: 27)
>
> Common property can be an effective means for allocating and conserving resources. It offers potential benefits over private property when interdependence is a fact of social existence and resource use. Its disadvantage lies in the potential for high transaction costs unless strong social self-sanctions exist.

Must property rights be 'unconditional'?

The second misconception is that for market instruments to work, property rights must not be subject to conditions that may reduce the ability of the owner to deal freely with that property.[2] The argument goes

---

2 A property right subject to conditions is attenuated.

that if rights holders feel their 'rights' cannot be protected, or that in future what they conserve will be taken away from them, their incentive is to maximise short-term use and to discount the value of future use. The result is harm to the resource.

This argument flies in the face of modern (as well as historical) reality. In a world where 'derivatives' such as options, futures, swaps and other interests are happily traded, it is hard to see how the argument can hold. Options, future, swaps and the like are based on an acceptance of risk and uncertainty. Options, for example, are a market tool enabling a person to acquire a right today to acquire ownership over some asset in the future. Option-holders take the risk that the resource will be of less value than the exercise price when the time comes to pay. If the resource is less valuable than the exercise price, then the options-owner will either have to forego his opportunity to exercise, or lose money in exercising. This kind of risk is justified if the gamble has a high potential return relative to the risk. There are also options where the exercise is contingent on some event outside the control of the parties, such as an option to purchase a property subject to rezoning.

The doctrinaire argument against attenuation also flies in the face of history. As noted above, the Crown has always had the right to take away any property interest. This has not prevented the development of the institution of property, nor to have prevented active markets, resource conservation, and all of the other behaviours which some claim can follow only from un-attenuated property interests. Market instruments will provide an incentive (to trade or conserve) when the perceived degree of opportunity to win resources, factoring in the perceived risk of not being able to realise that opportunity, is greater than the total cost (including the transaction costs), bearing in mind other opportunities that are available. Because the political risk that government will prevent the entrepreneur from realising their profit is sometimes perceived more adversely than some other risks, it may be desirable to reduce the possibility of government intervention to increase the perceived value, but this is far from a precondition to the effectiveness of market instruments.

Adaptability or absolute certainty

Nevertheless, agencies with the responsibility for creating market instruments tend to be influenced by the argument for absolute certainty. This pushes the debate towards full property rights, rather than triggering a more complex debate about relative incentives and costs of different forms of attenuation. This may be a serious mistake. The challenge of sustainability is about inter-dependence. Western property theory evolved under conditions of resource abundance where individuals could exercise their interest with relatively little impact on their neighbours. The modern challenge is to manage resources where impact on others and future generations is a real concern. Attempts to embed un-attenuated rights may inhibit innovation in recognising and managing that collective responsibility and interdependence.

The RCDM highlights that when looking at decision-making in society we are not dealing with fixed rules and principles. The game is fluid, and the ways in which it can be played infinitely variable. Property rights are a political institution to regulate the balance between the interest of owners and society's need to restrict activities that diminish the common wealth. As the social context changes and new resource challenges emerge, pressures will be reflected in the politics of property:

> [F]ull exercise of private property rights is now virtually impossible in an ecosystem setting. Air, water, inorganic and organic substances, and biota simply cannot be prevented from moving onto, off, or across one's property. Ecological 'neighbours', some as far as thousands of kilometers away adversely affect these migrant ecosystemic components that in turn affect what is ostensibly private property in some locale. The more intense and/or numerous such adverse systemic interconnections, the less complete will be the package of property rights in practice, if not in theory. Thus the 'dimensionality' of the domain of private property/closed access is caused to shrink with ecosystemic degradation. (Regier, Mason et al 1989: 115)

They highlight that things that are the subject of rights are in themselves not constant. Our understanding of them changes, and our valuation of them changes. There is a growing awareness of the inter-dependence of natural resources. For example, we now know that barriers like dams prevent fish swimming upstream to spawn, reducing the sustainability of marine fish resources. With increased knowledge of ecological inter-dependence, there is a growing emphasis on custodianship, sometimes attached to land and sometimes to cultural property. There is a reconsideration of the duties of property owners that attach alongside their rights. As the concept of environmental responsibility has taken hold, it has become important for rights owners to present themselves as responsible. There is also a reconsideration of what is valuable. For example, as the extent of unexploited natural areas diminish, there is increased interest in the non-exploitation of remaining areas.

Fortunately for the market system, our way of attributing or creating rights can also change. Flexibility in the definition of property interests provides us tools for managing changing social conditions. Market solutions have been created for a number of environmental problems by 'fraction-ing' natural values to enable market transactions. Carbon credit trading, tradeable water rights, fibre futures, SO_2 and NO_x emission rights, fishing quotas and licenses, and other property-like developments are emerging as solutions for otherwise intractable natural resource management problems. The process of creating tradeable fractions of the natural system will increase, as governments seek to create solutions that are not dependent on public funds.

Who bears the risk of change?

These observations about misconceptions about property rights lead us to a number of conclusions:

1. Real (land) property rights are the core of the tradition of property, but they do not define its boundaries. Within the concept of property are many fractions of interest spanning natural and cultural values of the environment. Increasingly, these fractions are being unbundled and managed and transacted as distinct classes of property.
2. New trading and economic instruments are emerging to meet economic and policy requirements. These deal increasingly with small fractions of the physical world, are traded internationally, and have significant aggregate economic value even thought the value per unit may be low.
3. Technology is a part of these developments, including new management, processing, measuring and trading innovations that make trading opportunities and markets feasible.
4. Politics is unavoidable in property rights. Property is a political concept. This encompasses both electoral politics and broader aspects of competing human interests embedded in the title owners.
5. Rights to physically exploit are the heart of traditional property institutions. Realisation of the physical limits to sustainable use, and cultural values attached to the physical world, and making exploitation more politically and legally contestable. Modern property institutions are increasingly concerned with non-exploitation and non-tangible values as part of the natural resource management mix.

Owners of interests in natural resources will naturally seek certainty, and as the context becomes less certain they will value this highly. Counter to this, as the pressures on the resources become more intense, society will value its flexibility more highly.

There is also a contest between those with a legally-recognised interest and those without. Resource users who are not rights holders have an interest in thwarting legal mechanisms that control their access. Creation of a rights-holder class has the effect of creating an interest in effective control, but simultaneously creates a class who have an interest in its subversion. The intensity of this competition will depend upon the price of access, perceived value to the excluded users and the ability to effectively implement exclusion.

Property is the battle-ground on which such economic, social equity and sustainability contests are being acted out. The desire to fix certain interests and to take them outside of this volatile arena is understandable. But from a systems perspective it is unrealistic and potentially dangerous.

Freezing one part of a dynamic system under pressure will always result in increased pressures and unexpected, typically undesirable results elsewhere in the system.

Compensation

Central to debates about property rights is the extent of the exclusiveness of the rights of the owners. Owners expect courts to exclude non-owners and to facilitate compensation if others cause harm to their property. What is more contentious is whether, and when, the right of owners should override the ability of government (which is the source and guardian of their interests) to adjust their interests. It is often unclear what compensation government should provide if it impinges on owners' interest.

In the US, compensation arguments have high status and operate within a framework of the unique US constitution. The constitution emerged from the US War of Independence – the heart of that conflict was resentment on the part of Americans at being taxed (deprived of property) to support a government not of their own making. The US constitution includes strong prohibitions against the taking of property without compensation, and this prohibition has been extended by American courts imbued with a strong philosophical commitment to defending the citizen against the government. Compensation arguments in Australia do not have the same legal, constitutional basis,[3] but still have political power. There are many property owners who believe that a similar sanctity of property should (or does) apply in Australia.

The strength of some peoples' beliefs about the sanctity of property gives rise to political pressure to protect this perceived right, which is translated into political action. This can result in demands that a particular state of interests (the current property right regime) should be entrenched and not changed without compensation. The effect of an entrenched right to compensation would be to increase the public costs of change and innovation, but to decrease some private costs of reforms that impact on property.

Advocates for compensation argue that this is desirable as it provides incentives for private conservation and also because of the dictates of fairness. They argue that a failure to compensate means that individuals bear an undue share of the cost of the collective good.

---

[3] The Australian constitution does give a limited version of a right to compensation for Commonwealth acquisition under s 51(xxxi) which requires acquisition of property on just terms. This limited right has been supported by a broad interpretation of the legal meaning of property, but falls well short of the US constitutional protection of private interests.

Arguments against a property-based approach

This argument about individual interests needs to be balanced against arguments about the needs of the community. Compensation from the state comes from the pool of taxation revenues. Any claim on this pool competes against all others, including other equity claims such as health, education, or pensions. It also competes against claims like support for economic growth (including infrastructures and subsidies for resource use industry) and national interests like defence. There is a strong argument for compensation for reduction of property interests, but it cannot be debated properly except as a claim against the common purse along with all of the other claims that need to be met. To frame the argument for compensation from government as a legal rights issue is to overstate it.

Compensation does provide an incentive for cooperation and may reduce some adverse economic impacts of adjustments towards sustainability. In Australia, this is a particularly important consideration when trying to reconcile the competing policy aims of supporting the rural economy while imposing restrictions to protect the environment from the adverse effects of some farming activity.

Part of the political impetus for strong property rights (particularly for rural resources like water or freedom to clear or use land or other resources) is the belief that better specification of these rights must lead to more generous payments for loss of use of a resource or constraints on that use. Those who fear that their use privileges will be taken away in the process of pursuing sustainability are attracted to an approach that might provide them financial compensation. This may reflect a misperception of legal compensation. Compensation is based on valuing what is lost, and requiring payment of this amount to the party who has lost the interest. Unless required to by legislation, courts can not pay a social adjustment or political risk premium. The low economic returns achieved by many Australian resource managers (for example, farmers, miners) suggests that the financial returns they would achieve from rights-based compensation may be less than could be obtained from a political adjustment mechanism. One has only to look at the approach to selective subsidisation of exiting sugar-growing to see how powerful claims for compensation can be when attached to politically marginal electorates, rather than to the economic value of production. If the political value of votes is higher than the economic value of resource use, then moving from a political to a legal valuation of loss of use rights may reduce compensation.

Will a change in venue from the political arena to the courts assist those who are seeing 'property' and 'rights' as the key to a better deal? It seems likely that it will provide more work for lawyers, but it is far from certain that it will make the situation better for these resource users. We have witnessed the inefficiencies of the explosion of liability actions as a means of achieving desired social outcomes (risk management). There is no guarantee that turning to property right litigation to protect use rights or to compensation will serve any better. If property rights advocates believe that the courts will value their interests more highly than the political system will, the pursuit of more rigid rights definitions may make sense. If not, then reliance on this approach may need further thought.

This argument does not downplay the importance of ownership, trading and compensation. Rather it highlights their association with property rights and the use of markets to support sustainability is not a *causative* one. The words 'property' and 'rights' do not of themselves address the need for improvement in the mechanisms for the constant adjustments between private and collective interests in society. Placing too heavy an emphasis on property rights as a solution may result in disappointment, and possibly make the achievement of some of the outcomes desired by its advocates more difficult.

Is the US model applicable to Australia?

In political debates about environmental regulation, it is sometimes suggested that a US-styled model of compensation when the use of land is restricted by regulation would be beneficial. But would such an adoption be beneficial? Concepts of property work within legal and economic institutional frameworks. These frameworks are slow to develop, and do not transfer well – and certainly not immediately – from one jurisdiction to another. There will be legal and administrative uncertainty and confusion while institutions and understanding develops. This will be reflected in transaction costs, and variability in outcomes. As learning develops, these problems will be resolved but the evolution may take decades. The way the issues are resolved will differ. In the US, where the same challenges in balancing the interests of the individual and society over resources are occurring, different States have developed different responses. Some place a premium on private interests, others are prepared to trade these off without compensation. This is in spite of strong constitutional statements regarding the paramount value of property rights. As a consequence, institutions and management strategies of the various States differ, as do the outcomes.[4]

One policy goal in institutional arrangements for natural resource management should be to minimise the drain on the government pocket, and to reduce bureaucratic intervention. This is an aim that is dear to many who own property and manage resources. Entrenching some resource-use interests above others, freezing the status quo, will create greater difficulty in the future in reorganising interests and responding to changed circumstances. A more legalistic approach to such adjustments may result in delay, and higher total cost (including legal costs as well as

---

[4] The following authors have provided a number of insights to the property rights debate in the US (Tully 1980; Rowley 1993; Meltz 1995; Pilon 1995), (Cupit 2000).

compensation) whenever administrative changes to natural resource access are needed to meet sustainability or other requirements.

It is important that the approach used to pursue sustainable resource use is fair, flexible and that it provides strong incentives. Overloading the property concept with the expectation that it will provide us with the 'magic bullet' solution is a mistake that will embed high transaction costs and inflexibility without necessarily benefiting those who have such faith in its power. Property rights are important and they should not be lightly interfered with. Neither should they be elevated as a simple solution to issues of sustainability and equity, which they are not.

Strengthening ownership responsibility

The common laws of negligence and nuisance require at least some degree of environmental accountability. Owners are obliged not to create environmental harms that affect other rights owners. However, the common law does not create an overarching responsibility to avoid harming the environment *per se*, nor any obligation to future generations. The implications of these common law underpinnings are discussed in Chapters 6 and 7. That is not to say that property owners do not accept a moral obligation to the environment and to future generations. But this is quite different from a legal responsibility going beyond the traditional concept of not causing harm to identified other rights holders.

Greater duties are slowly being grafted onto the Western legal system as society seeks more effective custodianship of the environment. The re-emergence of the concept of custodianship reflects the growing awareness of resource inter-dependence, and the limits of self-interest in protecting shared interests. It reflects a paradigm shift[5] which is causing society to deal with resources differently. As with all paradigm shifts, the new regime involves adjustments in economic interests and challenges previously unquestioned concepts of rights, driven by what will always be – in the early stages – not the view of the most powerful in society.

Farmers are particularly affected by this paradigm shift. Their emotional and economic commitment to the lands they work is strong. They have a resource ownership ethic, and are under increasing pressure to extend that ownership ethic to further embrace a custodial duty – requiring them to balance the needs of income production and environmental conservation. This is no small challenge. Policy and regulations designed to enforce a custodianship ethos have triggered anxiety and political action and can require actions that are a further drain on very limited incomes.

---

5   Paradigm shifts occur when a fundamental and unquestioned understanding of how the world works changes to a new way of understanding. An example is the Copernican revolution, when the understanding that the universe revolved around the earth was overturned. Paradigm shifts encounter strong resistance as they overturn entrenched beliefs and power structures (Kuhn 1974).

Some advocates of ecological responsibility see the political movement for compensation for perceived property right loss, for example, where lands have been subject to increased restriction such as requirements for stream banks to be fenced off (to protect waters) or areas be protected from clearing (to protect biodiversity),[6] as disguised subsidies to land owners for doing what they should already be obliged to do.

In recent times in Australia, political groups like the National Party, and the farmers lobby group, the National Farmers' Federation, have tried to restructure this debate by suggesting that with the redefinition of landholders' rights, there should be a clearer definition of environmental responsibilities, setting the boundaries for compensation for loss of rights. This is a constructive attempt to find a workable balance. It is part of the process of resolving who should bear the costs of environmental sustainability on private lands.

The social negotiation over traditional rights and new responsibilities, and over who should bear the costs, is a strategic issue for the future of sustainability. Once basic custodial obligations are well defined, the framework for compensation for any additional custodial requirements (beyond those defined as basic property owner's responsibility) will follow. A likely consequence will be gradual adjustment to the common law, incorporating standards accepted by the community in resolving these right/responsibility disputes. This process will begin through factual evidence of these agreements becoming a de facto standard, and over time acquire legal recognition. Eventually, new institutional frameworks will emerge to give effect to these decisions.

Rewards for good environmental management

It is possible to reward good environmental management. Consent-based custodial arrangements follow the trend towards financial recognition of property owners' role in providing resource management beyond their own production or legally-mandated requirements. Examples include payment for voluntary conservation of threatened species or habitats, or payment for implementing best management practice for water exporters in urban water catchments.

Custodial payments accommodate both the interests of resource owners and the community by providing an economic benefit to the resource owner who conserves. Typically the government, (but sometimes a private organisation) pays the resource owner a fee to preserve key values of that resource. These payments can take the form of fee-for service, compensation for expenses or foregone value, or a lease/license of the resource, frequently on commercial terms. They can also be provided as resource swaps (offsets) –

---

[6] Similar calls for compensation arise for foregone development opportunity through zoning prohibitions, but this is a different category of concern from custodial constraints on resource use within zoning.

Custodial payment schemes

The basic structure of a custodial payment scheme is illustrated by the first example below. However, as the other two US examples illustrate, it is possible to create custodial schemes with features like tradeability, and investment.

Under the Permanent Cover Program (PCP) in Canada, funds are provided to farmers to convert lands at risk of soil degradation by planting perennial forages for hay or pasture, or trees for recreation or wildlife. Applicants enter into long-term contracts for 15 or 21 years to ensure that the conversion is long lasting.

Eligible components can include: buffer strips of grass along watercourses and wetlands, with or without trees or shrubs; the retirement of flood plain land from agricultural production; block plantings of trees on highly erodible uplands, and tree windbreaks.

In the US wetland mitigation banks are created by a memorandum of understanding (MOU) among federal and State officials and a bank administrator. In most cases, the MOU describes the responsibilities of each party, the physical boundaries of the bank, how mitigation credits will be calculated, and who is responsible for long-term management of the bank.

Credits, which are usually denominated in terms of acres of habitat values, may only be used to mitigate development within the same watershed. Among established wetland mitigation banks, most MOUs allow the bank operator to sell credits only after the bank has actually accomplished wetland enhancement or preservation. About 100 wetland mitigation banks in at least 34 States are in operation, and more are in advanced stages of planning.

Initiated in 1986, Florida's Mitigation Park Program is the oldest fee-based wetland mitigation system in the United States. Fees paid by wetlands developers in lieu of on-site mitigation are deposited in the Florida Game and Fresh Water Fish Commission's Fish and Wildlife Habitat Trust Fund. These charges finance the purchase and subsequent management of large, biologically defensible Mitigation Parks, which range in size from 400 to 1,500 acres, are publicly owned but may be managed by either government entities or non-profit organisations.

There is some evidence that the scheme has been beneficial. Clustering individual mitigation activities into selected areas increases the viability of the wetlands. Moreover, the fact that developers have participated in fee-based schemes suggests that paying fees is more economical for them than conducting on-site mitigation activities on their own.

A number of US States and several counties and local governments have purchase of development rights (PDR) programs in place under which landowners are paid not to convert farmland to commercial or residential uses. In addition to objectives of food security and agricultural production, PDR programs have several environmental objectives, including the maintenance of habitat and resting places for wildlife and the aesthetic value of open space. Among the advantages of PDRs are the voluntary nature, which helps avoid the legal conflicts that can arise from zoning laws, and the low cost of this form of land protection for State and local governments as compared to outright land purchase.

exchanging the non-use of an environmentally-sensitive resource for the freedom to use another that is less sensitive. To illustrate, around 10 per cent of US rangelands are under voluntary conservation agreements and the demand for inclusion is strong. Voluntary conservation and custodianship has become part of the mix of land uses for many farmers.

Resource banks

Private conservation reserves have existed since kings set aside tracts for their private enjoyment, or plutocrats purchased estates for their exclusive enjoyment. National parks and reserves are versions of the practice of transferring large areas into protected catchments, for public good rather than private use.

These concepts have been refined as conservation trusts and land banks. Usually a fund purchases land – either on the market or via private treaty – for protection or rehabilitation. The lands are then held permanently, or later sold either as rehabilitated lands or as lands protected by covenant or zoned restriction. The eventual owners of the lands purchase them with full knowledge of the constraints, and at a market price that reflects this constraint. Reselling also allows the fund to move on to other sites. Variations on this approach include:

- The purchase of contaminated lands by an agency – either private or public – to rehabilitate under a shelter from liability. The lands are rehabilitated, perhaps developed, and then sold as uncontaminated sites free of liability risk. The arrangement may be purely commercial, where the developer provides insurance-based risk-management that achieves similar effects to legislated protection.
- The private conservation reserve, such as Earth Sanctuaries Limited. This company issued shares to purchase substantial areas as habitat for endangered species. It has taken the unique approach of pricing and reporting the value of the rare animals on its lands.[7] This is the most public face of a gradually evolving network of voluntary conservation reserves on private lands, where private owners protect their lands either by locking them up, or by imposing caveats or trusts for nature conservation.

The provision of a special custodial status by the Crown to environmental protectors is a further refinement. In both the US and the UK, environmental groups have been granted special ownership status for the protection of sensitive lands. This takes these lands out of public ownership, and puts them in private ownership or organisations whose purpose

---

[7] At a 2001 conference on property rights in Sydney, Wendy Craik explained the operation of the company and its relationship with shareholders (2001).

is conservation. This offers the advantage of removing the conflicts of purpose that can arise from publicly-owned lands, such as occurs in national parks that are often required to cater for multiple uses.

A new approach to conservation reserves

We are all aware of the conventional conservation reserves, like national parks or protected catchments. In Costa Rica they have gone one step further in combining conservation reserves with a novel carbon trading initiative. A project to consolidate and legally protect national parks and biological reserves in Cost Rica was recently approved by the US Initiative on Joint Implementation (USIJI). The project breaks significant new ground with its innovative financing approach, size of more than 500,000 hectares and national scale, and monitoring, verification and guarantee provisions. The USIJI pilot program encourages the US private sector to use its resources and innovations to reduce greenhouse emissions and promote sustainable development worldwide. The project will generate funds to purchase these lands from the sale of Certifiable Tradable Offsets (CTOs) or 'carbon bonds'. Each CTO will represent a third-party certification of 1000 tons of carbon the project sequestered the previous year. An experienced commodity trade monitoring firm will conduct detailed monitoring and verification of the carbon's sequestration, as well as the original baseline. The Costa Rican government will guarantee the CTOs for 20 years.

Indigenous custodianship

Custodian roles like 'elders' or 'keepers of place' are a cultural response to the problems of sustaining common property in societies where private property is not an effective means for protecting the resources of the community. The relationship between Indigenous people and the resources of the land and sea often involves a ritual custodial system. The removal of lands from traditional ownership has broken this relationship, or perhaps more accurately, has stopped it from being the practical basis of resource management.

The political movement to reinstate, to at least some degree, Aboriginal control of natural resources has the potential to re-establish some of the protective custodial rights and roles of Indigenous people. Many resource management agencies are building on land right recognition with programs to involve traditional owners in the management of lands and waters. Coupled with this, Aboriginal people are building careers as resource managers with national parks services, local government, and other agencies with a custodial role.

Aboriginal rights in biodiversity have been expressed at the international level through the United Nations Convention on Biological Diversity signed by over 180 nations, including Australia. Domestically these rights are articulated through the National Strategy for the Conservation of

Australia's Biological Diversity, and the *Environmental Protection and Biodiversity Conservation Act* 1999 (Cth). International developments in Indigenous custodianship provide some leads to the extension of this approach. In Canada, in particular, arrangements for co-management and more extensive Aboriginal ownership (in a legal framework very close to our own) have provided economic and environmental benefits and assisted to address claims for justice for Aboriginal people.

The basis of the challenge of sustainability is a problem of belief systems. Civilisations which found ways of living within a natural system resource base without the use of powerful technologies often did so by developing systems of responsibility to the land and to future generations. If, through reconciliation, our society can become re-attuned to sustainable ways of valuing our natural resources, this may have a significant beneficial effect.

There is ample evidence, ranging from the elevation of the intellect through the Cartesian revolution in philosophy, the French revolution fuelled by Voltaire, and the rise of modern views of the world fed by thinkers like Darwin or Keynes, that ideas, and beliefs based on ideas, do feed through into how humans interact with the world. A greater role for resource management based on Indigenous worldviews may be one of the paths for shifting the Western mindset towards sustainability.

Liability tracing and owner obligations

Chapter 5 discussed how the risk of liability can act as a means to develop the market for pro-sustainability products and services. By reducing the transaction costs of liability, liability instruments can be made more powerful.

Both ownership, but also non-ownership, carry with them rights and obligations. Those who purchase goods[8] have the rights to enjoy that purchase but do not have a right to interfere with others' enjoyment of their property. Non-property holders also have a duty, to allow the property holder to enjoy the benefit stream from that property, but do not have to accept consequences that affect their own enjoyment. The property holder would have a privilege, not a right to cause harm to the non-owner. Bromley explains the difference between a 'privilege' and a 'right', showing the correlation between rights and duties:

> The four fundamental legal relations [in property rights] are: (Static correlates XY) a RIGHT means that X has an expectation or assurance that Y will behave a certain way towards X. A DUTY means that Y must behave in a specific way with respect to X. DUTY and RIGHT are correlated. The second correlate is that of PRIVILEGE. X is free to behave in a certain way with respect to Y. The dual of privilege is NO RIGHT; (Dynamic correlates XY)

---

8   Goods, and to some extent services, may be considered as property of the purchaser, who has a right to enjoy the benefit stream from that purchase.

POWER means that X may voluntarily create a new legal relation affecting Y. The correlate is LIABILITY in which Y is subject to a new legal relation voluntarily created by X. IMMUNITY means that X is not subject to Y's attempt voluntarily to create a new legal relation affecting X. The correlate of IMMUNITY is NO POWER, means that Y may not voluntarily create a new legal relation affecting X. The legal relation is identical regardless of the position from which the relation is viewed. The difference lies not in the relation which is always two sided, but in the positions and outlook of X and Y which together make up the two converses entering into the relation. (Bromley 1991:17)

Pollution in its many forms is an externality that is a consequence of the use of goods by property holders who can be constrained by non-owners exercising their own rights. This right remains theoretical if there is no way of those whose rights are interfered with to enforce their interests. The problem of proving who is legally responsible for causing harm, particularly when dealing with companies where many people may be involved, creates a significant transaction cost in environmental regulation or the use of the common law to protect the public interest. Liability tracing reduces this impediment. The main forms of this approach are:

- *Technical tracing.* In such a system, controllers mark sensitive or harmful products with an indelible stamp of origin, or chemical 'signature', or require documentation that ensures that it moves from one custodian to another. In this way, the controller can track the product through to final certification of its proper disposal. Vehicle registrations are an everyday example of technical tracing. It is not unusual to have paper-based systems for tracking dangerous chemicals, or industrial oils, for this purpose.
- *Liability tracing* renders ineffective any artificial barriers to liability such as interposed companies or trusts, or the use of agents. The most common form of this is the requirement that directors of companies that have caused harm or breach of an environmental regulation will be personally liable for that harm. This is increasingly common in Environment Protection Acts.

Tracing can be powerful, by changing the risk-weighted cost of causing harm. If an individual director will potentially carry multi-million dollar costs of damage caused by a staff member and that director only achieves a small benefit from taking that risk (but will bear little of the cost of prevention) then it is likely they will be strong advocates of avoiding risk. Their capacity to create markets for environmental compliance systems, or for goods or services that reduce the risk of environmental harm, can be a powerful driver of demand. Liability tracing is as much an environmental industry development tool as it is a policing support.

Private property: problem or solution?

The word 'property' seems to have acquired a mystical political importance. This is understandable given the dynamics of resource use, but it adds little value in dealing with the very substantial underlying problems of resource conservation and the balancing of public and private interests.

Taking a view of property from the perspective of behavioural fundamentals suggests that many of the absolutes that are proposed politically are far more usefully understood as negotiable options. The focus needs to be on the detail of the situation, the details of the potential instruments to resolve that particular issue, and the strategies that will give the best outcome.

It is the case that every instrument that is used has the potential to adversely impact someone. That is unavoidable in a world of declining resource availability. Equity issues deserve to be debated as serious concerns involving many people, rather than having a temporary state of affairs frozen in time in the interests of protecting a myth of the status of property.

Resource owners who lose some or all of their interests have a cause for complaint, and deserve to have their interests respected. They deserve not to have to bear an unfair share of the costs of the social challenge of sustainability. Attaching paramount importance to a slogan 'property right' may assist some, but it will not achieve this equitable and principled sharing.

VOICE OF EXPERIENCE: PROPERTY

Angus Gordon spent many years as a coastal engineer in Australia and overseas. His role evolved to encompass the social and economic as well as the technical aspects of the interaction of humans and their environment, and now he is the general manager of a bustling local government area, with many coastal and urban environmental issues to manage. He has proposed a restructure of property rights as the key to solving the pressing sustainability and economic challenges of rising sea levels and increasing demands for coastal works to protect private property.

Why do you regard a property rights strategy as being pivotal?

We should first understand the problem. Coastal shorelines are always changing, and with sea level rise they will change more. Property rights support the mistaken perception that land is permanent and unchanging, because they are defined by governments as fixed points on a map. As a result when physical processes take away the land, the expectation arises that somehow government is responsible to put it back.

The definition of ownership is a statement about the relationship between people, government and the environment, in this instance the sea. If this relationship is misaligned it sets up expectations that government will either prevent the environment from reducing the uses rights of people or that government will pay if the right is reduced.

This is an economic nightmare. You cannot fight the sea with money. There is an interesting relationship here, because if you succeed in the short term, you can be sure that there will be greater and even more expensive challenges to come. Only if the asset you are protecting is of enormous, and rapidly escalating, value is this economically sustainable. There is a link between the environment and economics, which is made possible by engineering and made politically desirable by misguided expectations based on poorly designed property rights.

What we take from this is that inappropriate property rights create unrealistic expectations of what can be expected from the environment, or from government. So what needs to be done to bring this back into a more sustainable relationship?

We know that the boundaries of the sea and land, or other relationships between what is natural and what is owned or exploitable, will change. We know that if property is badly defined, this will lead to unrealistic and expensive expectations of government. We also know that engineering is part of the way that we shape how property is used, and use expectations. Unless government wants to be forever caught in an economic and political bind, it has to change the way in which property is defined, and the types of engineering that arises from the man/nature relationship we create with property. This is not conceptually difficult. Many other societies make ownership subject to natural conditions.

To illustrate, when I first began to work in Brunei, houses by the sea were portable. As the sea level changed, houses moved. Title and engineering were flexible. Then over time, land was more tightly defined and economic and other forces led to the construction of inflexible concrete and steel buildings. When the sea began to claim back the land, the government eventually was forced into artificially freezing the changes, by constructing expensive offshore islands.

In some other countries, they have realised this relationship is important, and have made property rights subject to the ebb and flows of natural conditions. This is far more effective than trying to achieve similar outcomes by design regulations and zoning, because once the degree of certainty is known people can design uses that take this into account. They can be very creative, even to the extent of designing homes that are modular and relocate-able.

I proposed a scheme like this for Byron Bay. They went further than I think was needed. Their rule is that if the sea claims back your land, to an extent that you no longer comply with the development rules, then you have to remove your house. I think that a more flexible approach was possible, but even so this rule has removed any expectation that government is accountable for changes wrought by the sea.

Given the value of the land involved, wouldn't this type of approach have a significant economic cost to landowners?

I think that is a 'yes' and 'no' issue. Certainly owners would be worried and would claim this, and in the short term they may be right due to an initial reaction. However, all you are really doing is clarifying that government will not step in to protect them from the sea. It is making clear the risk that they face. It is not changing any actual right to use and enjoy their land.

I expect that property values would rapidly recover. There may well be other actions taken, like the creation of investment or sinking funds to meet the costs, or to compensate for loss of land. I can envisage the market finding ways of dealing with this problem, to overcome the fact that the government would not be in the business of pretending to stop the march of the sea.

What prevents local government around the country from making these types of decisions?

Political issues, of course. But probably even more important is the absence of suitable institutional arrangements. State government controls property, and local government cannot reliably make these kinds of changes without the state providing the legal framework.

What I am proposing can be extended to other situations, beyond the boundaries of property by the sea. The property issue is about is how we set the boundaries of exploitation of nature by owners, whether those boundaries are set by the sea, or by some other condition like earthquake vulnerability, or even soil condition like salinity. If property operated within the boundary of the condition of nature, then many issues could be better handled. But to make this the case requires that we align the legal institutions of the state to the type of property regime that we want. If the state does not do this, it will continue to create false expectations, and be expected to pay when they are not met. If states do get this relationship right, then over time there will be a cultural shift that will make it a lot easier for government to pursue sustainability, without having to always think about compensation for unrealistic expectations.

You talk a lot about expectations that are generated by the type of intervention that government makes. Can you explain a bit more about this?

Expectations are what drives a lot of the issues we encounter. Expectations and rights are very close to each other. If you manage expectations or find ways of fitting into them, you can get far better outcomes than if you ignore them.

For example, I have been responsible for dune rehabilitation works. In the earlier times, the soils and plant staff would fence off an area, and then put in a scattered number of plants, and leave them to grow. This was the technically correct and theoretically cost-effective approach.

However, what would happen is that people would resent the fencing off, and could see nothing worth protecting behind the fence. They would break the fences, and subsequently damage the rehabilitation.

I changed the approach. We made the fences less aggressive and more people-friendly. We put in far more plants than were needed, so that people could see the landscape being created. We even fertilised them, to increase the rate of growth so that people could see something tangible. The result was that whilst we spent more than what was essential from a technical viewpoint, we got far better results because people respected and often grew to care a great deal for what we created for them. They could see the benefit of landscaping to them, and they could see the progress.

So what would be your advice to a strategist, thinking about sustainability and property issues?

You have to understand the basics before you think about the instruments. This includes understanding the nature of the natural constraints that you are working with, and the engineering possibilities, the economic relationships, and the expectations. You can do a lot to deliver economic and environmental sustainability if you can find ways to align use expectations with the capacity of the environment, and this can be done with careful design of property rights. It is a far more acceptable and efficient approach than trying to achieve the same things through conventional regulation.

Chapter 7

STRENGTHENING PRIVATE REGULATION

This and the following chapter take a 'helicopter view' of how actions by private citizens and governments can, and do, change the way in which other people's use of natural resources is regulated. This chapter discusses the private use of law to regulate for sustainability. Public regulation is discussed in Chapter 8.

The term 'private regulation' is used to describe the use of law by private citizens to regulate rights and relationships between themselves and other citizens. It is known in legal circles as civil or private law. It evolves through the resolution of conflict through the court system, creating precedents, as distinct from statutes which evolve through parliamentary political processes, though statute and precedent interact seamlessly in the operation of the legal system.

Precedent is a sophisticated method for balancing the demands of certainty with the need for flexibility in a changing world. Private law is fundamental to the operation of markets. Private agreement is the way enforceable obligations are created. Contracts are how people agree to transfer value, including property, services and natural resources, and can relate directly to the use or protection of the environment. A contract can include conditions to restrict harm (such as a caveat against multi-storey development attached to the sale of a property) or the quality of the environment may be an element in the contract (such as warranties on mineral deposits, or water quality). The underlying nature of what is transferred under a contract may be affected by environmental zoning. All market mechanisms are based on contract, and the range of natural matters becoming the subject of contract continually increases.

It is conventional wisdom that the role of the law is to resolve conflicts. Luhmann (1984), however, suggests that the role of law is to promote and channel conflicts in paths that are constructive for society. Conflict, played out through the often intense debates in society and the actions of courts, is fundamental to the way in which society evolves. Conflict and change are constant bedfellows.

Five categories of law are the most relevant to natural resource management:

1. *Contract* – the law of enforceable agreements.
2. *Tort* – includes many subcategories, for example, *negligence* – (protecting people from harm caused through the carelessness of others);

and *nuisance* (preventing others from harming the integrity of a person's self or property).
3. *Property* – the law of ownership, which also defines interests, transactions and mechanisms of transfer.
4. *Equity* – requires those with ethical obligations or duties with respect to others to act fairly and 'equitably', for example, the duty of a director to act in the interests of shareholders.
5. *Administrative* – concerned primarily with the right of the citizen to have decisions by government and government agencies made fairly and in accordance with proper process.

Courts continually redefine legal rights (and their corollary obligations), including property rights. Sometimes this redefinition follows parliamentary creation of statutes and sometimes it is solely through decisions made by judges. For example, the famous 1932 UK decision in *Donoghue v Stevenson*[1] extended accountability ('a duty of care') beyond individuals with whom one had a contract, to a broader class of people ('neighbours') to whom harm was foreseeable. Liability for negligence has been extended to encompass non-physical injury, such as economic loss, and the consequences of non-physical actions or inactions (such as liability for partial disclosures where the failure to completely disclose causes loss). With the advent of the corporation, artificial entities as well as people have become the subject of legal accountability. Statute and private action have worked together to create a network of legal responsibility.

The relationship between common law and statute law is complex. Many situations to which the common law applies are also the subject of statutes. Courts must apply both, with statute law generally overriding the common law. Some of these statutes are refinements of common law, such as the enlargement of the obligations of traders under contract by fair-trading and trade practices legislation. Others establish duties, which can be the basis for civil claims for negligence, and still others establish new rights and obligations for resource users and owners, that can be used by citizens to protect their private interests. These include rights to compensation (for example, in the event of forced acquisition of land by the state), or for recompense against businesses for harsh and unconscionable dealing.

Civil laws change risks

Private law is aligned to social standards. Because the rights of individuals are often bound up with access to or use of resources, environmental law and human rights are partners. This is why so much of the US

---

1 [1932] AC 562. A consumer, Donaghue, sued a drink manufacturer, Stevenson for negligence in selling her a bottled drink containing the remains of a snail.

constitution talks simultaneously of property and civil rights as interdependent. The claim 'no taxation without representation' was as much about freedom as it was about property.

Human civil and political rights and property rights are inter-related in complex ways, not least of which is the way in which litigation and the award of damages influences accepted standards of behaviour. Civil liability actions – actions in tort – shape the community's concepts of acceptable risk, and standards of risk management. Successful litigation can influence insurance company requirements of their policy-holders (for example, requiring site protection by holders of construction insurance), and lead to the adoption of defensive programs such as quality systems, more careful administration, defensively drafted contracts and insurances. Once courts decide that a duty and a standard of care exists and that those harmed are entitled to be compensated, a chain of events is begun. Insurers revise their risk pricing and contract requirements; lawyers warn clients; companies review policies; and potential litigants visit their lawyers. Civil action results in a mix of desirable and undesirable outcomes. It is desirable that polluting industries be liable to water users downstream, or that firms that are careless with dangerous chemicals find themselves paying penalties. These liability risks are an incentive to manage operations responsibly. But they come with a cost to the community; perhaps in increased costs of consumer goods, as well as a cost to the potential harm-doers who may, for example, need to pay higher insurance premiums to cover possible payouts for pollution incidents.

Claims of nuisance, where one person potentially interferes with the interests of another, (for example, from air pollution, noise, wandering cattle, to spillage of oil) establish rules that sit well with sustainable resource use. Often they require one person to refrain from emitting harmful by-products – noise, smell, pollutants – or losing control of something harmful. Feral animal control, noise and air pollution, water pollution and various other environmental harms are in part addressed by this tort, though environmental protection is not the original purpose of the law.

Judgments can also restructure interests in natural resources. Some judgments, such as the 1992 decision of the High Court in *Mabo*,[2] have implications for political and economic structures, and natural resource ownership, including the operation of property rights. The *Mabo* decision was a battle for land rights to protect the social and economic interest of a disadvantaged community. Respect for the environmental and cultural meanings of the land was at the heart of the claim. But, as with many social system issues, matters are rarely as simple as they might initially seem. While Indigenous groups may rely on the recognition of cultural

---

2   *Mabo v Queensland (No 2)* (1992) 175 CLR 1.

rights[3] as an alternative basis to secure protection of environmental values, it is not always the case that the recognition of such rights will be in the interests of the environment. Indigenous people may also use such rights to circumvent laws aimed at protecting environmental values – such as claiming their right to take protected fauna[4] through hunting. Even so, the legal principles are far from settled. In *Lockhart River Aboriginal Council v Cook Shire Council*,[5] the Aboriginal Council argued, unsuccessfully, that Indigenous people should be freed from the constraints of laws designed to protect environmental values, but in *Yanner v Eaton*[6] Yanner was successful when using apparently the same principles.

It is the received wisdom of the courts that decisions like *Mabo* do not create new rights and obligations, but recognise rights that have been hidden from view. However, the recognition of traditional ownership has triggered a shift in the political and economic power of Indigenous people, added to the transaction costs of resource exploitation, and accelerated moves to have Indigenous interests in natural resources reflected in how these resources are managed. Civil and political rights and property rights often strengthen each other.

Where might the evolution of the law take the interests of the environment? It is not hard to envisage that a form of property rights in native fauna could eventually be the basis for new legal developments[7]. Such matters as rights to cell lines, flora, or natural medicines could eventually depend on rights that are currently being identified.

Laws designed to protect consumers can also protect environmental values. For example, deception in environmental claims is actionable under the *Trade Practices Act* 1974 (particularly s 52), as well as under a range of State laws. Deception in relation to environmental performance claims is likely to come to prominence once environmental certification and environmental marketing become more evident in commerce. Civil action will be used to redress consumer losses in relation to the environment.

Resource scarcity driven by increasing population and greater demands on resources and the consequences of failures in caring for the environmental commons – such as depleted fisheries, salinity, reduced biodiversity – is likely to see a continued growth in civil action with ecological sustainability implications. It is likely that collective actions to protect rights will expand, spurred by the availability of class actions, contingent fees, and civil rights law (Martin and Verbeek 2000).

---

3   *John Bulun Bulun v R & T Textiles Pty Ltd* [1998] FCA 1082.
4   *Eaton v Yanner; ex parte Eaton* [1998] QCA 20, which involved the claim of traditional rights as a defence for an otherwise unlawful hunting.
5   [1998] QPELR 344.
6   [1999] HCA 53.
7   For a discussion of such issues see Kristin Howden, 'Indigenous Traditional Knowledge And Native Title' (2001) *UNSWLJ* 12 (1 January).

Accommodating the pressure to extend legal rights to protect the environment is causing policy challenges for the court system including:

- *Certainty versus responsiveness to change* – Certainty is based on a linear development of law. More radical interpretations are sometimes required to meet rapid changes in social conditions. The courts must weigh up the respective importance of these competing requirements.
- *Individual freedom versus community interest* – Determining the extent of individual freedom is a common concern in the arguments over regulation of resource use. Every case in which an administrative or zoning decision adjusts the exploitation rights of a landowner involves this balance.
- *Responding to emerging needs versus overburdening the courts by allowing too many cases* – Courts may restrict a legal remedy if it is possible that the benefits to the community do not justify the added burden on the court system.
- *Individual ethical choice versus maintaining the system* – This involves consideration of the extent to which matters ought to be decided by the individual's ethics rather than legal dictates. In the 1960s, conscription and conscientious objection raised such conflicts.
- *Societal cohesion versus cultural diversity* – The courts may have to decide whether to restrict a particular practice (for example, child marriage) that is accepted by a particular culture, but not generally acceptable to the dominant social ethic.
- *Enforcing community views versus respect for the individual* – Many of the issues above are encapsulated in a continual conflict between the freedom of the individual and the collective wishes of the community.

In a society that depends on diversity for its enrichment, a process for change is essential. Emphasis on one set of policy priorities may indeed make the law a straitjacket. A strength of precedent as a process is that it allows for both technical and policy development, and for gradual change to meet emerging conditions, while providing for reasonable consistency and predictability.[8] This is true in relation to natural resource management laws as for any other field of law.

Two factors will determine whether private regulation can be harnessed effectively to pursue sustainability. The first is the pattern of court decisions, since precedent will shape the law and policy applied by civil courts. The second is who can use the courts and for what purpose.

---

8   The seminal discussion of this elegant relationship is *Legal system and lawyers' reasonings* by Julius Stone (Stanford University Press, California, 1964).

Neither of these is strongly supportive of the effective use of civil law to achieve improved natural resource custodianship. Court decisions have tended to demonstrate an unwillingness of the courts to elevate sustainability issues over other (also legitimate) interests of economic freedom. The costs and constraints on the use of the law to support the environment have made it hard for individuals to exercise what rights there are in support of sustainability.

This is not to say that such patterns are unchangeable. Later chapters outline strategies to shift towards a more effective application of private regulation. But for now we will simply observe what patterns do exist in civil law and the environment.

How have courts dealt with sustainability principles

There are many statutes that nominally dictate that resource users and government agencies incorporate sustainability principles in their decision-making. It is clear from the cases that difficulties arise in interpretation and application by courts of concepts such as 'sustainability' and the 'precautionary principle', and in supporting actions for the implementation of sustainable practices. There is far less difficulty when the issues fall under more historically-established concepts, such as ancient property rights to land and water, administrative law compliance, or well established tort obligations. Our hypothesis is that this is because the paradigm of sustainability has not yet been 'bedded down' within the law, and that it will take further evolution through precedent before courts are comfortable with some of the essential concepts.[9]

For example, in *Bannister Quest Pty Ltd v Australian Fisheries Management Authority*[10] the court's approach to ecologically sustainable development was to focus on survival of fish stocks to be harvested in the future. Given that the legislation contained a separate requirement of maximising economic efficiency, it is hard to see why parliament would have inserted a sustainability requirement if they had not meant it to be a balancing consideration alongside – rather than subsumed within – economic considerations. Similarly when courts have considered the application of the precautionary principle they have found themselves lacking in supporting precedent. Cases such as *Nicholls v Director General of National Parks and Wildlife*[11] show that, generally, courts have fallen back onto more comfortable territory such as compliance with administrative direction rather than enforcement of sustainability concepts. For example, environmental principles are written into town planning, rezoning, licensing, and

---

9   With more than 120 cases dealing with environmental issues and the precautionary principle alone and volumes of books and articles on the substantive law, this brief survey of case can do little more than illustrate the complexity of the law, and the direction of its evolution.
10 (1997) 77 FCR 503.
11 (1994) 84 LGERA 397.

resource access regulations. Even in these cases there is no certainty that the environmental principles will be upheld. In *Randwick City Council v Minister for the Environment*[12] the federal Minister for the Environment made a decision that neither an environment impact statement nor public environment report was required for the operating plan for Sydney Airport. The court found that the Minister had acted within his legal rights. While the case is based on laws designed for environmental protection, the outcome was determined on the basis of compliance with administrative procedure. Administrative law provided the foundation on which the community sought to base claims for a stronger emphasis on the local environment. Other cases, including *City of Botany Bay Council v Minister for Transport and Regional Development*[13] and *Minister for Urban Affairs & Planning v Rosemount Estates Pty Ltd*[14] are also ultimately about defining the degrees of freedom of the administration when faced with requirements for environmental protection.

The situation becomes clearer for the courts when the law specifies liability, where wrongdoing can be readily identified by objective evidence, and where the cases are closer to traditional property rights (such as riparian rights) or tort situations. *McLennan v Holden*[15] provides an instance. In that case, Holden was convicted of polluting a river in contravention of the South Australian *Environment Protection Act* 1993. The courts also seem less sympathetic to authorities if clear standards, rather than environmental law principles, are the concern, particularly when human health is at risk as in *Ryan v Great Lakes Council*[16] where people became ill after consuming oysters from Wallis Lake which had been contaminated by sewerage – the regulation of which is the responsibility of council.

Rights to access the environmental commons are at the heart of economic activity – particularly extractive and primary production activities. As well as disputes over collective property rights, therefore, there are also legal conflicts between citizens (*inter-partes* actions) over resources. Contracts are the main legal mechanisms, but there are many other approaches in tort or equity. *Qantas Airways Ltd v Mascot Galvanising (Holdings) Pty Ltd*[17] illustrated how the right to protect property – in this case Qantas land – from damage from corrosive runoff from a neighbouring property can be upheld by the court. The civil right to protect land from adverse flows from neighbours is not limited to immediate neighbours. The ancient right to the flow of water through the rivers on (or bounding) a property can be a basis for the protection of broader environmental values.

---

12   [1999] FCA 1494.
13   [1999] FCA 1495.
14   Unreported, NSWCA, Handley JA, Sheller JA, Cole JA, 14 August 1996.
15   [1999] SAERDC 83.
16   [1999] FCA 177.
17   Unreported, NSWSC, 17 December 1998, No 3610/96.

This is demonstrated in *Van Son v Forestry Commission of NSW*[18] where Van Son succeeded in arguing that the Forestry Commission had been negligent in its operations where these adversely impacted water flows. It is interesting to note that the legal action succeeded on the broad basis of the duty to avoid actions that will interfere with the ordinary comfort of human existence. This is a very broad foundation for actions to protect one's rights to enjoy one's (owned) environment.

The right to obtain not only enjoyment but also value from the land is also upheld by the court. The case of *EM & ES Petroleum Pty Ltd v Shimden Pty Ltd*[19] is representative of cases where exploitative rights are considered by the courts, under a range of legal categories – contract, misleading and deceptive conduct and the like. In this case, EM and ES Petroleum attempted to rescind a contract on the grounds that it had entered into the contract relying on false representations concerning the environment.

This case also shows the intersection between civil matters and legislation. It represents the norm of how environmental issues come into dispute through contract. Exploitative rights are part of the value of land. If these rights do not exist or are compromised, either by legislation or by some physical constraint, then one can anticipate contractual disputes. These disputes may in turn bring other fields of law – such as negligence, Trade Practices, equity or tort – into play.

Information about environmental values also has an economic value and can be a source of conflict. *Armidale City Council v Alec Finlayson Pty Ltd*[20] and *Ryan v Great Lakes Council*[21] show the extent to which the laws of negligence have been extended to encompass duties to protect environmental utility and compensate for the consequences of environmental degradation and pollution. In *Armidale City Council v Alex Finlayson Pty Ltd*, the court found that the council had a common law duty of care when dealing with a contaminated site beyond that imposed by the *Environmental Planning and Assessment Act* 1979 (NSW). The statute does not set the limits to the duty not to cause harm to others as a result of causing environmental harm.

The courts have not taken a consistent approach to sustainability, although issues that are relevant to sustainability are often litigated. Where the issues reflect well-established common-law principles, the courts have had less difficulty in considering environmental matters. Where the cases have required adoption of sustainability principles which are new to the law, the courts have shown a limited appetite for change. In general, the environment continues to be a secondary interest in civil law. This indicates one area where reform could significantly alter the way in which natural resources are considered by the courts, and protected by the law.

---

18 Unreported, NSWSC, Cohen J, 3 February 1995.
19 Unreported, NSWSC, 1995, No 2483/92.
20 [1999] FCA 330.
21 [1999] FCA 177.

Suppressing voices for the environment

There are fundamental barriers to the ability of individuals with an altruistic interest in the environment using civil actions and taking political action to advance sustainability. These are the absence of rights to sue, an embedded economic imbalance against such litigants, and the risk of personal liability under the laws of defamation.

If you lack the ability to use the court system, it matters little whether you have a good argument about the substance of the issues you wish to litigate. The ability to use the courts to protect what you care about is an important civil right. The law recognises this right where conventional interests like property ownership, or physical safety, are concerned. In these cases there is a direct personal cost to the person whose interests are trampled upon, and the courts are happy to hear the matter. However, if the interests are the protection of the environment, where there is no personal economic interest to be protected, the courts are less likely to allow the concerned individual to sue. The absence of a right to litigate (or 'standing') acts to suppress the voices for the environment. Unless the environmental legislation directly confers standing upon those who do not have a direct economic interest, they will be frozen out of the legal system.

A further limiting factor to standing in the courts to support sustainability is the absence of a voice for future generations, or for the environment itself. The concept of 'intergenerational equity' is a component in the policies for sustainability but it has little meaning until someone can speak for the future. In civil courts there is no litigant to act for the unborn, except where a statutory right has been created for other interests to be heard.[22] Neither is there a basis on which the interests of kangaroos, dolphins, the humble snail or any other living creature apart from humans can be represented directly in court. The civil law is a forum for citizens to resolve their rights and, even if the unborn have rights, neither they nor non-human beings are counted as citizens. A limited voice for the natural world and for the interests of the next generation is only to be found in administrative actions and bureaucratic processes that may incidentally require taking sustainability into account in making a determination.

It is now common for government to have spokespeople for environmental interests on natural resource consultative committees. These voices are meant to balance the interests of industry, resource owners and resource users. However, unlike ownership and economic interests, these voices are not supported by the capacity to sue if the results of consultation override the interests that are being spoken for. They can make few

---

22 See, for example, *Byron Environment Centre Inc v Arakwal People* (1998) 3 AILR 16, where the right to have other interests considered under the *Native Title Act* 1993 (Cth) was considered. The court indicated that even where there is a legislative provision, the right to a voice is not on behalf of the environment. This contrasts with previous cases where interests such as fishing or sailing were considered sufficient to found a right to participate.

credible threats of recourse to law if the interests they represent are not fairly heard. The courts can require compliance with mandatory processes but this is weak compared with the right to force substantive consideration or to seek damage or other compensation if the interest is discounted.

The second major impediment is purely economic. There are hundreds of pieces of legislation to deal with sustainability issues.[23] It is virtually impossible for a person to be clear about his or her obligations and rights, within this morass. This is compounded by the fact that the common law on which many actions could be based is even less accessible. Principles are not codified and often so complex that it is not until after the court case that anyone can say with confidence that they had the right that was claimed. The transaction costs of using the civil law are substantial, which means that only those that can afford to risk losing these sums can consistently have access to the law. The costs of civil action, or the threat of incurring costs if litigants lose in court, often turn advocates for sustainability away from using the court system. In spite of the rise of industries such as eco-tourism and macrobiotic or organic foods, which rely on high-quality environments, we are still more likely to find economic interests aligned with degrading the environment than with conservation. The existence of an economic interest in resource use provides both the legal standing and the economic power to use the legal system, and at the same time is the basis of an embedded disadvantage for advocates for the environment to rely on civil action.

The civil law of defamation adds a third barrier. This law allows individuals (and companies) to protect their reputations, compensating them for the losses that arise from harm to that reputation. Frequently in environmental disputes, advocates of harm are pursuing commercial goals like property development or industrial activity. Arguments against harm will often at least imply that the harm advocate is self-interested and uncaring of the common good, or that their analysis is biased or incorrect – implying a lack of competence. This means questioning the good faith or competence of the advocate, and therefore, in theory, causing harm to their reputation.[24] The opponents of consumption are in many cases individual citizens or relatively poor environmental organisations who gain nothing economically from winning. Given the reality of resource consumption and wealth, advocates of harm are more likely to have a business reputation with economic value, and to have the resources to take legal action, and a strong incentive to prevent the spread of views counter to their commercial interest. They can stifle criticism by threatening activists with defamation if they call into doubt the good faith, ability or honesty of the advocate of harm.

---

23 See further Chapter 8 on public regulation.
24 While the citizens and voluntary organisations may value their reputations highly, the economic loss that they could claim for a loss reputation are likely to be far less, even if they were successful in any action.

SLAPPS

When a respected academic opened his mailbox a few years ago, he got an unpleasant surprise. In it was a letter, threatening him with defamation proceedings if he (and the environmental group of which he was President) continued to put forward arguments against a large-scale development in a sensitive site. He had just been hit with a 'SLAPP'. A SLAPP ('Strategic Lawsuit Against Public Participation') is the tactical use of lawsuits to stop environmentalist actions. In this individual's case, the process was stopped before it got too far, and without stifling what was eventually a successful defence of the environment.

Others were not so lucky, having to live through a number of years of stress and financial burdens. A small number of citizens fought on for many years before the litigation was finally stopped. The SLAAP tactic is a cynical abuse of legal rights, intended to prevent activists exercising their democratic rights in defence of the environment.

It is not only developers who use defamation laws. Ballina Shire on the North Coast of NSW used defamation action against local activists concerned with sewage discharge. The courts eventually threw out the council's action, but the time and effort that went into fighting on the legal front was diverted from other activities. (Beder 1995)

There are, of course, defences to such actions. However, the threat is often sufficient to stifle voices for the environment. The defences to defamation are complex and to mount them requires good legal advice. The transaction costs – legal costs and the stress associated with legal process – of defending oneself, the required effort and emotional energy, and the cost of failure to defend effectively – particularly given the risk of exemplary damages being claimed – are high.

Using civil tools to replace regulation

As already noted, avoidance of situations that would require incurring legal costs is a powerful motivator to avoid resource use that could harm others. The possibility of litigation, rather than regulation, has been the cornerstone of traditional protection of riparian rights, and other access and use rights of property owners. Advocates for private property regimes to protect the environment, such as the English author Elizabeth Brubacker (1995) point out that it would be more effective to rely on civil action based on property rights and the common law to protect the environment, than on statutory regulations. In a foreword to Brubacker's book on property rights, Anthony Scott writes:

> Property can be a weapon that victims use in their own defense. Those who care more about nature than about the glorification or vilification of government will find property protects it better than government does.
>
> Protection by property tends to avoid courtrooms as well as legislatures. Although legal professors too often forget it, property law does its job best when land is held and exchanged in an orderly way without litigation. A good standard property right works regularly and informally to keep disputes out of the courts; indeed knowledge of it prevents disputes from even arising. (1995: 8)

It is not impossible for a stronger voice for defence of the environment to emerge in the courts using the existing structures of the law. The indications are, however, that unless parliaments or other societal institutions – such as the State Supreme Courts or the High Court – intervene to clarify sustainability issues, emergence will be slow.

Litigation-led change?

The likelihood of being successfully sued is a risk. The likelihood of penalty for causing environmental harm closes the circle between harm caused by the individual and cost to that individual. Risk avoidance by resource owners and users is where 'the rubber hits the road' in the behavioural effects of private law. The landowner who puts in drains to prevent runoff entering his neighbour's property, or fences in his stock to prevent them running onto the road is often responding to financial risks created by law. The true measure of the law's effectiveness is not in the economics of wins and losses; it is the many risk-minimising choices that are made by resource consumers to reallocate resources to avoid the possibility of losses. These decisions are less influenced by court judgments than they are by other information dissemination processes that make court cases meaningful to them.

What strategies might support private action?

Individuals – including organisations legally defined as individuals – are the main actors within the institutional framework of the court system. Within that institutional framework are lawyers and judges who operate using prescribed modes of debate. People, including judges, tend to work more comfortably with things they understand. Matters of sustainability are not simple and obvious. It is far from clear to the uninitiated why, for example, allowing a waterfront property owner to replace native vegetation with grass can be a significant contributor to damaging shellfish; or why a compensatory wetland in a different location, which looks almost identical, may be no compensation at all.

These are some factors that cause law to be an expensive and uncertain medium to use to force someone who has caused environmental harm (or who proposes to cause harm) to bear the consequences. In addition to high costs and uncertainty, those advocating for the environment often have difficulty finding a suitable cause of action. There is no tort of 'harm to the environment' and no compensation for 'harm to the ecosystem'. While there may be a demonstrable economic or other harm to future generations, it is not compensable since there is no person with the standing to sue and the injuries are entirely prospective.

The discussion in this chapter leads us to a number of conclusions about the use of private law to support sustainability:

- Civil action is unreliable when issues are poorly defined and precedent and belief systems are not in place to guide the court in its deliberations.
- It is possible to increase the likelihood of success by clarifying issues through improved information, such as clarification of regulations, and education of lawyers and judges regarding environmental issues.
- It may also be possible to clarify the legal meaning of concepts of sustainability by declaratory action by the State Supreme Courts or perhaps the High Court.
- Increasing the legal resources of those who are advocating for the environment to use common law will accelerate the development of applicable principles and precedents in the court system.
- It would be possible to increase the use of common law to protect the environment by creating new torts – either through statute or precedent – and developing the right of a citizen to stand for future generations.
- It may be necessary to create some form of representative plaintiff to stand for the environment in court cases.

The next chapter examines public regulation, that is, direct action by government to protect the environment by penalising harmful acts and supporting restorative work.

Chapter 8

PUBLIC REGULATION

Public regulation refers to laws created by government and administered by agencies with the power to impose penalties or withhold access to resources. Agencies include policing agencies – such as the police, an Environment Protection Authority (EPA) or local government inspection and compliance sections – and land or resource management agencies such as State departments for fisheries, lands and mines.

Public regulation does more than control particular behaviour; it contributes to the evolution of social beliefs. Examples of this evolution include beliefs about slavery or child labour, which have been in part shaped by the laws outlawing these once traditional labour practices. The push for change was led by a relatively small, well-educated 'elite', and the practice was eventually outlawed. Only thereafter did these practices come to be seen as wrong and harmful. In today's world you could expect that a combination of community pressure, public regulation and private action for damages would be triggered by any attempt at slavery or child labour. Law both leads and follows community attitude change.

While economic instruments are typically more effective in stimulating innovation in the pursuit of least-cost solutions to problems, they are in themselves dependent upon regulatory regimes to establish the patterns of disincentives and incentives that shape markets. Cost-effectiveness is substantially a consequence of the aims of regulation and the way in which it is designed – poor design will result in low efficiency, regardless of whether the instrument is regulatory or otherwise. The discussion in Chapters 2 also explored transaction costs as a key aspect of regulatory (and market instrument) effectiveness. For these reasons, the authors do not accept the conventional economic wisdom that regulation is inherently less efficient than market instruments. However, neither do the authors dispute that regulation has not always delivered outcomes consistent with the policy aims of that regulation, and that it is a costly tool to use.

This chapter looks at some of the reasons why regulation has not been as effective as intended, and considers some ways in which regulatory effectiveness might be significantly improved. The chapter also highlights that regulation can be made far more effective, if improvements are made to the processes of law-making and law-enforcing.

In 2001, Arthur and Jeanette Conacher published an ambitious examination of the range of problems and issues associated with resource allocation, land use and environmental degradation in Australia. They complained that:

> [T]he rapid and uneven rate of changes in legislation, policies, agencies and nomenclature across all jurisdictions, often associated with changes of government and reform processes, has been a significant problem in researching and writing this book. (Conacher and Conacher 2001: xxv)

Other studies support their concern. The range of regulatory instruments include:

- Environment Protection Acts at federal and State levels, and anti-pollution laws, together with detailed regulations to implement them;
- Licensing of discharges and use activities;
- Controls over activities with substantial environmental impact such as land clearing;
- Local government regulations such as zoning, house and site requirements, and various health or social amenity requirements;
- Rules dealing with issues such as fire control, or health rules designed to protect water quality that have a significant environment protection aspect.

As well as specific environmental laws and statutes, much other regulation contains natural resource-use controls, such as industry-specific legislation governing land and water use, the management of national parks, the governing regulations of agencies and other sources. There are also supportive codes, such as State planning policies, which give effect to higher-level policies. There is no lack of formal law to support sustainability management, but this law is confusing and often difficult to understand (Martin and Verbeek 2000).

The clumsiness of regulatory structure

In the pursuit of sustainability we are now changing traditional beliefs and institutions, challenging simple concepts of ownership and the 'goodness' of exploitation as an end in itself. This transitional state is reflected in:

- The proliferation of participants in transactions;
- A welter of policies; and
- An explosion of legislation, designed to give effect to these policies.

A chaotic stage, though costly, is not abnormal in the introduction of concepts into society. The early stage (pre-paradigmatic) is often a period of confusion and accelerated learning about how to make new ideas effective in practice. The more pervasive the changes, the more complex the adjustment will be. The more that the new ideas fly in the face of established power structures, the greater the resistance that can be expected, and the greater the transitional disturbance. The introduction of machines with the industrial revolution, modern democratic choice with the French revolution, or the introduction of modern technology like the automobile, were all characterised by chaotic and sometimes violent periods of change.

Activist groups often press for more regulation to address environmental issues. But it is hard to see the value of more regulation per se. An increase in regulation could only be justified by a finding that the existing suite of regulations is ineffective and that new regulations would be significantly more effective, or that there are gaps in the network of rules that need to be filled. N Nelissen in his 1998 review of environmental law in the Netherlands (1998) concluded that:

- Environmental legislation alone is not capable of solving environmental problems, or significantly reducing them.
- Without environmental legislation, the environmental problems would probably have been considerably worse than it is now.
- The role that environmental legislation plays in attaining environmental goals is difficult to isolate from other influencing factors (particularly political, economic and social factors).
- Taxes seem to be a particularly effective policy instrument; subsidies, on the other hand, seem to be of little consequence.
- Consensual instruments in the form of covenants are only effective in certain instances, especially when obligations to achieve specified outcomes have been included.

In sum, effective regulation is likely to be efficient (low transaction costs), when implemented within a framework of policies and strategies that support and strengthen it (as part of a systemic behavioural strategy). It is a mistake to see more regulation per se as a 'solution' to natural resource abuse.

Regulatory process

The creation of legislation is triggered when information enters the parliamentary decision process. This information is typically provided by advocacy groups or by government agencies. This might be through formal submissions and petitions, through inquiries by parliament, the media, or direct contact with politicians. This information is mediated through the bureaucracy. Public servants scan the media, attend meetings, or are

A welter of policies reflecting a lack of synthesis

Policy is the first level of regulation by government. This is not to say that resources will necessarily flow to the implementation of policy, nor does it mean that specific law will be enacted, but it does signal political attention and will to address the subject matter. Following is an incomplete listing of policies applicable in 2004 in one State (NSW). All are meant to regulate resource use. The list is a mixture of State and national policies. Local government and State agency policies would also apply but are not listed. There are equivalents in all States to most of these policies.

- Weirs Policy
- State Rivers and Estuaries Policy
- State Wetlands Policy
- Estuaries Policy
- Sand and Gravel Extraction Policy
- State Soils Policy
- State Trees Policy
- State Groundwater Policy
- Stream Management Policy
- Riparian Zone Policy
- Riverine Plains Policy
- Wild and Scenic Rivers Policy
- Environmental Flow Policy
- River Recreation Policy
- Water Quality Policy
- Flood Prone Land Policy
- Policy and Guidelines Aquatic Habitat Management and Fish Conservation Policy
- Policy for Dredging and Reclamation
- Policy for Marine and Estuarine Waterfront development
- Policy for Bridges, Roads, Causeways, Culverts and similar structures
- Policy on Introduced and Translocated fish
- Habitat Rehabilitation and Environmental Compensation Policy
- Australia's Oceans Policy
- State Environment Planning Policy – Coastal wetlands
- State Environment Planning Policy – Urban Bushland
- State Environment Planning Policy – Littoral Rainforest
- State Environment Planning Policy – Hazardous and offensive industry
- State Environment Planning Policy – Maintenance dredging
- State Environment Planning Policy – Operation of mines and extractive industries
- Coastal Policy

What is most striking is not the number, but the fact that they are dealing with essentially the same issues, in a fragmented way. This exposes the reality that governments are coping with emergent issues, rather than developing comprehensive, principles-based strategies for dealing with sustainability. The lack of synthesis in sustainability policy is a barrier to simplifying and strengthening the regulatory approach.

It is difficult to determine which policies are 'active, as policies are rarely formally revoked. More typically they lapse into disuse. The resulting uncertainty contributes to transaction costs.

briefed by interest groups. The information is then changed – distorted or interpreted – in the parliamentary system in both the advocacy and the political process. Some of these processes are formal. Agencies are often charged with the task of investigating possible regulatory reforms. This is likely to mean that they will carry out their own investigations, as well as carrying out stakeholder analysis. Through these processes the agency will typically contact the stakeholders with whom they commonly deal and marry this to contact with groups pressuring for reform. The process establishes a structure for a debate or conflict out of which the agency will distil its advice. The agencies become parties to the advocacy, and their views are often powerful in the shaping of its outcomes (Lazarus 2004).

In the period between advocacy and implementation, there are opportunities for distortion of intent and outcome. This is particularly when the issues are new and there is little experience about the difficulties that may be experienced in implementation, and little agreement in society about the necessity for the legislation. Those who provide information include the media, power brokers, attitude research companies, government agencies and lobby groups. There is no guarantee that these groups will be operating from the same information base or define issues in the same way. Information accepted by parliamentarians is dependent on believability, which in turn depends on the pre-existing belief systems of parliamentarians as well as the arguments advanced. This filtration process was discussed in Chapter 2.

As draft legislation goes through the political processes it is refined, distorted or manipulated, in response to political data that includes perceptions of what voters will value, budgetary implications of various choices, information about impacts on allies and enemies, and rumour and horse-trading[1] associated with the parliamentary system. Democracy is a stage on which self-interest is legitimately acted out.

---

1   There is a market for political power. That market operates through complex transactions. The outcomes are determined through political bargaining, which involves politicians, agencies who may have a stake in the outcomes, and 'insider' stakeholders. Apart from the obvious political considerations, institutional issues such as departmental boundaries, budget availability, and the personal power of participants in the process, all determine what regulatory direction will be taken.

How regulatory process can distort intent

In *Economic Dynamics of Environmental Law*, David Driessen studied the process of rule formation in the US. Based on extensive investigation he highlights how the process is likely to introduce sources of regulatory ineffectiveness, even when the regulatory issue is as fundamental as promoting innovations to control pollution.

> Agencies have substantial incentives to avoid decisions that will disrupt existing industries, for such disruption can lead to political pressure on the agency. For this reason an agency may prove reluctant to introduce an innovation, especially radical environmental innovation that may change the winners and losers in the marketplace ...
>
> The biggest existing polluters receive most of the regulatory attention. Agencies do not regulate by figuring out what clean technologies are out there and then asking the developers of these technologies what regulations would help them to find a market, hopefully at the expense of the dirtier competitors. Rather, regulators focus on the dirtiest existing industries and use regulatory proceedings to get them to clean up. So, a major party in most rulemaking proceedings has a great financial stake in continuing the use of the current technology.
>
> Many environmental entrepreneurs will not participate at all in rulemaking proceedings like this. Many of them will get their innovations to the market, if at all, only through selling their innovations to the regulated companies. They are therefore frequently anxious not to alienate their potential customers by advocating more stringent limits on pollution based on the capacity of their innovations. (2003: 117)

Driessen provides further illustrations of the problems of entrenched economic and political power, and the process of rule formation.

These include the way in which even the selection of consultative groups to help shape policy will typically be biased towards those who have the greatest interest in the status quo, placing those who are not yet entrenched and who question that status quo at the periphery of regulatory design.

This is because the government agencies will readily identify the existing population that they regulate as key stakeholders in the new regime. Other stakeholders (such as those who are not in the 'industry') are less likely to be identified, nor are they as likely to have the same degree of economic incentive or economic power to lobby for their interests.

The author suggests that the more 'heated' the debate on issues becomes, or the more complex the issue, the less likely it is that the outcome will be a brave decision in favour of the environment. What is more likely under such circumstances is a decision to consult further, rather than take a political risk in the face of uncertainty. In the US there are various regulatory review processes such as 'cost/benefit assessment' and 'regulatory impact assessments' that further skew the regulatory process in favour of the status quo.

All of these are illustrations of an aspect of path dependence – the extent to which the ability of a society (or an organisation) to make marked change is constrained by its many forms of dependence on the existing order.

The impact on problem definition on solutions

Out of this process, through the prismatic perspectives of politicians, their advisors and technical experts, is defined a problem in need of a solution. Any environmental problem can be defined in different ways, and the precise definition will impact on the solution that will be sought. The destruction of a sensitive wetland can be defined as a environmental problem in need of regulatory intervention, an engineering problem in need of capital works, or a problem of political alliances and voter perception requiring a negotiation across a range of issues (of which the wetland is only one) or perhaps some 'spin-doctor' investment. The definition of a problem automatically defines the possible solutions that are likely to be invoked.

Specialists in regulatory drafting are involved once many important decisions have been made about the approach to be taken. It is rare to find (for example) economists and educational psychologists being seconded into the regulatory drafting team or for regulation to be put in the context of an overall behaviour management strategy. It is also the exception rather than the rule that the design of regulatory instruments is linked to the budgetary and human resource processes of the agencies responsible for implementation. Remoteness from stakeholders and implementing agencies raises the risk that what is designed may be technically good drafting, but impractical.

As a result, the passing of regulation can often be characterised as a behaviour management plan without the benefit of an integrated strategy – it is rare that the passing of regulation is married to a total program of market initiatives, education and incentives carefully designed to ensure well-defined behavioural results. Unfortunately, the system also embeds a framework of political winners/losers, which may result in swings in policy and difficulties in creating an integrated approach to cultural change or the implementation of a strategy on a sustained basis.

Implementation

The implementation of regulation creates further possibilities for a variance between intention and outcome. When agency managers are confronted by new regulations, they will look at whether they have the resources and knowledge to implement the regulatory requirements. Resources are always in short supply. Agency managers will naturally try to fit the implementation of new regulations into ongoing operations and to structure that implementation into existing modes of agency operations. When effective implementation requires the agency to restructure then, potentially, the preference is to defer implementation until the organisation is ready to change its structure and processes. Changing priorities requires both an incentive to change and knowledge about how to make that change – which may mean restructuring coordinating and control mechanisms within the organisation, or introducing new technologies for implementation and monitoring.

Many regulations require agencies to detect unwanted behaviour, and trace it to the perpetrator beyond reasonable doubt. To avoid wasting funds on unsuccessful prosecutions, enforcement agencies add internal prosecution guidelines that are often even more demanding, so that often only those potential prosecutions with an almost certain likelihood of a legal victory are pursued. The effect of these management decisions is to require intensive and expensive detection. Effective implementation also incurs transaction costs. For example, if a regulation requires traditional policing and prosecution, the responsible agency will incur significant costs for every successful prosecution. However, if the design of the applicable regulation establishes a *strict liability*[2] offence, uses innovative monitoring technology, or in some way transfers the costs to others – such as by full-cost recovery policing – then the cost structures for the agency will be markedly different.

The net effect of complex evidence requirements is threefold:

1. It requires substantial expenditure to put enforcement officers where they can observe offenders and collect evidence that will stand up to scrutiny;
2. It imposes a time and cost burden for each offence identified; and
3. It creates disincentives to prosecute and increases the incentive for 'soft' policing, such as advisory notices or informal counselling. This in turn creates further disincentives to enforcement.

As we saw in the preceding chapter, the court interpretation of regulations does not necessarily follow the original intent of the law-maker. Courts seem uncomfortable with some concepts of sustainability where the contests may be between well-established ownership rights and the demands of the inhuman environment. Only through refinement do complex concepts develop sufficient clarity to be applicable in individual cases. In the previous chapter we noted the tendency of the courts to redefine some issues into economic sustainability considerations. In part this is because a concept that is useful in political debate or in policy formulation may be too broad for application by the courts at this case-by-case level.

If judges are not fully aware of the severity of the consequence of breaches of environmental regulations, they are likely to adjust penalties downward, reducing the signalling effects throughout the system. The end effect of a strong penalty is to signal the importance of the issue to those subject to the regulation. It is for this reason that it is important that the legal community (judges and advocates) have a sophisticated understanding

---

[2] Strict liability offences are proven merely by the facts, without any requirement for proving intention.

of the natural system issues that the law is dealing with, so that they can understand the significance of harms being done to the natural system.

Following the enactment of the *Trade Practices Act* in 1974, it took over a decade of experience for the courts to become comfortable with concepts of market and competition. A similar lag was seen in the adoption of anti-discrimination laws. It may take courts some time to come to grips with sustainability principles. It is therefore important that those with a social change agenda do not limit their effort to promulgating regulations, but also ensure that lawyers and judges have a well-developed understanding of the implications of breaches, and of the significance of the environmental harms the regulation is attempting to ameliorate.

Effectiveness

Regulatory effectiveness relies on the capacity of a government to take away resources or privileges from those who do not comply. Compliance is more likely if the resource that can be taken away is of substantial value and if the threat of removal is credible. But this is not simple.

The penalty, the risk of being caught, and social acceptability of the illegality are important elements in the effectiveness of regulation. If a valuable opportunity to gain access to a resource can only be realised by breaching rules, for example, mining in a protected, environmentally-delicate riverbank area, then the probability-weighted chance of what can be won (the resource) against the probability-weighted chance (risk of being caught) of what can be lost (the eventual penalty). The risk-weighted cost of prosecution must be higher than the value of the breach of the law to the organisation or individual, if a regulation is to work. Policing and prosecution are at least as important as legal drafting. The person, in effect, gambles on whether the regulation will be effective.

The more that the unlawful use of resources is socially acceptable, the less likely will be compliance. Popular examples are the ineffectiveness of soft-drug regulation, minor tax avoidance and past efforts at liquor prohibition. In these instances the law-breaker is supported in their choice by the lack of strong social sanctions against the behaviour, and by the perception of a low risk of successful prosecution.

An alternative explanation is that for the majority, compliance is based on acceptance of the responsibility of the citizen to comply with the law. It is through perception of the legitimacy of the power of the state, and of its capacity to enforce meaningful penalties, that regulation has its effect. If individual beliefs diverge with the values embodied in the regulation, there will be conflict. If a regulation requires a significant behaviour change, the signals will have to be far stronger than in situations where no belief-conflict arises. Credibility of the regulations within the community is important to effectiveness.

Factors affecting compliance

The International Network for Environmental Compliance and Enforcement puts forward a summary of the types of things that will impact on compliance.

Factors motivating compliance	Barriers to compliance and factors encouraging non-compliance
Economic	
➢ Desire to avoid a penalty ➢ Desire to avoid future liability ➢ Desire to save money by using more cost-efficient and environmentally sound practices	➢ Lack of funds ➢ Greed/desire to achieve competitive advantage ➢ Competing demands for resources
Social/Moral	
➢ Moral and social values for environmental quality ➢ Societal respect for the law ➢ Clear government will to enforce environmental laws	➢ Lack of social respect for the law ➢ Lack of public support for environmental concerns ➢ Lack of government will to enforce
Personal	
➢ Positive personal relationships between program personnel and facility managers ➢ Desire, on the part of the facility manager, to avoid legal process ➢ Desire to avoid jail, the stigma of enforcement, and adverse publicity	➢ Fear of change ➢ Inertia ➢ Ignorance about requirements ➢ Ignorance about how to meet requirements
Management	
➢ Jobs and training dedicated to compliance ➢ Bonuses or salary increases based on environmental compliance	➢ Lack of internal accountability for compliance ➢ Lack of management systems for compliance ➢ Lack of compliance training for personnel
Technological	
➢ Availability of affordable technologies	➢ Inability to meet requirements due to lack of appropriate technology ➢ Technologies that are unreliable

Source: Table 2.1, Chapter 2, Principles of Environmental Enforcement, International Network for Environmental Compliance and Enforcement, at <www.inece.org/enforcementprinciples.html>

The ability of the public to understand regulations is another important element in their effectiveness. If those being regulated cannot understand or give effect to the regulation, compliance will also be weak. Or if a rule requires complex technical choices for which those subject to the regulation are ill-equipped, then compliance will be difficult and resentment likely. If a regulation requires overturning power structures, change will be less likely to be rapidly adopted. In some cases regulations may require reversing past decisions, and developing the decision-making capability of those affected by the regulation so that they can adopt new approaches. This is often the case with new sustainability requirements.

When regulations introduce new concepts, there will be a lag between the creation of the regulation and its widespread acceptance. In the interim, those being forced to comply face uncertainty and may resent the imposition of the regulations. This will increase transaction costs for regulators and may cause them to – in practice – modify the regulation or cease to implement it. To illustrate, regulations banning vessels discharging sewage into estuaries may be down-played by regulators because many vessels are without holding tanks, and because of the belief by some vessel users that receiving waters are not significantly effected by discharge. The capital costs of retrofitting, some safety concerns associated with this, and natural resistance to doing so, all act to retard implementation. Coupled with the practical difficulty of detecting breaches in regulation, it is easier for regulators to simply to ignore implementation until there are at least sufficient new boats with holding tanks.

Might regulatory costs be better understood as a price?

Using regulations to encourage sustainability is expensive because of the cost of the judicial and the parliamentary systems, and costs to the agencies and those regulated. The high cost is one reason why some people argue that regulations are not effective ways of achieving change. This is part of the reason for the call for de-regulation and for more emphasis on market-based instruments. However, to look at the costs of regulation and on that basis determine that regulation is not a cost-effective strategy for promoting sustainable resource use would be misleading. Another way of looking at regulatory cost is to see it as a price of undertaking undesirable activities. If the cost is mis-allocated (to the regulator rather than the activity-doer) there will be a distortion of the market and will result in perverse outcomes. However, if the price is appropriately set, and allocated to where it will provide an incentive to avoid doing the harm, then this price (like any other price in any other market) can be an effective rationing tool.

Society uses regulations to ration scarce resources or protect valuable resources from the impacts of exploitation such as pollution. Regulations, such as State environmental planning Acts which legislate for environmental impact statements, control immediate exploitation, or require the exploiter to bear some, if not all, of the costs of harm to the environment. These regulations thereby redirect exploitative effort towards resources that are less scarce to resources where the secondary costs (externalities) will be less, or to technologies that improve the cost-effectiveness of resources or reduce the side effects of resource use.

Regulations are ways to support transactions society wishes to encourage and, in effect, tax activities it wishes to discourage. Taking this view, the regulatory cost imposed on organisations is also a mechanism for exercising control – by making it more expensive to risk harm to the environment where community values are sensitive. When the cost-effectiveness of regulations is judged without taking into account their systemic effects, their contribution towards encouraging sustainable behaviour is ignored. When a narrow perspective on regulatory efficiency is taken, it assumes that resource exploitation is the collective end of social activity. This is clearly an incomplete picture of the aims that society pursues.

On the other hand, some proponents of greater reliance on the law would argue that the legal system is efficient, and that it is this system that is the source of much of the liberal reform in society. Such a perspective is blind to the substantial costs and inefficiencies of regulatory systems. Narrow assumptions about the role and interaction of law and economics are incomplete reflections of a more complex reality. Without statutory underpinnings, market mechanisms and common law would be largely ineffectual. However, the pressure to find more cost-effective ways to pursue social and environmental responsibility, and greater flexibility in the instruments we use to do so, is a well-justified and positive force for innovation.

Better regulations?

The observations in this chapter lead to the following conclusions:

- Regulations are not optimal strategies for behavioural change when issues are poorly defined, and social structures and belief systems are not in place to support the behaviour required by the regulations.
- It is possible to increase the effectiveness of regulations by allocating significant resources to their implementation, provided that there is clarity about the issues being regulated. Without this clarity other social institutions, predominantly the courts, may reduce the effect of regulations.
- Complementary programs that change belief systems will enhance the effectiveness of regulations. Education and communications are important companions to regulation.

- The extent to which the complementary programs will enhance the effectiveness of regulations will depend on the delay between the regulation and the achievement by both the regulators and the regulated, of capabilities for implementation.

To put it briefly, to make regulations work better their design must align with the underlying incentive structure of both regulators and the regulated, and the practicalities of being able to implement change. This is difficult in new fields, such as sustainability, but several tactics may be possible.

Principles of regulatory design

The USA EPA has a long history of developing and implementing regulatory programs to control pollutants. They have developed a range of principles that they use in evaluating regulatory design. These are summarised below:

> First, enforcement programs should be strong enough to have an impact on the regulated community, to change behavior so that environmental compliance becomes standard practice among industry. To accomplish this objective, the program must reach enough violators to pose a credible threat of enforcement against all violators, it must assess sufficient penalties to deter future violations, and it must effectively communicate its results to the regulated community.
>
> Second, enforcement programs must be efficient to establish a presence within the regulated community despite limited resources. Enforcement must use all its available tools, administrative, civil, judicial, and criminal remedies. Where feasible and appropriate, multi-media approaches can address environmental problems comprehensively, potentially delivering greater environmental benefit than would likely be achieved otherwise. Similarly, risk-based targeting enables an enforcement program to devote its resources to addressing emissions or discharges that pose the greatest threat to public health and the environment.
>
> Third, enforcement should be creative, by striving where appropriate for environmental results that go beyond compliance. For example, the government can seek through enforcement to induce a violator to conduct a pollution prevention or pollution reduction project, in addition to coming into compliance.
>
> Finally, enforcement should be fair. If the government treats similar violators in a similar way, industry will have greater confidence in the government and is likely to abide by the consequences of enforcement more readily. (SF Fulton and EJ Gilberg, US EPA, *International Network for Environmental Compliance and Enforcement*, conference paper, February 1999)

To read more about regulatory design, the International Network for Environmental Compliance and Enforcement provides extensive information about this issue, including many case studies and paper <(http://www.inece.org>.

Fundamental to the design of a strategy to make regulations effective is a realistic assessment of the decision systems of the agencies and those whose behaviour is regulated, and a commitment to changing these systems to ensure that the regulation can work. To simply drop a regulation into a network of decision-making systems, and to expect it to work, is an abdication of responsibility.

The importance of feasible design

It is important to regulatory effectiveness to provide the resources to increase regulator and regulated capability, and for detection and compliance. The extent of resources required depends on community attitudes, the nature of the matter being regulated, and the transaction costs of the regulation. One way of achieving a reduction in the costs of implementation is to shape evidentiary rules designed for easy administration. For example, use of exclusion zones; where an offence is proven simply by its undertaking (strict liability) with no need to prove intent or rights to 'aver'[3] – the enforcing agency claims sets of facts based on initial evidence, and the defendant must then provide evidence to overturn this. These minimal evidence designs restrict flexibility but are justifiable when the injustice that may be created from application of strict rules is small compared to the benefits that may be achieved. Typically such situations arise where the environmental value being protected is very important, and/or where the inconvenience to the regulated group complying is small.

Regulatory design should also acknowledge the possible contribution of technology. Technology can be used to reduce transaction costs – for example, the use of speed cameras and parking meters in traffic management. It is possible to insert 'traces' and dyes into chemicals or liquids, to have genetic or chemical or electrical signatures, and to use automatic metering and monitoring to reduce supervision costs and increase the certainty of identification. 'Privatised' monitoring – where a private agency provides the technology and obtains a share of the penalties – would remove the investment risk of providing this capital from policing agencies. The EPA has successfully used this approach in managing electricity generation emissions in NSW.

Regulatory instruments should have measurable goals and transparent evaluation, enabling agencies and individuals to know whether they are achieving their targets. There should be an incentive for the regulated to make the regulations work. As noted earlier, where both the transaction costs of enforcement and the risks of failure all fall on the regulator, then the odds are stacked against the regulator. A better system is one in which the good operators in the system also have an incentive to assist the regulator to control the bad operators. This requires some care in design. One method is to have credible penalties, which will more than compensate the regulator for the transaction costs of enforcement. Another is to have a default outcome so that all of those in the regulated group are aware that if the regulation (or other control on abuses) proves ineffective, all potential harm-doers will be denied access, or have access only on very restricted conditions. The *Green Dot* program already described is a useful illustration of this principle.

---

3   Widely used in anti tax-avoidance legislation

VOICE OF EXPERIENCE: REGULATIONS

Neil Gunningham is the author of S*mart Regulation: Designing Environmental Regulation* (with Grabosky, Oxford University Press, Oxford, 1998) and a leading academic and advisor in the field of regulatory design. He is also a consultant to the Organisation for Economic Cooperation and Development (OECD), to the United Nations Environment Program (UNEP) and to various environmental and occupational health and safety regulatory agencies in Australia.

If a catchment manager asked you for guidance about how to regulate better, what principles would you suggest they bear in mind?

The starting point for any design should be 'will it work?'. While this should be an obvious point, it is clear that often effectiveness is sacrificed in the pursuit of political acceptability. Often you end up with weak education or voluntary programs, which don't offend anybody but usually also have very limited positive impact. So you have high political acceptance and very low effectiveness.

Of course, you can't have everything. There is a tradeoff to be considered, between issues of acceptability, social equity and effectiveness. Sometimes what you think might work will not be politically practical, such as a strong 'polluter pays' approach, if the affected industry will mount such a strong opposition that the politicians will not back it. This is one of the reasons why it can be very valuable to accompany negative regulation (sanctions) with incentives, so that the people being regulated do have some positive choices available to them. Positive incentives offer a lot of flexibility.

Your strategies reflect a pragmatic approach to the politics of communities, as well as the practicality of instruments. Could you give us some more detail about this aspect of his thinking?

Political practicality also can guide the choice of instrument. To illustrate, environmental taxes, to be effective in influencing behaviour, may have to be set at such a high rate that there will be a political backlash and for this reason may not be a good choice.

There is also value in thinking about how to soften the introductory stage of a regulatory approach. For example, South Australia led the way with the protection of native vegetation. They phased this in, beginning with an education and voluntary approach, moving through incentives to bans on clearing. However, even when they introduced bans, they provided a financial benefit (that is, compensation) for protecting vegetation when a clearing licence could not be obtained. This made it more acceptable. The price was however quite high, creating a $61m hole in the South Australian budget, and so after about ten years, the financial incentives were phased out.

Clearly there is some sort of priority sequence in the approaches you take to regulation. Could you please outline this in some more detail?

There is a hierarchy in how you approach regulation. For example, if you have decided that regulation is necessary then the next key issue is what type of regulation will work best.

The first level of this is to regulate on an outcomes basis, regulation by results. This is the closest to managing the impacts you want to manage, but often it is not possible. For example, managing non-point source pollution – you simply can't measure it directly so a performance standard won't be possible.

The next level you move to is mandating some forms of specified technology or standard. A simple example is to require fencing to protect a river bank. This has the advantage that you can see whether it has been done – it is easy for the administrator, and for neighbours, to verify compliance.

If this is not feasible, then you move down the hierarchy to requiring some process to be in place. This might be an environment management system (EMS) or a code of practice, or the implementation of a prescribed best management practice. The difficulty with this approach is the risk that this will descend into tokenism.

You have not mentioned much about policing and enforcement, is this because of the costs, or for some other reason?

Enforceability is absolutely essential, you simply cannot get away from the necessity of enforcement because regulation will rarely work without it. If enforcement is not effective, then your whole approach will lack integrity and people will not support it.

This issue can be politically difficult (as well as practically challenging). Politicians may want to avoid the problems, and back off on enforcement. My response to that is that if this happens, then we are being unfair to those who do the right thing. We create a 'free rider' on the back of those who do comply, and give an advantage to those who choose not to.

That is not the same as saying that enforcement has to be harsh. I would often prefer to see a softly-softly approach. In the early stages, people are given advice on how to comply. If they continue to be uncooperative, an administrative notice can be supported by a personal visit and an offer of assistance or advice. The offender can be told that there will be a follow up to see how they are going. Only after this has proven to be ineffective do you move to the harsher side of enforcement.

In Neil's approach, regulation is nested within a broader social change framework. The challenge is not merely the technical design issue of making regulation that is cost-effectively enforceable, it is also the management of the political context, and the creation of a staged approach that will be fair, and be seen to be fair, by those whose behaviour is being regulated.

Chapter 9

Influencing the rate of change

The RCDM described in Chapter 2 highlighted that in the pursuit of sustainability, only the two flows – resources and information –can be changed to affect resource-use outcomes. The strategies explored in this book harness the market to provide a different pattern of price signals to encourage conservation, or use regulation to discourage particular resource consumption actions or generate or support a market. Two observations are at the heart of the strategies discussed. First, that it is possible to change the structures that shape these flows by managing institutional arrangements. Secondly, that innovation is central to achieving the desired efficiencies in resource use while delivering desired services.

Effective strategies have a character of permanent change. Markets are created, regulations imposed, and institutions reformed to achieve long-term strategic outcomes. Over time these changes give rise to new patterns of incentives, new information flows and new belief-based ordering and decision-making, through the mechanisms described in the RCDM. The reinforcement of the desired patterns is ongoing.

Sometimes it is necessary to oil the wheels of progress, and tactical influence strategies allow this. The term 'tactical' is used here to describe interventions that are not intended to be permanent, intended to achieve specific aims rather than more fundamental changes. Education programs and incentives for particular works are tactics for the pursuit of sustainability. These tactics are never likely to be reliable tools to reverse the effects of the incentives and information flows of a consumption-focused society, but can be important as part of a process of change. The nature of systemic change is that it is often incremental and cumulative, and the combined effect of tactical interventions can be to eventually inculcate knowledge, beliefs and behaviours that will be significant.

Two types of influence program

This chapter deals with two types of influence. The first is tactical intervention in resource flows, through incentives. The second is intervention through information (education and marketing).

It is important to make a distinction between incentives and information as tactical interventions, and market instruments, regulation and institutional reform as strategic interventions. It is natural for government to be nervous of radical interventions that may upset the powerful stakeholders in the status quo. It is therefore unsurprising that government will often elect to use the least threatening, and usually reversible, interventions.

A targeted incentive or education program often fits this description. However, such tactical intervention is not an efficient replacement for more radical strategic change. Tactical interventions (unless in support of strategic change) typically cannot be sustained except by continuing public expenditure, and if they run counter to mainstream incentives and signals they must overcome filtration effects and 'friction' to be significantly effective. For the sustainability strategist, tactical interventions are important, but they are second-best alternatives in rebalancing the relationship between humans and the natural world.

Types of incentives

Incentive schemes reward, and therefore promote, desired behaviour. They also have the effect of helping to change attitudes and increase the knowledge of those who participate in the scheme and also those who observe outcomes for the participants. People who take up incentives and succeed in their projects provide credible evidence to others and this assists the recruitment of subsequent waves of those who are prepared to act on the incentive. Landcare, Coastcare and Bushcare are all programs that have successfully blended incentives with recruitment through examples of clear benefit to participants.[1]

Incentives can be financial or non-financial. They include:

- *Public recognition*, such as through awards, or 'credentialing' the person or the works. For example, putting a sign on the gate to private land acknowledging the owners have established a voluntary conservation reserve under Landcare provides public recognition.
- *Social reward*, such as is gained by participating with a group of like-minded people engaged in good work. Often the social networks are the main reason why individuals remain engaged in groups, such as 'care' organisations or environmental groups.
- *Opportunity*, such as becoming pre-qualified for different treatment or included in a preferred supplier program as a result of acting in a certain way. For example, the US EPA certification of firms as superior environmental performers, rewarding them with less onerous audit conditions, preference in projects, and (reflecting the lower cost of their compliance monitoring) reduced fees.
- *Cash*, either as a direct incentive payment or as a reduction in an obligation through tax deductions, lower tax rates, or avoidance of other expenditures.

---

1   In Chapter 3 we outlined the operation of the individual subsystem. The psychology that drives individuals, explained in Social Cognitive Theory, makes each person open to modelled behaviour – especially when it is the behaviour of peers.

- *Capital*, such as providing funds for infrastructure work like riparian area fences, stock-watering points, changes to manufacturing technology, remote area solar-power systems, or improved sewage treatment.

It is possible to set up incentive schemes to influence the input, the process or the output of a particular endeavour. Under an inputs-focused incentive scheme, participants in the scheme qualify by providing proof of the adjustment of inputs. For example, a resource user might qualify for a tax credit or a certification by removing a riparian area from production, adopting chemical-free farming, or agreeing to forego fishing in a spawning area. For process-focused incentives, scheme participants need to adopt a certain process, for example, life-cycle assessment for products, cleaner production techniques, or changes to fishing methods to reduce by-catch. When the incentive is focused on outputs, incentive schemes are rewarded for particular outcomes, such as bounties for fox carcasses or rewards for reporting new Argentine ant nests.

As well as using incentives to influence the behaviour of natural resource users, they can be used to change the information or decision-making resources of users. For example, it is possible to use incentives to provide training to users, increase their access to technical expertise, or focus research and development on to particular topics – such as is done through Cooperative Research Centres (CRCs).[2]

Subsidies as incentives

The line between subsidy and incentive schemes is blurred. Generally, we think of subsidy schemes as those that partially or wholly compensate for the costs of a private activity. They can be paid to cover the cost of new activities, or to compensate for expenses or lost opportunities. For example, a subsidy may compensate for the voluntary surrender of land to an environmental trust, or the establishment of a conservation reserve on private property for environmental purposes; the surrender of fishing licenses to create a conservation zone; expenses incurred in acting for the benefit of the environment such as purchase of herbicides for weed control, or traps for feral animals, or additional costs of measuring and reporting emissions.

Subsidy schemes often harness the good will of the community, targeting people whose beliefs or self-interest makes them attuned to carrying out beneficial works. These people may have a 'good citizen' ethos, or a commitment to the environment. Allocating even relatively small financial support may provide the additional comfort they need that their work has community and government support and build their confidence to proceed.

---

2   CRCs – Cooperative Research Centres – established by the federal government in the early 1990s to provide the infrastructure to encourage cooperative research and development in various fields between the public and private sector.

Privately subsidising conservation

Some utility companies help consumers reduce demand for their products. It is in the utility company's interest to do so when the demand for their product outstrips supply, and/or the cost of supplying the resource is restrictive.

The Kalgoorlie-Boulder area of Western Australia is one example. Water is transported by pipeline over 500 kms to service the remote mining towns of that region. As a result the operating and capital costs associated with supplying this demand are amongst the highest in Western Australia. Population in the towns is increasing, resulting in even greater demand.

The utility company was not able to meet the demand, necessitating water use restrictions during summer. This led the water corporation to conduct a water efficiency education program. The program consisted largely of engineering and design strategies to reduce demand.

It included:

- Retrofitting 6/3 litre dual flush toilets – free of charge;
- AAA-rated (9 litres per minute or less) water efficient shower heads – installed free of charge;
- Fitting of flow restrictors/aerators to tap spouts in internal sinks and basins – free of charge;
- Leaking taps repaired – free of charge;
- Air-conditioner bleed valves fitted – free of charge;
- Garden reticulation systems checked and adjusted plus minor repairs – free of charge;
- Tap timers discounted from $AUS20 to $AUS8;
- The supply of free WaterWise (drought tolerant species) plants up to the value of $AUS80; garden mulch up to the value of $AUS200 in exchange for lawn reduction and new garden establishment in the WaterWise theme;
- WaterWise garden assessment and information brochures – free of charge;
- Free water audits for the premises of 150 commercial and institutional customers with annual demand greater than about 1,000kL/a; [and]
- Two WaterWise demonstration gardens which incorporate information on low maintenance and low cost landscaping.

The financial analysis of the program suggests that the financial benefits in reduced operating and capital costs will more than make up for the costs. There will also be a major financial benefit to customers in reduced water bills and also energy bills due to reduced hot water usage. Based on the original budget, the projected savings to the Water Corporation are $AUS3.5m, and $AUS2.8m to the customer over a 2.5 year period.

Source: Jodi Smith (2004)

Alternatively a subsidy may simply provide the leverage needed to bring some tasks forward in time or work priority. It may be that the subsidised work fits with other tasks and can be carried out at less than the full cost of the work when all tasks are combined. In this case the offer of subsidy may allow the resource user to justify bringing the subsidised work forward into a total work program. An example would be where a government catchment authority wants to carry out an extensive weed eradication program, and seeks to have adjacent land managers participate. Offering a selective subsidy may be sufficient to bring them into the fold, allowing some efficiencies of scale. In the case of weed or feral animal control, these efficiencies can be fundamental to effectiveness.

Perhaps a subsidy scheme may reduce the price of some input, for example, the subsidy on solar energy may encourage people to adopt the technology.[3] A recent example is the domestic subsidies for the use of solar water heaters, or (in many States) the subsidisation of domestic rainwater tanks. Another reason some people or organisations take up subsidies is their expectation that the works being subsidised will provide some advantage, such as a higher value of a property, a public relations benefit, or perhaps improvement in how the resource is managed for profit. A subsidy may perhaps overcome a cash-flow problem, giving a reason to bring forward work, or swing the economic balance in favour of the works, or fit with opportunities to carry out the work at low cost, by accessing underemployed labour, or providing carryover work between more profitable activities. The range of situations where subsidies could help is enormous although unfortunately the funds for such subsidies are always limited.

Advantages to government

Harnessing any of these reasons for carrying out works to improve sustainability offer substantial cost savings and public relations advantages for agencies:

- Voluntary works are often more politically palatable than work imposed or carried out by government. When government provides subsidies, it is supporting, rather than controlling the private citizen and entrepreneurs, creating opportunities for positive relationships and positive messages.
- Avoiding legal and political barriers to works on private lands can reduce costs. When an owner voluntarily takes up a project, there is no cause for compensation, and no sense of violation of rights. The subsidy is seen as supporting the interests of the rights-holder.

---

3   Note that production subsidies, fuel rebates, a super-phosphate bounty, and subsidies which support economically marginal farming in sensitive environments also have the effect of promoting resource use, which may be counter to sustainability.

- The costs of work carried out by voluntary groups, or by organisations who take up subsidy offers, can be lower than that of works done by agency-employed staff:
  - Volunteers do substantial work without being paid and, because of high motivation, may be less costly to encourage and supervise than paid workers;
  - They can sometimes lend capital equipment (such as farm equipment like tractors) so the project does not bear depreciation and other costs associated with equipment use;
  - Specialists may provide technical support on more favourable terms than for paid 'commercial' projects, when they are supporting a volunteer effort.
- Budget management can be easier for the administering agency. Typically, subsidy payments have a fixed value. If conditions for the payment are not met, there is no obligation to make that payment. Contract supervision is easy when all you have to do is certify completion, ignore day-to-day supervision, and when the party doing the work has no choice but to complete the job if they want the payment.
- Limiting the subsidy can control budgets. Unlike programs where the agency carries the staff and capital obligation (and the political cost of incomplete works), there are no ongoing obligations. Subsidy programs can be increased or decreased with funds availability although there may be some political costs. They can be adjusted depending on response. There are typically few risks of budgetary over-runs. Although this flexibility is an advantage for the agency, it can be a significant source of inefficiency for those working within the subsidy scheme. Intermittent funding means that projects commenced when a subsidy is available may not continue if funding is reduced. Learning, goodwill and effort may be lost in the process.

The costs of subsidy schemes

Unfortunately, individuals who carry out work under subsidy schemes are sometimes managed as if they were dubious claimants of public support. There are many examples of 'burnout' by Landcare and Coastcare, and other community champions who cite constant battles with bureaucracy as the cause of their disillusion. Often the problem is that when agencies assess the costs of the subsidy they administer, they do not adequately recognise the non-direct financial benefits being provided by the recipients. Unpaid salaries, depreciation on capital and lost production borne by those who take up the subsidy, all act as cross-subsidies of the agency budget. The result is that the value being contributed by the community may be poorly recognised, and the sense of partnership can be undermined.

Subsidy schemes, for all of their substantial benefits, do have costs to the agencies and the community that can make involvement unappealing. The transaction costs embedded in subsidy schemes can be substantial.

There is a cost in making bids for support – incurred whether a bid is successful or not; there are infrastructure costs ranging from the costs of regulation-making through to the costs of scheme managers, materials production and printing, marketing to applicants, political relationship management, dispute and inquiry management; and the costs of explaining the benefits of the scheme.

In addition, the uptake of subsidies depends on the motivation of individuals and organisations. This increases the risk of crucial elements in a sustainability strategy not being taken up. For example, an agency may be trying to encourage farmers in a catchment to rehabilitate the riparian zone. To be effective, all landholders in the catchment should participate. If some do not, especially if they are in the upper catchment, the outcome of the efforts of downstream farmers may be suboptimal. Regulation has the advantage that no one gets a 'free-rider' gain by choosing not to be involved, whereas voluntary schemes can be plagued with the problems of some members of the community choosing not to participate.

There are also issues of economic efficiency in voluntary works. Subsidy uptake by scattered groups who do not share their knowledge or resources may mean that it is more difficult to gain economies of scale and learning. The same mistake (like choosing the wrong species, ill-advised weed control, or other basic errors) can be made in different places, even when the cures are known elsewhere. Suboptimal capital equipment may be employed because the fixed costs of the right equipment cannot be efficiently spread. Of course it may be possible for the agency sponsoring the works to overcome some of these difficulties. For example, many agencies now publish case studies and hold forums where they bring together community groups to share experiences.

Creating effective incentives and subsidies

The effectiveness of incentive and subsidy schemes is highest when they fit with the preferences of the target group. For example, the Waste Reduction Grants offered by the NSW EPA provide opportunities for small to medium-sized NSW businesses to extend waste reduction, tapping into their business motivation. Individuals and organisations in NSW can apply for grants up to $100,000 for innovative and proactive approaches to waste reduction. The EPA disbursed some $5 million in subsidies between 1997 and 2002, funding projects such as:

- A computer take back scheme;
- A waste education/promotion Internet site;
- The distribution of food waste to charities;
- A radio program about waste reduction called *Talking Absolute Rubbish*;
- The use of recycled waste materials in concrete.

Effective schemes ensure that the key elements of the RCDM are working together – resource and information flows, information-structuring and beliefs – to strongly reinforce attitudes and behaviour. Good design ensures that the hurdles – transactions costs – for all parties involved in the schemes are as low as possible.

To attract participants to an incentives program, the level of the incentive and the probability of reward have to be sufficient to outweigh any transaction costs and to justify involvement. One method of gaining more participants is to reduce the transaction costs. Encouraging agents to promote a scheme and assist potential applicants is a proven approach in commercial settings. It is not unusual for accounting firms or consultants to become promoters of business development schemes, taking a percentage of the subsidy as their payment. There are organisations that specialise in providing information about incentives, and others who help to make applications for grants.[4] This type of support is less common in incentives for sustainability than in business, but can be cost-effective in increasing uptake.

The staged uptake characteristic of incentives is generally poorly understood. Incentives and subsidies pick the 'low hanging fruit' first, and then move (with increasing cost and difficulty) towards addressing the most intractable challenges. Given this characteristic, an ideal design may be to begin with relatively small incentives to attract those who are on the edge of commitment, gradually increasing the incentive as the easy wins are taken and the more difficult problems come to be the focus of attention.

Our examination of subsidies and incentive schemes suggests that often the inverse of this rationale occurs in practice. It seems that if the initial results are encouraging, it is sometimes assumed that the incentive is fully effective. The agency may decide to cap the incentive or reduce its budget, assuming that shaving the incentive will have only a marginal effect. When the incentive loses its effect, the agency may assume it has run its natural course. The alternative approach would be to increase the extent of incentives as their uptake declines, thereby moving deeper into the less tractable applications of the incentive. It would be easy to test the alternative hypothesis that the incentive has only just begun to take effect

---

4   The Australian COMET program takes this to the extent of building in a percentage of the equity value of the enterprise that is supported as remuneration for the agent.

Funding volatility creates outcome risks

Tactical interventions are usually dependent on government funding. They bear a risk of volatile funding, due to political decision-making with scarce resources. The cost of this can be the failure to achieve the desired benefits even after substantial investment is 'sunk'. An example of this scenario is the Georges River Foreshore Improvement Program (GRFP) in Sydney. In 1999 the NSW government promised to fund a program to halt and reverse the degradation of the Georges River. In four years, the Program allocated $5.6 million for 40 projects and generated over $11 million in partnership expenditure. In 2003, the government decided not to allocate more funding to the program, announcing that it had achieved its aim. This was not the view of those directly involved, who (while proud of the results to date) were convinced that a reduction of funding would 'snatch defeat from the jaws of victory'. Their view was most of the work over the past four years had been to establish the task structure and harness community support. In their view, the incentive was poised to truly prove its worth, and that removing the grants funding would undo this good work.[5]

It is difficult to know when or whether to close down any taxpayer-funded program. The choices are inherently political and this is a fundamental problem with the use of tactical approaches such as project subsidies and education to achieve strategic goals. This problem is pervasive of natural resource management programs across Australia.

by increasing the budget and gauging whether uptake increases. It would also be possible to conduct in-depth interviews to get a good sense of whether the incentive scheme is indeed moving from the low-hanging to the higher-hanging fruit.

It may be possible to improve incentive scheme outcomes without significantly increasing costs by:

- Combining the demonstration effects of successful adoption with community education about the issues being addressed, and the solutions demonstrated by the works. To some degree this is being done with the public relations activities of government, where subsidised successes are promoted through the public media. However, this is a passive way of winning support from late adopters. As we will discuss later in this chapter, the key to educational effectiveness is engagement. Merely providing messages does not deliver this. Voluntary programs supported by incentive schemes can provide credible examples of community action, and support educational messages in the general media. To take full advantage of this requires that the educational strategies are sophisticated and effective.

---

5   Personal communication, Georges River Foreshore Program team.

- Using competition to leverage limited funds. It is possible that those who demonstrate the behaviour sought by an incentive scheme can be advantaged in winning funding. Forms of rewarded involvement might be undergoing or delivering training, or obtaining the support of partner organisations by becoming accredited. It is easy to envisage an incentive scheme in which there is a basic reward for entry-level activities but a potentially far higher reward for those who have demonstrated in practice that they are committed to the principles that are being promoted. This is consistent with the economic case for high salaries at the 'top end' driving a disproportionate amount of effort at the base levels of an organisation. The pursuit of the possibility can generate effort disproportionate to the cost of the upper level incentive. The effectiveness of leveraging depends in large part upon whether the reward for effort is attractive.
- A further opportunity is to use incentive payments to negotiate advantages for the environment. For example, subsidies and incentive payments supporting industry or farming or recreational activity could be coupled with negotiated environmental management obligations, or the allocation of incentives could be on the basis of demonstrated environmental performance. It is easy to envisage a structure in which either funding for recreational facilities such as sporting fields or special uses (dredging or boating facilities, or swimming pools, or cultural facilities) requires demonstration of the effectiveness of regional sustainability strategies, or is tied to new initiatives for the environment. In recent months the Australian government has begun rewarding Indigenous communities who achieve benchmarked levels of participation in education and work, with subsidised infrastructures like swimming pools.

Support through subsidy and incentive payments is often treated as if such payments should be permanent arrangements. This makes sustainability a fragile creature, in much the same way as permanent reliance on government support (tariffs and subsidy) can generate a fragile business sector.

During the period of transition to sustainability, direct financial support from government, and a substantial amount of support, is essential. This should be within a clear program to wean action for sustainability off the public purse, through effective regulation and harnessing of market power. A robust program for sustainability should view transition supports as temporary.

Information as an influence for adoption

One has only to visit any local council chamber, or most natural resource related government offices, to find glossy brochures, reports, videos and self-help guides aplenty. Even more common is the public announcement of the commencement of some subsidised project, complete with local dignitaries and a ministerial statement. This passive information provision is often preferred over more intensive educational approaches because it is relatively low cost (the labour and expertise cost is minimal), not threatening to those who do not want to hear the messages, and does not require that anyone really engage with the topic. It also has the benefit of being able to carry various brands, such as the logo of an institution or the photograph of an official.

It takes only a little reflection about one's own decision-making to realise that little of this passive information will have any marked impact on those who most need education about the how and why of sustainability. Rarely will the uncommitted feel motivated to scan this material, and even if they do it simply will not engage them and lead to new behaviour. As explained in the RCDM, inconsistency with self-reinforcing (rewarded) beliefs and knowledge is a powerful filtration mechanism.

Education is a deceptively simple term covering many meanings. Its dimensions include a diversity of aims (technical, attitudinal or informational), targets (children, the general population, or specific vocational targets) and a myriad of forms (passive forms like brochures through to high-engagement approaches like experiential or real life training). It is any information flow which is intended to shape the decision-structuring approach of people. The outcome can be any combination of changes to decision-structuring (either in the decision-making process, or on the values that are attached during these processes), or it can be changes in the information that is available as inputs for decisions. This relationship is somewhat circular because as structuring mechanisms change, the information that is required as an input also changes.

Empirical research shows that information on its own is not a powerful change agent, as demonstrated by several examples in Chapter 2. Passive education programs about resource conservation often has negligible impact on resource-use knowledge or behaviour. Information provision is most effective where targeted consumers are already interested and committed, or where the balance of effort and reward is sufficiently strong that the information will be sufficient to lead to adoption of the change. Though even in this instance, behaviour changes do not have a strong likelihood of 'sticking' in the absence of a sustained flow of economic or informational reinforcement.

The need for reinforcement

In one experiment (E Aronson, and M O'Leary, 1982-83) focused on water conservation behaviour, researchers placed signs next to the showers in a sporting change room. The sign asked people to *Conserve water: 1. Wet down. 2. Water off. 3. Soap. 4. Rinse.* Over 90 per cent of the users of the showers noticed and understood the signs. Only around 6 per cent complied.

Passive information provision had relatively little effect. However, when this was reinforced with a peer group demonstration (a researcher posing as a student and exhibiting the behaviour) the outcome lifted to almost half, and this rose to over two-thirds when more than one demonstration was provided. Information, plus modelling by a member of the peer group, provided a far more powerful stimulus for the desired behaviour.

In another experiment (reported by McKenzie Mohr and Smith, 1999: 39) researchers placed brochures under the windscreen wipers of the cars in a parking lot. They conducted experiments to see what affected littering. In the first instance, a researcher walked by as people came to their cars and decided whether to discard the paper or putting in the bin. Around a third took the littering option. However, if the researcher demonstrated picking up a piece of litter and put it in the bin, littering was very rare. The experiment also showed that if there was a lot of litter, people littered more than if there was very little.

Such experiments show that mere information is not what will shape behaviour, except in the case when all that is lacking is information on which to act. Other forms of reinforcement are also necessary.

From the wealth of sometimes inconsistent research on behaviourally-effective education and information recurring themes include:

- Having a clear behavioural aim;
- Knowing the target group and understanding their motivational triggers.

Building on these themes (Hernandez and Monroe 2000: 12) suggest that different strategies are required for different levels of a target group's environmental understanding. The levels are:

1. Precontemplation – Not considering or not knowing about an environmentally-friendly behaviour, or actually engaging in an environmentally-unfriendly behaviour such as dynamite fishing.
2. Contemplation – Beginning to think about adopting or changing to an environmentally-friendly behaviour.
3. Action – Trying out an environmentally-friendly behaviour.
4. Maintenance – Making the adopted environmentally-friendly behaviour a customary practice.
5. Advocacy – Multiplying the behaviour by encouraging others to do the same.

Different types of educational messages therefore have differing impacts. 'How to' information is not likely to be much use in the earlier stages of understanding, and information about 'why to' is likely to be of limited value once people have moved to the latter stages.

Creating information that works

As we've noted, information and education are most effective when they fit within an overall strategy to change to the balance of incentives, and when they align with the decision-structuring mechanisms that are in place in the subjects. Subsidies, incentives and regulation all form part of this, as does sophisticated design of messages, and the use of peer groups and illustration to show the social desirability of the sustainability actions. There is little evidence that promotional pamphlets change behaviour!

Educational design (in which we include environmental marketing) is a sophisticated field in its own right and there is a wealth of readily accessible information available.

Social marketing guides, like commercial marketing instruction, always begin with a fundamental principle: understand the people you are selling to! Unless you have a clear understanding of their decision-making, and the available points of intervention in that process, how can you design a behaviour change strategy, particularly with limited resources? If the sustainability strategist is not prepared to put in the effort to really understand the people they are intending to educate and inform, they are in effect saying 'I am prepared to gamble whether this approach will work or not.' That is not strategy! In order to change others' behaviour, a strategist can only manipulate information that flows to them, and the resources that they might secure from their environment. The RCDM identifies how behaviour is shaped by a persons values and experiences. There are no strategies that can directly adjust internal processes. However, by understanding and taking into account decision-making approaches, we can predict what strategies will work, and adjust how we manipulate information and resources to shape the outcomes.

Environmental marketing that works

Doug McKenzie-Mohr is an international leader in social marketing for environmental purposes. He provides a distillation of what is required to make environmental education work. Some of his principles reflect the implications of the RCDM.

> ➢ It is not enough to get people to listen or read – they must make a commitment. That can be symbolic, such as agreeing to take a particular simple action ('I will check the bottom of the next container I intend to throw out, to see if it can be recycled'), or it can be substantial, such as a public promise by a corporation to move to a 'zero-waste' method of operation. The stronger the commitment, the more likely that behaviour will follow.

- Passive receiving of information is a weak means of changing behaviour. Active involvement works better. This can be through the use of on-site workshops, or involvement in clean-up campaigns, children's education, or simply a bushwalk coupled with education. The greater the involvement, the greater the likelihood of change.

- Messages that conflict with existing beliefs or decision-making structures, have lower probability of being accepted. Unpalatable messages can be reshaped to seem more consistent and appealing, such as by framing sustainability in themes like 'the future of your children' or 'winning businesses adopt sustainability'. Messages can also be reframed by changing who delivers them. A sustainability message from a respected farmer is more likely to be accepted by rural people than the same message provided by an urban environmentalist. The more consistent the message with the thinking of the recipient, the easier it is to introduce.

- Prompts and reminders are important, because people easily forget messages until they become incorporated into their internal decision-making. Prompts should be simple, clear and proximate (in time and location) to the decision. A prompt might be a sticker placed next to the light switch, reminding people to 'turn off', or a wallet card on 'actions I can take for the environment'.

- Make sure that the action you want has easily identifiable social support, and that it is well demonstrated. Good examples of this in action include Landcare and Clean Up Australia day. If people know that others see the activity is good, they are more likely to implement it.

- Within these frameworks, the information needs to be interesting and engaging. Make it memorable, whether by creating interest, or by the power of the communication. Facts and figures rarely engage people, but entertainment, shock and surprise do.

- Feedback is important to sustain interest. An example of feedback might be a self-assessment checklist ('how well are you going on recycling?'), or it might be a notional monitor (the equivalent of the fund-raising 'thermometer' that may be used by a hospital charity).

- Build in accountability and a quality cycle. There is ample evidence that a process of setting and measuring performance against targets and using objective performance reviews makes a difference to management outcomes. The same applies to social marketing and educating. The statement 'if you don't measure it, you are not managing it!' is as true in sustainability strategy as in any other management domain.

Doug McKenzie-Mohr's website <www.cbsm.com> provides extensive information and case studies. Further case studies and detailed support guides are available from the Fostering Sustainable Behaviour web site at <http://www.Toolsofchange.com>. There is a step-by-step workbook (complete with pro-forma programs and case studies) *Tools of Change: Proven Methods for Promoting Environmental Citizenship* prepared for the Canadian National Round Table on the Environment and the Economy by Jay Kassirer and Doug McKenzie-Mohr This is also available for download, at <www.nrtee-trnee.ca>.

What steps must be followed?

Fred Emery (an Australian pioneer on the international arena of 'purposeful' systems) provided a dynamic view of what is needed to market a product. Emery's heuristic marketing model traced the steps involved in the marketing process from consumer ignorance about the existence of a product, through to the point at which the product is the preferred choice of the consumer.

The question to which Fred Emery directed himself is what information and environmental changes are necessary to move a consumer to move from this initial state, (ignorance or the available product) to the final state, (preference for the product)?

1. There must be a message which the target can discern. We know that most messages are filtered out. There are three requirements.

    (a) The concept must somehow fit with the target's existing values and preconceptions. If the message conflicts, it will be filtered. It is, however, also important that the message has a sufficient degree of novelty to be memorable. This balance is difficult with sustainability, which is why environmental messages are often tied to more sympathetic concepts like 'looking after the fish, so you can catch more' or 'protecting the air you breathe'.

    (b) The message should not disappear nor fragment in the mind. Simple messages are frequently powerful. Think for example of the slogan for Coca Cola ('Coke is it') or 'When you're on a good thing stick to it' (Mortein) or any memorable slogan or brand. When dealing with sustainability, complexity can be a trap, leading to detail that merely confuses.

    (c) The message should contain identifiable images which trigger memory when stimulated by a symbol or cue. Thus, for example, displays of 'Tic Tac' confectionery may trigger recall of the advertisement and/or the message which those advertisements carry.

2. The message must enable the target to learn something which creates a desire. Unless the features of the concept presented in the message are relevant to the needs of the consumer, the message will be ineffective. Often sustainability means avoidance of future harm to the collective interest, and this can be a difficult message to sell. Recasting the message as looking after children, or recreational or economic interests may make the messages more relevant.

3. It must be possible for the target to act on the message. We have seen earlier that actions for sustainability can be limited by matters like the lack of information ('green' purchasing), infrastructures (public transport) or gaps in knowledge (sustainable farming). Unless barriers are removed, the outcome will be frustration. Implicit within this is the need for detailed understanding of the steps which

the potential customer will have to take to effect the transaction and of the factors which will lead or deter them from effective action.

4. It is essential that the target, at the time of making the relevant decision can discriminate between available alternatives to choose the desired approach. In a crowded environment, the preferred choice must be made distinctive, and the unique appeal of the product must be made clear. Often the resource user lacks meaningful support for more sustainable choices, from everyday consumption issues (that is, 'which food product is most sustainably produced?') through to lifestyle choices like 'where will I live?' or 'what kind of recreational activities will I do?'

5. To ensure commitment it is essential that the effected transaction provides satisfaction. When the benefit is to the planet or future generations, this is difficult. Effective education often sets up proximate goals like 'you will know you are a responsible citizen because you recycle', in the hope that the act will provide at least that emotional satisfaction to the actor.

6. It is desirable that this positive experience is conveyed to other people providing 'word of mouth' promotion for sustainability. With sustainability, the media 'green radical' imagery stands in the way. There are many people who do not want to be associated with a group whom they think may be socially unacceptable. Replacing this image with less challenging ones like families, community leaders, or even sporting heroes, is one possible approach.

Why target and segment?

We know that a person's situation significantly affects the way they behave, and the choices they make.

Marketing gurus, organisational change specialists, and sales trainers suggest that we should 'stand in the shoes' of our target groups and see the world from their perspective. Understanding our targets requires an understanding of what motivates them – what their values and capabilities are, their environment, filtered through. Only when we understand can we develop effective tactics to affect their behaviour.

Groups may be segmented by their attitude towards the environment (for example, from indifference, to emerging interest, to personal commitment, to active promotion of sustainability), or knowledge (for example, from ignorance to deep knowledge). They are segment-able by their role in relation to natural resource issues (for example, domestic consumer, industrial manager or operator, agency employee). What different groups want or need in sustainability information will vary accordingly. Taking a 'one size will fit everyone' approach is likely to result in a 'no size will fit anyone' outcome. Education and information strategies are likely to be effective proportionate to their precision.

The power of precision

Precise targeting of promotional messages is cost effective. One illustration is the chartered accounting firm which grew from being at the bottom of the 'big 8' ladder amongst chartered accounting firms to being in the upper part of that list, in only five years. A key to its highly successful promotional strategy was the use of highly targeted communications:[6]

- A series of current event publications, such as discussions of the Taxation Summit or the White Paper on Taxation, or the Fringe Benefits Tax. These publications were prepared and mailed within twenty four hours of the information being available, hitting the desks of potential clients at a time when they were most concerned about these issues, and conveying the message of the firm's expertise and efficiency.
- Public relations releases on events of topical interest, timed to hit the media while the issues were still 'hot'.
- A specialist market research of chief executives, published in conjunction with Business Review Weekly, focusing upon current issues and made available to the senior executives with further information sent upon request.
- A number of direct mailings and publications, timed to reach the decision maker at the point where the issue has become a question of concern, and highlighting the firm as the source of a solution to that issue.

The key to success was in focusing the right message at the right time, rather than relying upon the weight of a substantial advertising expenditure. Precision, rather than expenditure, was the tool.

---

[6] Personal communication, senior marketing consultant.

VOICE OF EXPERIENCE: EDUCATION

Dr Jodi Smith is expert in strategies for educating people to change their behaviour in relation to the environment. Among her many projects are studies of what approaches are most effective to ensure business and government implementation of environmental safeguards[7].

What works, and what does not?

The methods that many educators use are effective in raising awareness, but not in obtaining behaviour change. This became clear to me personally working with 1500 businesses in the 'Changing Streams Pollution Reduction Project'. A wide range of techniques were used including brochures and case studies, site visits and audits, seminars and training, grants, awards, and other forms of recognition. We published regular newspaper articles and educated the public to support those businesses that were taking action. We started an industrial resource exchange helping the companies to use each other's waste as raw resources. The outcome was well short of the aims. There were knowledge and attitude outcomes, but relatively little change in practices. So I began more intensive research to find out what works and why.

If I was trying to introduce a sustainable practice into business, or government, what would you tell me to do?

That you must involve your staff throughout the whole initiative. They need to understand why the change is important, why it will be worthwhile, and how to do it. They must believe that it is achievable. They should have the opportunity to ask questions and suggest options for action. Together you should choose the steps you will take to implement the change, when it will occur and how. This way the staff will have some commitment to the change and be motivated to do it. If this does not occur staff are likely to simply resist or ignore the initiative.

I would also tell you to carefully consider what level of action you want to take. There are many different possibilities for making your business more sustainable. I see sustainability not as an end point to reach, but as a journey. The end point continues to move as technology and our capabilities improve. Best practice is typified by a business whose management and staff are doing as much as is possible for their industrial sector at any particular point in time while also researching how to improve practices further.

---

7 For details, the web site is <www.une.edu.au/cwpr/people/Jodi.html>.

In your thesis[8] you consider interventions targeting outcomes from simple reactive changes, to holistic proactive ones. Can businesses choose the level they want?

Yes they can, but it is important to realise that over time each business will need to implement the more complex sustainability approaches. Business personnel will be pressured to do so by stricter regulations; customer, investor and community demands; bank and insurance company policy requirements; competitor cost savings and marketing advantages; and market access pressures, to mention a few.

If business wants initiatives to succeed it requires creating a learning organisation or change-supportive culture. This means you need to ensure that staff members have time allocated to learn about the changes, to implement them, measure their impact and refine them. They have to be encouraged to admit when something isn't working or when they don't know what to do. Any mistakes or problems that occur need to be seen as learning opportunities so that staff members feel safe enough to admit to them. If a safe space is not made staff members are unlikely to risk making the changes or suggesting improvements for fear of the consequences. If you really want them to bring energy to the project it's also advisable to provide forms of recognition and reward for their efforts.

Let's say you were given such a project. Tell me the steps you would go through, and highlight the things that you think would be essential to success?

This is an adapted version of John Kotter's eight-step approach to leading change.

Step 1: Establish a sense of urgency, making sure that people understand why it is essential to change.

Step 2: Create a guiding coalition of people who do care about what you are trying to achieve, and get them to lead the change.

Step 3: Develop a vision and strategy, based on understanding the people in the organisation. We would set ourselves specific goals, and make sure that we have the ability to achieve them, and then work hard to have everyone commit to them.

Step 4: Communicate the change vision and continue spreading the word about sustainability. Everyone should know what we are doing, how we are doing it and where we are up to. Making sure that people stay informed and feel a part of the process is important.

Step 5: Empower broad-based action. I'd ensure that people have time to work on the issues. I'd promote the process as one of continuous improvement. I'd ensure that individuals were not blamed if things went wrong. We would look for the systemic reasons that led to the problem and change the system to prevent it reoccurring.

Step 6: Create and celebrate short-term wins. By having wins throughout the process it helps to keep people motivated and committed to the project. I would ensure that all stakeholders know the wins we are making. It's important that wins are celebrated not just documented.

Step 7: Consolidate gains and produce more change. I'd keep communicating about the issue and our progress to ensure that staff and management stay focused on it.

Step 8: Anchor new approaches into the culture. Ideally I would ensure that the people who are hired or promoted are advocates for sustainability. I'd ensure that reporting on sustainability initiatives is included in all staff meetings. The staff of each

---

8 *Redesign of government sustainability education programs for business personnel – from awareness raising to changing behaviour*, University of New England 2004.

department or work area should be working to improve their own practices as well as being a part of the larger initiative. I would conduct regular surveys of staff to identify any needs that they have, any barriers to the process that exist and take action to remove them. This may involve changing policies and structures in support of sustainability.

Given this organisational change focused and systemic approach, what should government or other sustainability strategists think about when they approach these change issues?

There is no simple, quick fix. Getting any audience or targeted stakeholder group to change their behaviour requires significant commitment of resources and time. It requires a multi-faceted approach.

Most government initiatives I have evaluated have involved one or two focuses. They may have focused on legislation and penalties or on awareness raising and case study development. Some tried grants and incentives while others tried developing voluntary codes of practice. There has rarely been a coordinated approach.

Awareness raising on its own has proven to result in little behaviour change. Likewise a reliance on legislation and penalties has been shown not only to achieve little behaviour change, but it has often led to a reluctance in business personnel to work together with the government in the future or to move beyond basic compliance. Similarly, the use of emotional appeals to protect the environment for its own sake, with wonderful images of animals and plants, has had limited impact on behaviour. Why? I believe that it is because on their own these approaches do not address the specific beliefs that the targeted stakeholders hold. They do not identify or remove the barriers to change that they may face or explain how to and help them to implement the changes to their practices. The initiatives do not meet the targeted stakeholders needs.

In order for sustainability strategists or government staff to be successful with their efforts they need to work with the targeted stakeholders. They have to find out what the targeted stakeholders believe, what barriers to change they face and what support they need. They should then design their policy and programs to meet these. This can only be achieved through participative problem solving and focused education and policy approaches. In essence they have to ensure that their efforts help the targeted stakeholders to see why the issue is important, why it is worthwhile for them to take action, and that they can successfully implement the changes. They have to believe it is achievable.

This suggests that a wide range of policy and education approaches should be used. Individual tools or approaches can be seen as pieces of a jigsaw puzzle, each of them is an important part of the picture, but it is only when they are all bought together that the picture is complete. Likewise the various policy and education approaches can be seen as complementary. We need legislation and enforcement, we need incentives and role models, we need awareness raising and consumer pressure, but we also need training and coaching of the targeted stakeholders, not only in sustainability methods, but also in the skills of leading change. We need to make it as easy as possible for business personnel or any targeted stakeholder group to change their behaviour.

There are lots of educational initiatives taking place but they do not seem to have a major impact. Is this because they are too simplistic, or just not resourced?

I believe that in order to make it easy, we need to actually look at not only the educational and policy methods that we use but also our organisational structures. At the moment there are many different agencies and government departments that are each running education programs and other initiatives on a wide range of different environment related topics: water, air and soil pollution; biodiversity; climate change; and waste management to mention a few. Targeted stakeholder groups such as business personnel and residents are bombarded with information from different agencies and do not know who to listen to or what to do first. The government programs compete against each other and minimise their own success.

In order to remedy this, I believe we should have a whole-of-government approach with a single government sustainability program that addresses all issues. This way the targeted stakeholders would only have one person or agency to listen to or to contact when they want help. Local Agenda 21 attempts to do this at the local level, however at the State and federal level there are many different agencies involved, all spending significant amounts of money on projects. A lot more could be achieved if these funds were combined and used to produce a single, multi-faceted, whole-of-government education and assistance program that helped the targeted stakeholders to address their needs, built their capacity to take action and coached them with their efforts.

The three levels of government could still be involved just having specific roles to reduce duplication and maximise effectiveness. For instance the federal government sustainability agency could research sector specific solutions, work to alter federal legislation and market conditions to encourage targeted stakeholders to take action, and finance mass-media awareness raising campaigns. The State government could deliver training to local level educators and provide networking and support services to them. In addition to this they could alter their State legislation and the operating conditions within their State to make it as important and worthwhile for the targeted stakeholders to take action. While local government would actually work with the business personnel to implement the changes – to make them achievable.

Are there any other things you want to bring out?

I'd like to reemphasise that all the different policy mechanisms are required to make it as important and worthwhile as possible for the targeted stakeholders to take action. Problem solving focused education methods and coaching can then be used to make it as easy as possible for the targeted stakeholders to achieve the changes. It is my opinion that no single mechanism will be effective on its own. They are all important pieces of the jigsaw puzzle.

PART 3: IMPLEMENTATION

Chapter 10

HIGH-LEVEL DESIGN CONSIDERATIONS

The preceding chapters of this book have been about strategies. This chapter presents some broader policy issues and puts forward some 'big picture' ideas about the reforms that are needed as we move towards sustainability.

Broad policy issues that impact on strategy design

Any strategy that changes how people access and use natural resources will have secondary effects. It will impact wealth and the ways that people create wealth. It will impact the patterns of belief in a society for, as we saw in Part 1, these are shaped by the patterns of reward. Questions of fairness and the spread of opportunity in society will arise in response to any change of wealth and access to resources. For these reasons it is not enough to consider only whether a strategy will achieve specific natural-resource management outcomes. Whether a strategy has secondary adverse effects or can be shaped to deliver benefits outside of the narrow confines of resource management should be an important concern.

Accordingly, it is worth testing any strategy against the following four policy considerations:

1. How costs and benefits are allocated, taking into account the economic and cultural patterns that might be promoted by the strategy.
2. The need to take into account social justice and equity in the design, so that the strategies strengthen social as well as natural resilience.
3. The fact that due to financial and political constraints, government is limited in its capacity to implement systemic change.
4. The need to account for path dependence (discussed in Part 1) which limits the rate and amount of change that is feasible (except when there are radical shocks from the environment). Sound strategies will need to consider how to reduce the inevitable lags, and account for the delays that cannot be removed.

Allocating the costs, benefits and social impacts

It is important to consider how the costs and benefits from any sustainability strategy are allocated, taking into account the economic and cultural patterns that might be promoted by the strategy. Depending on which mix of instruments is used, there will be different secondary impacts on:

1. *Culture.* For example, through having an impact on the perceptions of freedom and restraint within society, or attitudes to authority and neighbourly relations. Different societies have varying attitudes towards authority, the use of natural resources and personal responsibility. We have seen in Part 2 that cultural frameworks result in markedly different responses to market and regulatory instruments.
2. *Economic flows.* For example, the pattern of funds flow and the accumulation of wealth, the degree of social equity which prevails, and economic growth.
3. *Innovation and entrepreneurship.* For example, how innovation and entrepreneurship are rewarded, and the resulting extent of environmental entrepreneurship. The demise of the Soviet system illustrates the problems that arise in an economy that relies upon regulation and frustrates innovation. If the circumvention of law is rewarded then this will probably occur. If good paperwork is rewarded, then efficient administrators will abound. If sustainable use is rewarded, then this is more likely to happen.
4. *Public institutions.* For example, the amount of pressure on the public purse. The 'affordability' of a natural resource management strategy is at least as much about the choice of instrument as it is about the amount of tax revenues to pay for the strategy. If there are limited tax revenues available, or if those revenues are volatile, then strategies that depend upon public expenditure bear a high risk of failure.

Table 10.1 highlights the behaviours promoted by various approaches, and shows how instruments allocate the burdens. The choice of mechanism affects social outcomes as well as environmental sustainability. For example, the behaviours promoted through a regulatory or subsidy strategy are markedly different to those promoted through the use of markets. This is not to say that one is inherently better than the other. Rather, it indicates that in choosing an approach the strategist needs to consider how the instrument will work and whether it will shape behaviours and allocate costs in a way that is desirable.

The social cost of conservation

Social justice and equity are aspects of the design of sustainability strategies hopefully so that the strategies strengthen social as well as natural resilience. This is important because incremental improvement in resource-use efficiency will not alone achieve sustainability, it is also necessary to limit access to resources, and in some instances prevent use of these resources altogether. There is a cost of conservation and therefore issues of fairness arise.

Table 10.1: Mechanisms, costs and behaviour

Instrument type	How does the instrument work?	What behaviours are promoted?	Who bears the cost?
Markets	*Through market transactions* The price of scarce resources increases Consumption is therefore curtailed by choice or inability to pay.	Market entrepreneurship Trading or Improved resource access or value.	Consumer of the resource bears the cost of consumption
Civil litigation	*Through private litigation* Harmful effects are compensated for. Harm to third parties is therefore curtailed by the choice to avoid risk.	Avoidance of third-party harm and 'neighbourly' negotiation of interests	Offending user bears costs of avoidance of harm. Affected neighbours may bear costs of un-avoided harm. Both bear negotiated costs.
Public regulation	*Through penalisation* Specified behaviours are made expensive. Consumption is therefore curtailed by choice to avoid risk.	Compliance, focused on least cost to avoid the risk.	Regulator bears the costs of enforcement. User bears the cost of compliance.
Incentives	*Through contract:* Desired behaviours are rewarded; Conserving behaviour is thereby promoted.	Administrative entrepreneurship to - win grants - satisfy requirements	The granting agency plus grant applicants under cost sharing.
Education	*Through communication:* Attitude or knowledge change leading to Conserving behaviour.	Civic responsibility	Volunteers who adopt the learning.

The setting aside of resources and areas – as a buffer against future needs and as a means for disciplining wasteful use of limited resources – is a useful strategy. For example, protected rainforests or 'no take' zones in fisheries deliver significant value that is not reflected in the short-term economic contribution that may be made by their exploitation. It is clear that such protected areas make a major ecological contribution. The continued protection of such areas is important for our future resilience.

Society is slowly making use of unspoiled resources expensive. Many activities now carry the risk-weighted cost of prosecution, the administrative burden of getting approvals (if possible) and the license or other fees that attach to the right to use. For example, water contamination or waste dumping carry an increasing financial cost (in the form of either the risk of penalty, or a price for legal disposal). Erosion on private land is no longer a matter of private concern alone, as delicate riparian areas are becoming valued for their non-use values, with the price for production use increasing as controls become tighter. In many catchments, there are penalties for abuse of riverside areas, and financial incentives for fencing off and protecting these. The price for their use is a mixture of possible penalties for doing so, and the foregone rewards for protecting them.

Declining access as a result of deterioration of the environment and our actions to protect what remains, embeds potential problems of social justice. Those incapable of getting a license for access due to lack of funds or administrative wherewithal will be disadvantaged. However, those prepared to risk prosecution are potentially advantaged as they bypass the restrictions that others must observe. Virtually any strategy to conserve or increase the efficiency of use of natural resources will add to the problem of lack of free access.

Some commentators suggest that the use of market instruments avoids the social costs of restriction of resource access. It is hard to see how this is the case, (even while accepting that a market-based strategy is more likely to support innovation). Market competition transfers wealth and opportunity to those who can exploit efficiently. It shifts resources from those unable to maximise wealth to those who can. Those who can typically already have the capital to implement technological solutions and the information and education to manage a technologically and capital-intensive production process.

Water in communities

We sometimes hear that it is possible to assist marginal regional communities and contribute to conservation by implementing tradeable water allocations, untied to land. The argument is that water will be reallocated to the most efficient users and overall economic benefits will be maximised. However, this strategy has broad social effects, not all of which are positive. If farming in a region is of marginal economic value, local farmers may choose to exit production if they are able to sell their water rights. Less profitable owners may sell their water interest, lease it, or hold it as an asset for later sale. They may choose to trade their right to another region. As the production activity of such landowners reduces, the regional economy suffers.

If the policy aim is community development (as distinct from entrepreneur enrichment), then a different instrument approach may be needed.[1] This could include the use of regional 'bubbles', limits to trading outside geographic boundaries, or restriction of trading to short-term leasing of water. Alternatively, pursuit of social equity may require a regional adjustment strategy, accepting that the water trading will add to regional viability problems. Reliance on the one instrument to achieve all three aims (social equity, economic growth and sustainability) may be a risky strategy.

---

1   See, for example, Carolyn Lochhead 'Farm Bill kills farming', *San Francisco Chronicle*, 20 May 2002: 'As costs rise, bigger farms buy up smaller farms. Small family farms begin to disappear. Agriculture consolidates into enormous industrialized operations covering thousands of acres. The countryside depopulates. Towns vanish'.

Apart from strategies that voluntarily curb consumption, virtually any strategy to protect the environment carries the potential for reducing resources available to the less well-endowed, prohibiting un-priced uses and strengthening private property interests.

Traditional strategies to attack inequity also have an economic or an environmental cost. Asset redistribution, through taxation and subsidy means moving resources from the most economically productive to users who are not as economically productive, for example, by endowing them with land or other assets, or by providing subsidies. Shifting assets to less productive uses will reduce the total wealth available to support the disadvantaged, or to reward the advantaged, and to invest in protecting and developing our natural capital. There is a complex relationship between pursuing wealth and curing disadvantage, even when the goal is reallocation to the less well off. There are few free lunches in social or economic policy.

Equity requires fair distribution and ownership of the fruits of natural resources. This suggests that strategists should make choices about natural resource management instruments within a framework of three overlapping social justice considerations:

1. Achieving integrity in the way in which Aboriginal interests are reflected in our natural resource use system – as in other aspects of society;
2. Creating opportunities for less-advantaged individuals to have meaningful and enjoyable lives; and
3. Ensuring that communities who might otherwise be disadvantaged have sufficiently robust economic and social infrastructures to support the people living within them.

This may require attention to social risk reduction, targeted subsidies or waivers, or other interventions that may, in turn, impose further economic or environmental costs. Some of the examples outlined in Part 2 show that smart strategists can successfully tackle this challenge. It is possible, for example, to provide Indigenous people with an 'as of right' allocation of tradeable interests in natural resources and allow them to benefit directly from the market (the indications from the economic literature are that this ought not inhibit efficient allocation provided that transaction costs are low). It is feasible to create limited exemptions to otherwise restrictive laws, or to require those who benefit to achieve defined social outcomes as part of the price of their privileged access.

None of the triple-bottom-line goals of sustainability, wealth and fairness can be fully achieved within the present paradigms of resource use and resource sharing, nor through the natural resource governance system we currently use. Innovation in technology has to be matched with innovation in social institutions to encourage entrepreneurial behaviour in the interests of the environment. While technological innovation is often lauded, innovation in social institutions is perceived as risky since it means disrupting a status quo to which we have grown accustomed. It is more comfortable but Pollyanna-ish to believe that we can keep the structures intact and somehow achieve different outcomes.

Over-reliance on government may be a mistake

To what extent can we rely upon government action to counter private consumption or inaction on sustainability? There is a tendency for advocates of conservation to insist upon more regulation, perhaps coupled with subsidies from government, and for those whose uses will be restricted to seek compensation from government. While government controls regulation, the levers of taxation, distribution of public funds, and a substantial workforce, it is quite limited in pursuing change of the magnitude that is needed for environmental sustainability. 'Affordability', 'acceptability' and 'effectiveness' are difficult for governments to achieve.

Private market activity involves an exercise of the right of an owner to set price, and to control access as a privilege of ownership. Individuals choose to bargain about ownership, access and price, and come to agreements that they can accept. Most government action involves an exercise of power (often limiting the use of private property). It is rarely based on voluntary consent, except in the case of subsidies or education. One byproduct is that government action and private action are viewed differently in society, with action by government being more readily disputed than an exercise of an owner's rights. For example, it is considered reasonable to contest a government when it increases the price for some service such as raising resource prices, such as mining or forestry royalties, whereas a similar price increase by a private owner does not give rise to such protest. Part of the motivation to use private market instruments rather than direct government action has been that private owners can 'get away with' more use restriction and price increases than can a government.

There is a second aspect of perceived legitimacy of actions by government. Violation of a private owner's right is not undertaken lightly in our society, whereas outwitting the government can be a matter of pride and hero worship, often celebrated (witness the status of Ned Kelly, or Robin Hood, or even 'smart' entrepreneurs who limit their tax bills). It is rare to hear people boasting about how much they have stolen from other people, but relatively common to hear about how they have circumvented government controls or imposts. This game of avoidance is made easier by the fact that while ownership is a relatively well-understood social concept, government action depends on technical legal interpretations, which can be (and frequently are) contested in the courts.

Government incentive schemes are tax-dependent for funding, and therefore will always, directly or indirectly, encounter resistance.

Environmental regulation is not self-funding for government, nor are incentive schemes. Government investments in sustainability compete with national defence, social security, healthcare, the arts, industry development and other demands on the public purse. As a result, it is not unusual for funding to be adjusted to allow for other demands, or because political priorities change. Promoting green taxes or increased expenditure on the environment is rarely a recipe for political success. It may be possible to vote in a regulation, but voting in the expenditures to make the regulation effective seems to be far more difficult.

Market instruments, on the other hand, involve a balance of 'wins' and 'losses', since for every buyer there must be a seller, and for every expense to someone there is an income for someone else. There is generally someone with the self-interest to drive and maintain pressure for full implementation. The incentive to protect the interest remains regardless of the whims of politics and increases commensurate with the demands for exploitation.

Table 10.1 indicated possible effects of over-reliance on government driven strategies. They are vulnerable to political changes in resource use, they embed patterns of behaviour which are likely to be less innovative in problem solving, because there is no gain to the individual from solving the problem. It suggests that sustainability strategists ought to consider how to leverage government intervention to drive change, rather than rely on ongoing government intervention (whether in the form of subsidy or policing). The use of regulations to embed or strengthen positive incentives for private action in support of the environment seems in this light to be a sensible design approach.

The following example of an integrated approach using regulation and markets, illustrates this concept. The example also highlights the need to consider the time and incentives needed to achieve change, which reflects an acceptance that transitions to sustainability are not readily achieved.

Addressing path dependence

Why is it that Australians consistently overshoot the sustainable level in our use of natural resources? We can easily point at greed and stupidity as the culprits, but, realistically, we cannot accuse all the people who try to use the land sustainably and fail of having these vices. We might be better off to acknowledge that our ability to use resources sustainably is constrained. In Chapter 2 we described the nature of the constraints, citing the experiments by Moxnes with fishers and herd managers. To quote Moxnes:

> There seems to be a general tendency that decision makers misperceive feedback in that they undervalue the importance of delays, misperceive the workings of stock and flow relationships, and are insensitive to nonlinearities that may alter the strengths of different feedback loops as the system evolves ... (Moxnes 2000: 327)

An integrated strategic approach

Neil Gunningham[2] provides an example of an integrated approach for the Swan-Canning river system. It had been identified that neither conventional regulatory approaches nor reliance on voluntary action were effective mechanisms for controlling pollution from a large number of widely-spread sources.

Gunningham outlined a range of possible approaches and an implementation program. The implementation program illustrates the integration of different approaches and the exercise of caution. The implementation has been designed to take place in stages in order to minimise adverse impacts and maximise effectiveness.

A suite of approaches might be used in concert, such as:

- Defined process standards, which specify what landowners are to achieve in terms of process outcomes, but allow them flexibility about how they might achieve them. Standards might be set on bases like a nutrient balance or for particular aspects of land use. Methods for encouraging compliance might include mandatory requirements, and incentives;
- Controlling business inputs (like fertilisers) to minimise the adverse effects of their use. This approach, however, is seen as potentially expensive and cumbersome to implement.
- Landscape-scale management could form part of a program, including use zoning and activity restrictions. It might conceivably mandate particular practices (such as contour ploughing) for particular use zones. Implementation could be achieved through various combinations of regulatory requirements and subsidy for desired practices.

All approaches have drawbacks and for this reason the strategists have focused on implementation as a key part of strategy in addition to the choice of instruments. They suggest implementation by a staged process, comprising:

- Persuasive approaches mixed with positive incentives. In this stage, performance benchmarks would be announced, along with a clear indication that if stage 1 does not achieve performance, more stringent controls will be introduced. A mixture of farm plans, capacity building, and incentives would provide the impetus for implementation of improvements.
- Stage 2 would come into effect if Stage 1 fails to achieve benchmarks. Stage 2 involves stringent mandatory controls and permits. Interestingly, it would also create a clear duty of care for the land (opening up the possibility of private regulatory action in defence of the environment).

---

2   Personal communication.

Three path dependence issues should be borne in mind in shaping our moves towards sustainability. We have touched on this concept earlier, but some more explanation is provided below.

Signals for change are not always effective

Natural resource yields are the result of factors that fluctuate. Physical elements – seasons, temperature, rainfall, presence of other species, and the interactions of all of these – cause yields to vary, providing weak natural resource condition signals for managers to respond to (while providing powerful economic reasons to try to increase production). Changes in management techniques, such as the application of new technology or the restructuring of holdings, can mask declining yields due to environmental degradation. Natural resource managers use capital and technology, such as bigger, more efficient fishing vessels, sophisticated cattle herd management and plant genetic manipulation, to increase natural resource yields. This investment is intensified as yields become more difficult to win. Such investments increase the fixed capital commitment of the resource user and financial obligations become locked in through borrowing. Decline in production triggers more intense use, as repayment of the capital becomes the driving concern. A cycle of debt, stress, and abuse of the environment, is generated. For many, action to reduce pressure on the ecosystem is available only at enormous personal cost.

When the accumulating injury is so great that further effort and capital can no longer compensate, the ecosystem and dependent economic system collapse. This is seen with the long-term patterns of rural responses to salinity in South Australia, where for many years farmers worked harder and harder, with greater efficiency, to yield wheat from increasingly saline soils. This is an illustration of the vicious cycles that lock in commodity markets and environmental harm, along with poor economic returns and social harm.

A good strategy should tackle the problem of ineffective signals. Part 2 highlighted examples of information and education programs designed to sensitise resource owners and users to the signals that are being sent by nature. Community-based programs like Landcare or Clean Up Australia help to achieve this, as do user education programs and scientific studies when they are understandable and communicated to the affected public. These programs do not, however, address the capacity to change which may require tackling fundamental problems of economic or personal capacity to shift to a more sustainable approach. Again, Part 2 showed examples where subsidies, or enlisting the support of financial and other private market institutions, have become a cornerstone of a strategy. If capacity to change is not addressed, otherwise sound strategies for sustainability will fail or be abandoned because of poor early results.

Beliefs rarely support paradigm change

Beliefs are at the heart of the resource overuse. Changes in beliefs occur slowly in response to new information and patterns of reward. Beliefs form filters against disconfirming information. James Doyle reviewed the psychological literature on cognitive systems and concludes:

> Psychologists have documented a wide variety of errors and biases in people's observations of data, and the judgments and interpretations based on them, that result from 'bounded rationality'. For example, when deciding what evidence is relevant to testing a hypothesis, people often ignore crucial information such as base rate probabilities and potentially disconfirming information. When examining data, people often perceive correlations that are not there, fail to perceive strong correlations that are there, perceive patterns in data that are in fact random, and see what they expect to see whether it is there or not. When drawing inferences from data, people sometimes conclude that the data supports their theory even when it strongly supports the exact opposite theory and are too willing to base firm conclusions on information that is incomplete or unrepresentative. (Doyle 1997).

It takes time to change

The experiments by Moxnes' show that even when harm from resource use is evident, change to reduce the harm is still difficult to achieve:

> In reality, there is an additional and time-consuming process of developing and agreeing on institutional arrangements. This process is likely to further delay the necessary actions, hence worsening over investment and overexploitation. In addition, the double-loop learning required to develop institutions to solve the problem is likely to be weak. New institutions depend on agreement among resource users, politicians, and in many cases the electorate. Many of these actors have limited knowledge, and in many cases, weak incentives to spend time and money on learning. Thus they are likely candidates to suffer considerably from the misperceptions revealed in my studies. With threatened interests at stake, considerable frustration, and incongruent views of the problem, it is no wonder that the process can take too long, be violent, and lead to less than perfect policies. (Moxnes 2000: 333-34)

It makes no difference in substance whether we are talking about boatowners dragging up seagrasses over diminishing *Posidonia* seagrass beds as they anchor, a farmer continuing to clear lands even as the economic return declines, or a city dweller choosing to water their garden while the catchment suffers from drought. Those on an unsustainable resource-use path are often locked in to behaviours they have little incentive or know-how to change.

Path dependence can lock a society into economic structures that do not satisfy either its economic or social goals.[3] Changing the path requires a lot more than the desire to do so. It often means:

---

3 For a summary of the field see (Marceau, Manley et al, 1997), particularly Chapter 4.

- Flying in the face of conventional wisdom;
- Putting up with the ridicule of being seen as impractical;
- Taking on the risks of innovation;
- Not being able to access appropriate local knowledge and expertise; and
- Doing so without the infrastructures that others who follow the main path enjoy.

Changing a society and an economy means adjusting resource flows and knowledge, and shifting the emphasis from the old to the preferred structure. It also requires building complementary assets like appropriate capital, investment mechanisms, educational institutions and markets to ensure that those who pioneer have access to what they need to be successful. Above all, it requires that there be sufficient incentives to individuals to counter the risks that are perceived in any change.

This requires a commitment to understanding and systematically reducing the risks that will be borne by the early adopters of change. It is too late to try to rectify the problems once the early adopters have been destroyed, and the socially-accepted wisdom is that the behaviour you want to see become widespread is seen as a sure path to failure!

Careful thinking about the barriers to change and what is needed to support the pioneers and to create a market for sustainability informs the more sophisticated strategies for sustainability. Regulation and market-creation go hand-in-glove with developing the capacity and resources needed to make the market work.

Barriers to innovation

Earth Sanctuaries Ltd (ESL) is the world's first-publicly listed company with the core business of conservation. Listed on the Australian Stock Exchange in 2000, ESL restores and manages natural environments to conserve Australian wildlife. It has innovated in many ways, from its approach to conservation areas and the protection of species, its funding approach, and even its accounting so as to be able to demonstrate to shareholders the value in investment.

This type of innovation is needed to harness the markets to sustainability. The effects of barriers to environmental innovation are apparent from its history. In its brief life it has encountered legal problems in being allowed to keep and conserve endangered species, major stock market compliance issues in achieving listing, and has been engaged in ongoing battles over accounting methods for valuing its wildlife 'assets'. Recently it has undergone a restructure in the face of financing difficulties, but it still survives as an illustration of the coming together of markets and conservation.

THE VOICE OF EXPERIENCE: INTEGRATION

Ian Coles is the CEO of EcoRecycle Victoria[4] and the President of the Waste Management Association of Australia. Ian works at the cutting edge of waste and litter reduction. We began by asking him about the strategies that EcoRecycle is using to tackle the challenge of a still-growing stream of waste, in its *Towards Zero Waste* strategy.

We asked him why the strategy did not set zero waste as the target.

I hope that with advances in technology and with changing attitudes in business and the community, in a few years I will be saying that we can get closer to zero waste. A large part of our strategies are about how we bring about change to make this possible.

We aim to reduce the flow of waste, in particular diverting as much as possible from landfill to reuse. Our forecasts are that the annual volume of waste will increase on average around 1 per cent over the next few years, but waste strategies will see almost 80 per cent diverted from tipping, into recycled product, compost, and energy. Innovation in technology and management, coupled with better processes, better education, and attitude change will make this possible.

Of course we are working on reducing the waste stream from the source, but we cannot see how we will stem this tide until there are significant changes in consumer attitude, and new ways for industry to produce and present products. For this strategy we are setting up the situations that will encourage business and consumers to make the changes that are needed.

So your approach tackles all of the waste streams, using a range of tools to suit the particular type of problem, and the type of 'customer', you need to manage?

We definitely use a mix of strategies. We use incentives such as grants and supporting funds, advisory schemes and partnering with industry and local government. This is coupled with a very active communication and education program. We back this up with regulation and creating conditions where the price of *disposal will be a stronger incentive to avoid disposal. However the way the mix is applied depends a lot on* the segments you are working on.

The waste stream is quite segmented, and your strategies need to reflect this. An equal volume of waste comes from commerce and industry, and from construction and demolition, and slightly less from municipal sources. As you can imagine, the most effective mix of incentives, technology, communication and other approaches is quite different depending on which of these streams you are trying to deal with. Even within the streams there are different issues. For example, the management of litter differs greatly from the management of green waste. We are working on all fronts, and so we use a diversity of approaches.

---

4   See <www.ecorecycle.vic.gov.au>.

Our program is staged, and we have created partnerships to ensure that the program is workable and practical to implement. We have created different approaches for city, country and regional settings, and for different types of waste. You have to be prepared to tailor the approach to the people and the situation that you are faced with, if you want the strategy to work.

It is clear from our research that the results of different instruments vary greatly depending on the situation. What are the types of local conditions that have influenced this strategy?

One of our challenges is that around Melbourne there is a great deal of potential landfill available. In other States they simply have not got the landfill opportunities available to them. Since there is not the same supply constraint that exists elsewhere, this reduces the ability of the normal market to set a price that will lead to reduced disposal. We will have to continue to create conditions that stop it being too cheap and easy to continue to dispose of waste.

On the positive side, we have the great advantage of a reliable flow of funds from the waste levy. That has meant that we can commit to longer-term programs, and that we can give industry and other partners some assurance that we will be working with them on a continuing basis. That is very important.

You do not seem to have embraced some of the instruments that have been successful in other places, like container deposit legislation (CDL). Why not?

Victoria has looked carefully at CDL, compared to improving the efficiency of kerbside recycling, and other ways of supporting industry to overcome packaging waste. Our studies showed pretty convincingly that on a life-cycle cost basis, CDL did not come out terribly well. You can see the studies for yourself; they are on the EPA web site. Of course, that decision reflects our strategic aims, which was primarily the efficient recovery or resources. CDL has been more effective in litter control than in waste reduction, and we have other programs working with industry that deserve to be tried fully first before we re-consider CDL.

We believe on the evidence we have that our approaches are very cost effective compared with other programs internationally. For most of what we do, we are quite stringent in carrying out economic and other evaluations, to make sure that our approach is strategic and well designed. We invest a lot in supporting innovation and market development to give industry a positive reason to make the changes it needs to, and we work on helping attitudes to change. Regulation and pricing are part of the mix, but heavy-handed regulation is not usually the most productive approach. You have to lead as well as push if you want to change industry, or the community.

Chapter 11

IMPLEMENTATION

The seminal strategist, Kenichi Ohmae, states:

> The object of strategy is to bring about the conditions most favourable to one's own side, judging precisely the right moment to attack or withdraw, and always assessing the limits of compromise correctly. Besides the habit of analysis, what marks the mind of the strategist is an intellectual elasticity or flexibility that enables him [or her] to come up with realistic responses to changing situations ... one first seeks a clear understanding of the particular character of each element of a situation and then makes the fullest possible use of human brainpower to restructure the elements in the most advantageous way.
>
> No matter how difficult or unprecedented the problem, a breakthrough to be the best possible solution can come only from a combination of rational analysis, based on the real nature of things, and imaginative reintegration of all the different items into a new pattern, using nonlinear brainpower. This is always the most effective approach for devising strategies for dealing successfully with challenges and opportunities, in the market arena as on the battlefield. (Ohmae 1982: 13)

Natural resource management is complex. It involves decisions about ways to change entrenched behaviours. This in turn demands a sophisticated understanding of not only behavioural management but also social and economic systems that shape that behaviour. It also requires an understanding of the types of instruments that have been discussed in this book, and the capacity to use them creatively to develop elegant solutions to complex problems.

The process outlined in this Part follows the conceptual approach that Ohmae recommends in forming a strategy:

- First, evaluate the physical and social phenomena with which you are concerned;
- Secondly, group these phenomena and develop hypotheses about what causes the behaviour you observe in the system;
- Thirdly, consider what options are available to effect change towards the outcomes you would prefer to see;
- Finally, use creative problem-solving (that is, strategising) to find a way of resolving the issues, and plan the implementation of your strategy, carefully.

While step-by-step guidance to process can be provided, useful guidance about how to be creative cannot. This essential element is more a function of the abilities and flexibility of the strategy team, than it is of the process. However, without imagination, the process will not yield the types of strategy that are essential to the effective pursuit of sustainability.

Good strategic thinking about complex behaviour requires a substantial investment of time and skill, coupled with extensive investigation and analysis. To short-change the processes is merely to increase the risks of failure of an already challenging task. Natural resource strategy development is often under-resourced, compared to commercial strategising. For important commercial decisions, it is normal to assemble a strategy team from different disciplines, and to support them with consulting and research resources. Behavioural expertise (from a marketing or an organisational perspective) is typically coupled with financial and operational skill, to ensure that the issues are comprehensively considered. The processes of analysis are guided by well thought out understandings of the 'right' way to think about strategy, when the issues are important. Months of analysis and planning and substantial investments in research are the norm for major projects like product launches or organisational change programs. This preparedness to invest is a result of sensitivity to the risks from a failure to properly manage strategy design and implementation.

In the newer field of natural resource strategy, awareness of the risks of under-investment in preparation is not as well developed. It is not unusual for the sustainability strategy to be left in the hands of a narrowly-constituted group, unaided by a well-developed 'conventional wisdom' about the issues to be considered and the disciplines to be applied. It is relatively rare to see in-depth behavioural evaluation as part of the approach, even though, in essence, natural resource management strategy is behavioural. Market and organisational research is often non-existent or limited to stakeholder meetings.

The purpose of this Part is to help bridge the gap between the theory we have explained and its implementation. Implementation approach depends very much on the situation and on the resources (including time) available. A series of processes are outlined, designed to be conducted by multi-skilled teams led by a skilled facilitator. A team approach lends itself to brainstorming and debate which assist the understanding of complex issues, and in finding creative solutions to intractable challenges.

The processes are designed to be part of a project that stretches over months and is supported by sufficient research and preparation to make the approach meaningful. For each process, there is necessary background work. Team creativity unaided by careful preparation is far less powerful than team creativity supported by thorough and skilful analysis. A grudging investment of time in dealing with complex problems is rarely likely to result in glorious success.

The investment should be proportionate to the importance of the result and the complexity of the issues. Sustainability is vitally important, and the issues are extraordinarily complex when fully understood.

Investment in professionalism is sometimes seen as unrealistically costly, however, as the cost of ineffective behaviour change strategies becomes more evident through experience this mistaken perception may decline.

The processes are a template for the strategy team and facilitator. It is expected that they will be modified to suit the needs of the team. The workload for each process is substantial, with many issues to be explored. None of these work sessions could be completed with less than a very full day of intense work. Depending on the importance of the issues, the complexity of natural resource-use systems, and the quality of preparation and support available to the strategy team, many of these sessions may extend over substantially longer periods.

The processes partly mirror commercial strategy development approaches, modified to reflect the nature of sustainability issues. The steps address:

1. Creating strong foundations for a natural resource strategy project.
   The aim is to develop an understanding within the team about the behaviours to be created, and the behaviours the team will demonstrate itself in achieving this.
2. Objectively evaluating natural resource management performance.
   Being clear about the shortfall between what existing policy says should be happening, and what is actually happening.
3. Carrying out the initial evaluation of the issues.
   Understanding what natural resource management and behavioural issues need to be managed.
4. Narrowing the range of possible strategies.
   Filtering the possibilities down to a more manageable level.
5. Reviewing existing institutional arrangements.
   Developing a clear understanding of the structures that shape natural resource use and how these might be changed.
6. Brainstorming instrument possibilities.
   Thinking creatively about the range to techniques available to change how resources are used and conserved.
7. Developing sensitivity to the behavioural issues.
   Increasing awareness of the underlying causes of the behaviours that need to be changed.
8. Brainstorming behavioural interventions.
   Thinking creatively about the range of approaches that might be used to change behaviour.
9. Filtering and prioritising possible strategies.
   Narrowing the range of approaches to be considered in detail.
10. Moving towards implementation.
    Turning good ideas into actions with impetus.

There is a natural tendency for any group to find new processes strange, and to revert to known approaches. When the issues themselves are difficult, this tendency can be even more pronounced. For this reason the facilitator should ensure that they understand the processes before attempting to implement them, and that they modify processes that they do not think will work for them or with the strategy team. However, the modification should not be at the cost of comprehensive evaluation.

Process 1: Setting up the strategy team to succeed

Outcome

A strategy team that has agreed:
- the specific outcomes they are aiming to achieve;
- the 'rules' they will work to; and
- how they intend to fill the gaps in the team makeup and the intellectual resources they can draw on.

In most cases creating a strategy should start with a multi-skilled team. The first task is to get them working effectively. This means making sure that all in the team understand their own aims and those of their co-workers and allies, and have agreed the 'ground rules' to work within. The essentials are to:

1. Understand everyone's motivations and goals;
2. Establish the collective goals of the strategy team;
3. Document the team's aims;
4. Agree behavioural 'rules' to work within; and
5. Review the gaps in the team and take steps to fill them.

If well run (with keen participants) this process will take between one and two days for a diverse team. A preliminary survey is useful preparation. Each participant should arrive at the session well briefed about the overall purpose and scope of the sustainability strategy project and the reasons for their involvement.

Some of the examples below are from the creation of a catchment management strategy[1] where some of the recommended approaches were applied. Other approaches are drawn from business consulting and team building.

---

1 The Southern Catchment Board Region of NSW is one of the Australia's population growth centres. It covers approximately 9,000 square kilometres, encompassing the Shoalhaven, Kangaroo, Minnamurra and Hacking River catchments, South of Sydney.

Step 1: Explore motivations and goals

Sustainability issues bring together strange bedfellows. Around any issue there might be a coalition of farmers, 'deep' and 'light' green activists, businesses marketing a preferred solution, academics, lawyers, politicians of various hues, and the occasional egotist out to make a name for themselves. If the strategy is being developed within government, different departments and different levels of government may approach the same issue with varying aims and approaches.

A strong team is likely to present many points of view. Ideally, the team should represent the key dimensions of the sustainability challenge, with a diversity of skills (social science, economic, legal, managerial, and behavioural) and in-depth understanding of the issues and stakeholder interests.[2] This diversity can be a strength, but also a source of conflicts if not well managed.

Time spent exploring desired outcomes and deciding how the team will work together can replace time spent later in trying to hold together a coalition that lacks a firm foundation.

The exploration starts with an 'exposure session'. Plenty of time should be set aside for the team to discuss interests and perceptions and get to know each other. It is important that no outcomes are proposed at this point other than building better understanding of 'team rules' or principles within the strategy team. It can be useful to begin with a survey of everyone's issues and perceptions.[3] The results should be circulated before the first get-together, providing a solid basis for developing awareness. If properly handled, exposure sessions accelerate trust building and generate a clear, shared agenda.

This is not always easy. Sometimes people have not yet thought through their own positions, or may be unsure about what they ought reveal to those they do not yet know. Some may express themselves in ways that raise fears or concerns in others, perhaps making provocative statements to test the group. It is not unusual for participants who later prove to be the backbone of the process to start out with apparently antagonistic positions – these should be treated as indications of commitment rather than a definitive example of how that person will behave as the plan is developed. It is surprising how often honesty builds trust and how friendships can be generated out of early disagreements. It is important not to create a false sense of coalition, but to build a reality of consensus even if this is narrower than some would want.

---

2   In reality, most teams are assembled in a more haphazard way, resulting in gaps in the knowledge base and a potential bias in the interests considered. This weakness should be addressed early in the process.
3   We have used Delphi surveys to identify key issues and likely future issues. Individual survey results are collated to ensure anonymity. When the results are circulated, a discussion can take place without issues being tied to personalities. We have also had success using Value Management Workshops, where the participants determine what mix of activities and outcomes will deliver the greatest value at least cost to team participants or their organisations.

The focus of the discussion should not be the sustainability issues for which the team has been assembled. It should be about 'how can we begin to work as a team?' Moving too early into a contest of ideas (rather than discussion of shared aims) can erode the basis for coalition. Some people try to avoid personal exposure by moving immediately to raise abstract issues or proposing their preferred solutions. If this is not controlled, the underlying issues may never come to the surface and later problems can arise.

It can be a great icebreaker to link this exposure session to some constructive activity that provides a common ground, and supports cohesion. This might be a set of briefings by different stakeholders or technical experts, or a 'team-building exercise'.

Team formation

At the formation of a new catchment management organisation, few of the members knew each other. They represented wildly different perspectives, with farmers, environmentalists, city people, local government and departmental staff. There was ample opportunity for distrust and conflict.

Team-building began when the Chairman filled out a detailed exposure survey and sent the same questions to all the other members, asking them to do the same. The questions were about each person's background, family, reasons for involvement and perceptions and concerns about the process. Team members were also asked about the challenges that they thought the catchment would face, and the issues that they thought would be important. The results were collated and circulated to everyone. This was done in a way that made it hard for anyone to know who had nominated what issues, preventing stereotyping of the responses.

An experiential workshop on Aboriginal culture was used to increase cultural sensitivity and to provide a shared experience for the team. A two-day meeting was held, focused around information sharing and learning activities that would not directly raise conflict, but which would require collective creativity. There was discussion about 'how do we want to work together?' and the team was invited to set the rules to govern the work of the Chairman.

At the end of the two days, there was a much greater level of trust. Within six months, people were prepared to tackle tough issues without taking things personally. Two years later, the members of the committee had created an ambitious strategy, and moved to implementation, without once having to take a vote.

Template 1: Questions to consider at an exposure session

➢ Who are you? (including your background and everyday activities)
➢ Who do you represent?
➢ What do you/they want or need from this strategy?
➢ Why? What are the issues, problems, or opportunities driving your involvement?
➢ What resources or networks do you/might you bring?
➢ What are the outcomes that you would not want to see occur?
➢ What are the principles or rules you think we should agree to govern our work together?

Step 2: Establish the goals

Once everyone has begun to get to know each other, it is possible to consider the next question: 'What do we want this strategy to achieve?'

Brainstorming allows anyone to put forward any idea they want and others take it up and build on it. Criticism of others or their ideas is not permitted. Well run, brainstorming is constructive and can be very creative. It helps build cooperation. However, it does require skill and discipline to run a good brainstorming session.

Only after many ideas about the possible goals of the project have come forward (and everyone's creativity is exhausted) does the group move to refining and culling and then to reaching agreement. It is better to pursue agreement at a separate session, a little while after the exposure session, so that people can acclimatise to each other.

As discussed in Part 1, the outcomes of natural resource management are behaviour changes (even if the aims are biophysical). Teams can mistakenly jump from stating the biophysical or economic or social problem into immediately trying to propose solutions without focusing on the people and their behaviours at the heart of both problem and solution. Behavioural outcomes must be central. A goal matrix, like the example below, can ensure that the behavioural aims are clearly set for the strategy project.

To create a goal matrix, the team is asked to propose a goal of any type (biophysical, social, economic or behavioural). Then the team considers how this goal will be reflected in the other dimensions. The aim is to ensure that the team has clearly considered the different dimensions of what they are trying to achieve, and focused directly on what behaviours they will have to create to achieve the other goals.

Template 2: A goal matrix

Biophysical outcomes	Social outcomes	Economic outcomes	Behavioural aims
For example:			
40% environmental flows return to river	Viable catchment communities, with adequate employment	Profitable water-efficient farming and industry	Consumers: 30% reduction in non-potable use. Industry: Adoption of 'best practice' water conservation leading to 25% use reduction. Landowners: Voluntary minimisation of water demand, and implementation of water quality safeguards to maintain current supply with less seasonal variation.

Clear behavioural aims provide a focus and a test for the strategies proposed. The strategy team is forced to identify the people or organisations whose behaviour has to be changed, and the type of behaviour that has to be achieved, in order to deliver the environmental, social or economic outcomes being pursued. This is an important step as it moves thinking to the specific question of 'how will we get these people to change their behaviours?' Behavioural aims (like any other target) can be renegotiated as the team develops a deeper understanding of the issues. It is not unusual for the behavioural focus of a strategy to shift as new ideas and information come to light.

Step 3: Debate the team's guiding principles

A strong team is founded on more than political expedience. It needs to have a clear and high-minded vision of what it is trying to achieve. This provides a values-based glue for the work of the team. The team ought agree the basic principles that they intend to use to guide their decision-making. These will reflect the sensitivities and interests of the team participants. Having principles clearly stated can go a long way to minimising conflicts, and is also of value in explaining the basis of any strategy that is developed.

> **Example: A statement of principles**
>
> - Reducing the pressure on our natural resources can only be achieved by changing behaviours. The Board believes the approach must be equitable and innovative to bring about new attitudes and practices. Mechanisms for change should demonstrate a strong preference for incentives, education and compensation rather than rules and sanctions.
> - Natural resource planning must light a path towards reconciliation between Aboriginal and other Australians.
> - Our strategies should reflect a serious attempt to listen to, and take into account, all interests.
> - Overlapping programs, confusion and insufficient funding of programs all result in wasted efforts. The Board is committed to reduce this waste.
> - Management should be based on objective analysis, and the success of plans and programs should be objectively measured against clear targets.
>
> Strategies must not only prevent deterioration of our natural resources, but also provide positive examples of sustainable approaches to productive use.

It is worthwhile to have all of the participants sign off on their foundation statements of aims and principles, and to regularly review where the strategy team are 'at' compared to them.

Step 4: Agree 'rules' for the team

Deliberative groups need 'rules' about how they intend to work together. This is because people have differing expectations of how one works and what is acceptable. For example, some team participants may believe that attendance at meetings is optional, whereas others would consider it mandatory (and see failure to attend as an insult). Some may believe that 'what is discussed in the room stays in the room', while others believe that it is part of their representative role to canvass issues more widely. A failure to agree on the process rules can lead to misunderstanding, demotivation and conflict. While the team is forming, it is useful to discuss what is, and what is not, acceptable and to document this. It is also possible for the team to resolve how possible problems might be overcome in advance of these arising.

The process rules that were agreed by the catchment management team (and modified over time) are set out below, as an example.

Example: Team rules

Any team member can signal their disagreement with a possible decision with a code 'orange' (I am not ready yet to decide), or 'red' (I am not able to agree). They will not be required to justify this, if they do not want to. No decision will proceed for so long as a red flag is up. The Chairman may elect to take a vote on matters where an orange flag is up, but only once all other avenues for agreement are exhausted.

All discussions are absolutely confidential, but all decisions are to be public after the draft minutes are reviewed and agreed.

Guests are welcome at meetings, but any team member can require that any discussion be held in confidence, and that request will be automatically honoured;

No more than three meetings in a year can be missed by any team member without a formal 'show cause'.

Step 5: Evaluating the team gaps

A multi-facetted approach to sustainability requires many skills and a variety of high-quality information. Any gap in the team's resources means a risk that the decisions will be poorly informed. It is worthwhile work out ways of offsetting any deficiencies in the team.

It can be useful to draw up an 'inventory' of the ideal team and the ideal analytic resources that are needed to make that team effective. There are many dimensions to what a fully-effective team needs. The strategy team should consider both the generic analytic requirements (such as needing *someone who understands statistical method*, or *a skilled environmental scientist*), and task-specific capabilities (such as *knowledge of the local stakeholders*, or of specific *biodiversity issues*). In specifying the ideal analytic resources, the team should consider what raw or processed information they would ideally have (such as *attitude surveys*, *economic analysis* of affected industries, or *species population data*), and the processing support that would be needed (such as *computerized mapping*, or particular *data processing* requirements).

The assessment should takes into account the need to have access to both state-of-art theoretical understanding, and practical experience in dealing with the issues. Theoretical knowledge is important in providing conceptual depth, but this is best married with practical experience to refine its application.

After evaluation of the perfect team composition and the ideal information and analysis resources, the team is able to see how far short of this ideal they are. The main gaps can be characterised in ways that help the team think about the approach that they will use to ensure a complete team. The team will define the resources they need as:

- Accessible by the strategy team from their own resources or networks;
- Accessible from an identified source, by negotiation or purchase;
- Inaccessible – if a gap cannot be filled, the team should consider the implications for the reliability of the final strategy, and how any adverse effects may be countered. For example, an incomplete team may use a panel of stakeholders and experts to test its conclusions before the strategy is finalised.

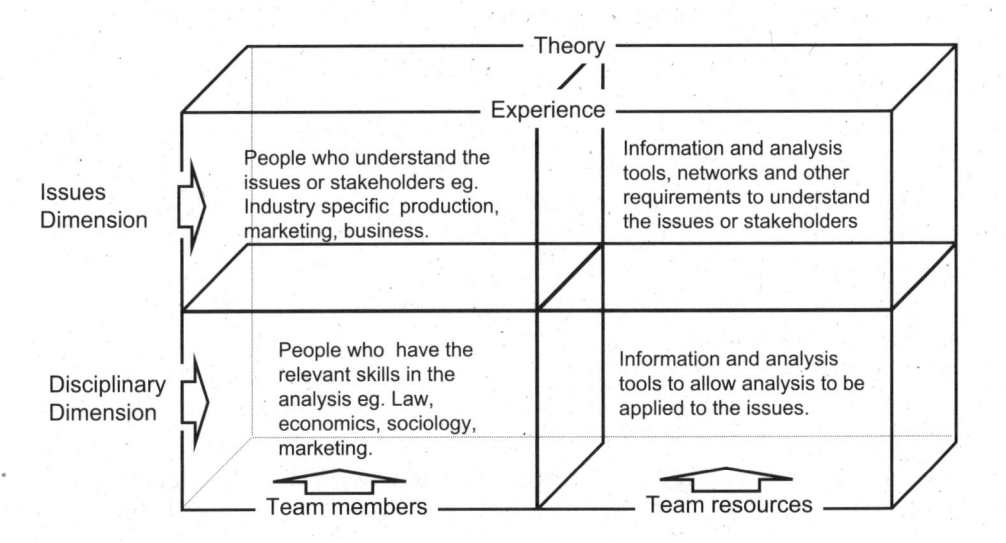

Figure 11.1 The dimension of a complete team

	Team members	Team resources
Issues Dimension	People who understand the issues or stakeholders eg. Industry specific production, marketing, business.	Information and analysis tools, networks and other requirements to understand the issues or stakeholders
Disciplinary Dimension	People who have the relevant skills in the analysis eg. Law, economics, sociology, marketing.	Information and analysis tools to allow analysis to be applied to the issues.

(Theory / Experience axes)

This approach will focus the whole strategy team on trying to plug all possible gaps before the project gets underway, instead of ploughing on in blithe ignorance of hidden deficiencies. Awareness of gaps helps reduce the risks that come with that gap.

Peter Schmigal (see Chapter 1, p 24) provides an illustration of the type of thinking that is done before embarking on the strategy development project.

> To be able to create an urban water strategy, it would be desirable to have a deep understanding of the issues. That would mean having strategy team members or consultants who work every day with, and understand conceptually as well as practically, the water sector. It would be best to have access to expertise in water supply (back to the catchments) through to water consumption (industrial and domestic) and disposal. It would be best to ensure that this team was informed about the economic and social aspects of water use, and with good market research and other data to guide analysis.
>
> Coupled with this, it would be desirable to have the involvement of people with economic and social analysis skills, sound legal understanding, experience in and links with government, and with strategy skills. They should be armed with the latest information relevant to their expertise.
>
> If there will be critical gaps that cannot be filled, then the strategy team is faced with the realisation that its work may be flawed. It is possible to put in place safeguards (such as expert reviews or further consultation) to minimise these risks, or alternatively to reconstitute the team or redefine the project to better fit the available resources.

Once this is done, the team is in a position to create a project plan, and to allocate responsibilities.

Step 5: Document the agreements

The preceding steps arm the team with behavioural aims, principles that will guide strategy formulation, an understanding of how the team intends to operate, and a specific set of gap-filling initiatives that they intend to take.

Documentation makes explanation easier, and less exposed to errors or distortion. It also provides a touchstone for the team, reminding it of its commitments and purpose.

The document need not be complex or bureaucratic. A simple statement of the behavioural aims and the agreed parameters for the strategy will serve. Converting the goal matrix to an agreed 'Mission' is a constructive step if there is sufficient consensus to do so.

Any agreed principles to govern how the team will work should be documented so they can be referred to when needed. Any constraints on what the project is to do, or sensitivities to be noted, should be carefully documented so that later mistakes are prevented.

The team is now ready to grapple with the issues, by developing a clear understanding of the system that they are setting out to change.

Process 2: Understand the system to be changed

Outcome

A systemic understanding of the issues through:
> Analysis of the issues that the strategy will have to address; and
> Mapping the elements, actors and relationships that drive the system.

Understanding the resource use system is a prerequisite for good strategies. This involves understanding who participates in the resource use system, how they interact, and the decision-making roles that they serve.

At least an initial day of concentrated work from a keen team to build awareness is required – a system mapping workshop or workshops (a half-day to a full day each), intense work by the facilitator to structure the results of this work, and discussion by the strategy team to deepen their insight. Preparation includes background interviews to obtain non-documented intelligence, and preparatory reading by the strategy team. It is possible to improve the process by using a series of such workshops with different participants, with the facilitator and the strategy team consolidating the results in a final workshop.

The approach is conducted in two phases.

Stage 1: Issues evaluation

An issues evaluation is a five-step process. It can be carried out by a small team, ahead of Stage 2 which is more effective with a range of views.

Step 1: Review what is written about the issues

This desk research involves obtaining every document available that relates to the strategy issues. This can be tedious, but is typically informative. There are two types of documents the team will need.

1. Documents that establish the management standards that ought be applied in the resource use system being evaluated.[4] These include:
    - Policies (international, federal, State, and local);
    - Statutes (federal, State, and local);
    - Regulations under these statutes;
    - Plans, which can either be advisory or have legal status. Typically these will have been created by the agencies that are responsible for implementing policies, statutes and regulations;
    - Advisory reports, from scientific or resource management bodies, or from stakeholder groups; and

---

[4] The use of these documents is explained in Process 3 below.

- Relevant private sector equivalents to these documents, such as corporate plans, policies or management guidelines from corporations, voluntary organisations or associations, who own, control, or who have use of or manage important resources.
2. Documents that outline the state, pressures and anticipated state of the relevant natural systems. These are likely to be of two basic kinds:
   - Scientifically-verified studies, typically coming from mainstream government agencies or research bodies; and
   - community information (which may be just as important and reliable as institutional information), such as reports, or even anecdotes.

The key sources include the agencies that have scientific or management responsibilities, corporations, and research and community groups that have particular interests (such as environmental groups, or resource user interest groups).

Step 2: Identify the 'data-pockets' who know about the issues

Data-pockets are people or organisations that, by virtue of their role and experience, can be expected to be a collection point for valuable knowledge. They may be people who have previously researched elements of the system, or who have frequent interaction with the actors in the system. The strategists begin this identification by picking out key actors and asking themselves 'who provides information to this actor?' and then 'who takes information from this actor?' The process is conducted by looking at those who deal directly with the actors (like suppliers, purchasers, advisers, and the direct media), and then second order and increasingly remote providers and receivers (such as academic institutions, or government agencies). At different levels of relationship, the nature of the knowledge available changes. You can expect, for example, that those with primary contact knowledge will understand more of the subtleties of the actors' behaviour, whereas those whose knowledge is based on formal research will have a more remote but aggregated and systematic awareness of the actors and the issues.

Step 3: Tap the data-pockets

Face-to-face conversation is the most effective way of capturing the knowledge of data pockets. Some of the most important insights will come from informal comments from people who have already thought deeply about the relevant issues. This is a process of making appointments and having a chat. An ideal team must be prepared to put in the time talking to people, whose aim is not always to assist. This is a learning process and the team members' state of mind and receptiveness will be crucial to the outcomes.

Step 4: Document the issues

Issues can be documented in a database, spreadsheet, report, file-cards or an exercise book. They should be captured in a way that makes it easy to structure use of that information. A database or spreadsheet will allow flexibility in the way the team sifts and present the issues, which may lead to boons as they explore and learn about the issues.

Step 5: Brainstorm the relationships between the decisions and actors

The more the team 'turns the pile' of information over, the richer will be the result. Sitting around and talking about how and why issues arise, and the role of the actors, can free up thoughts. If the strategists can brainstorm the issues and relationships with people who represent opposing views, the likelihood is that their understanding will be far richer. The outcome sought in this process is not an answer, it is a deeper understanding of the issues and the system that the strategists need to change. The aim is expansive, not restrictive.

Stage 2: Map the relationships

The preceding steps outline 'who' and 'what', but say very little about 'why?'

The process below outlines how to map issues and relationships. Fundamentally this is a sloppy process of drawing lines to represent what the team understands about flows and relationships. The trick is not to be too concerned about the diagram and to be more concerned about learning. Issue and relationship maps are never accurate. Reality is far richer and more complex than can be represented on paper.

A systems map is a way of setting out what the team thinks is true so that they (and others) can question and interrogate the logic. It helps the team to see the complex relationships and to explain them to others. It helps the team to see if there are actors or relationships that they are missing in thinking about the issues. The map is the tool that is used to provide focus and to assist in remembering and communicating. It does not have to be objectively 'true', merely useful.

There are many different ways of going about this process, some far more sophisticated than the approach outlined below. However, this simple approach does work, and can be run without requiring any special expertise.

Step 1: Assemble a system mapping team (or teams)

The team(s) should represent a diverse range of views on the topics being investigated. It can often be difficult to involve people with widely different views on the issues but in this process diversity is strength. The aim is that issues be understood, relatively uncontaminated by particular biases, and the best approximator of a bias-free team is to involve people who will 'strip-out' biases by contesting them. This is why the team(s) should represent a diverse range of view on the topics being investigated.

Step 2: Inform everyone

The team's desk research will result in a lot of information. Either by access to documents or by well-structured briefing the team should ensure that everyone is well armed with knowledge about the issues. Good preparation leads to a higher quality understanding of the issues.

Step 3: Brainstorm the system elements

The team can open up the process by having everyone nominate the issues that they think are relevant to the sustainability challenge the strategy team is concerned with. This is a simple brainstorming process. Do not allow criticism or commentary beyond adding more issues. List these issues on a white board or butcher's paper, and keep going till there is an extensive list. Carry out a review, asking people to add anything that is missed. Post this list where it can remain on view.

Having set the scene, the facilitator asks the team to nominate:

- Who are the key actors in the system, related to these issues?
- What are the decisions that they make, that relate to these issues?
- Who or what influences these decisions?

As these are nominated, they are written up on sticky paper and placed on a board or wall. Push the team hard to come up with suggestions. Once the strangeness of the task diminishes, suggestions should start to flow. Enthusiasm and energy from the facilitator can make a world of difference! The team should then group the issues in ways that make sense to them. This acts as a stimulus to consider relationships between elements in the system.

Keep going until the group is satisfied that they have identified the bulk of the relevant actors and decisions and influences.

Step 4: Create the landscape

The landscape is a metaphor for the physical aspects of the resource-use system being studied. Choosing the right metaphor can be surprisingly difficult, but it is important because the strategy team is deciding what sort of spatial relationship between the issues will be most meaningful in interpreting that system. The choices for arranging the issues include:

- Physical landscape (eg, arranged from mountains to the sea);
- Temporal landscape (eg, arranged from first event to last event);

- Political landscape (eg, arranged around relationships and alignments of interests).

Draw a 'map' that represents this landscape on a very large piece of paper. Since whiteboards are not portable, they are often not the best medium for this. 'Roll-up' whiteboard paper is efficient but butchers' paper works as well.

Step 5: Populate the landscape

Using sticky notes, write down the decisions that have been identified in Step 3 and place them on the map close to the aspect that they impact upon. For example, the decision to release water from a dam would be placed close to the downstream flow that it impacts.

Once decisions are located in the landscape, locate the actors who are most concerned with these decisions around them, and then the influences around these. In this process the team may find many more actors and influences than identified in Step 3.

The team can expect that this process of locating will trigger discussions about who influences what and whom. Expect that the team will move sticky notes around quite a bit, until (through a process of elimination) they are reasonably comfortable that they have mapped out the key flows and relationships. In effect, the team is jointly learning and negotiating how they want to understand the system, prior to thinking about strategy. The facilitator may have to encourage the team by reminding them that they are creating and learning about the issues at the same time. Some confusion, complexity and uncertainty is not only inevitable, it is also beneficial as it pushes the team to try harder to clarify and understand.

Step 6: Draw the relationships

The team can then draw lines on the map to show the important relationships. These relationships might be information flows, resource flows, or 'affinity' and power structures. A good idea is to specify the nature of the relationships, as this will help with Step 7. Different coloured pens can be used to show different types of relationships.

You can expect that at this point the process has generated a messy arrangement of actors and relationships that confuse

- Information flows;
- Economic flows;
- Power relationships; and
- Physical flows.

It is worth spending time to cull and group the information, with an aim of simplifying. The facilitator asks the team to consider how the decisions and actors might be reduced in number or complexity without losing the essence of the map. Usually issues can be reduced by deeper investigation of what is causing them, and finding common causes. The facilitator can also ask the group to reduce the number of relationship lines by wiping out those that they consider are not vital.

While it is possible to achieve further clarification and simplification in a group, our experience is that there are diminishing returns once the group has done so once. Usually it is better to delegate the next stage to the facilitator, a suitably experienced member of the strategy team, or a sub-group of two or three.

Step 7: Map the system

The task is to convert the messy material into an insightful map of the actors, decisions and relationships. This can take a couple of days and a few false starts.

The following is a useful hierarchy by which to order the material.

- Create a diagram of the underlying natural system of bio-physical elements (such as the physical flows of the river to the sea, and the elements such as contaminant flows that impact).
- Arrange the activities of man that give rise to impacts (such as industrial extraction, release from dams) within this diagram.
- Write in the decisions that govern these activities at the relevant points.
- Then locate the actors who make these decisions on the map.
- Identify the secondary drivers of the decisions of these actors towards the outer edges of the map.

Only then, draw in the lines. Our approach uses two types of line. One type is to represent the physical movements through the system, and another is to represent causal relationships.

Figure 11.2 (next page) is an example of the output from this process.

Step 7: Talk about it

Once the map is complete, discussion adds value. The strategy team can be re-convened to review and discuss the causal links, and also to lay the foundations for the sessions that follow. The map is a tool, and unless those who are meant to use it understand it, it will not be useful.

IMPLEMENTATION 237

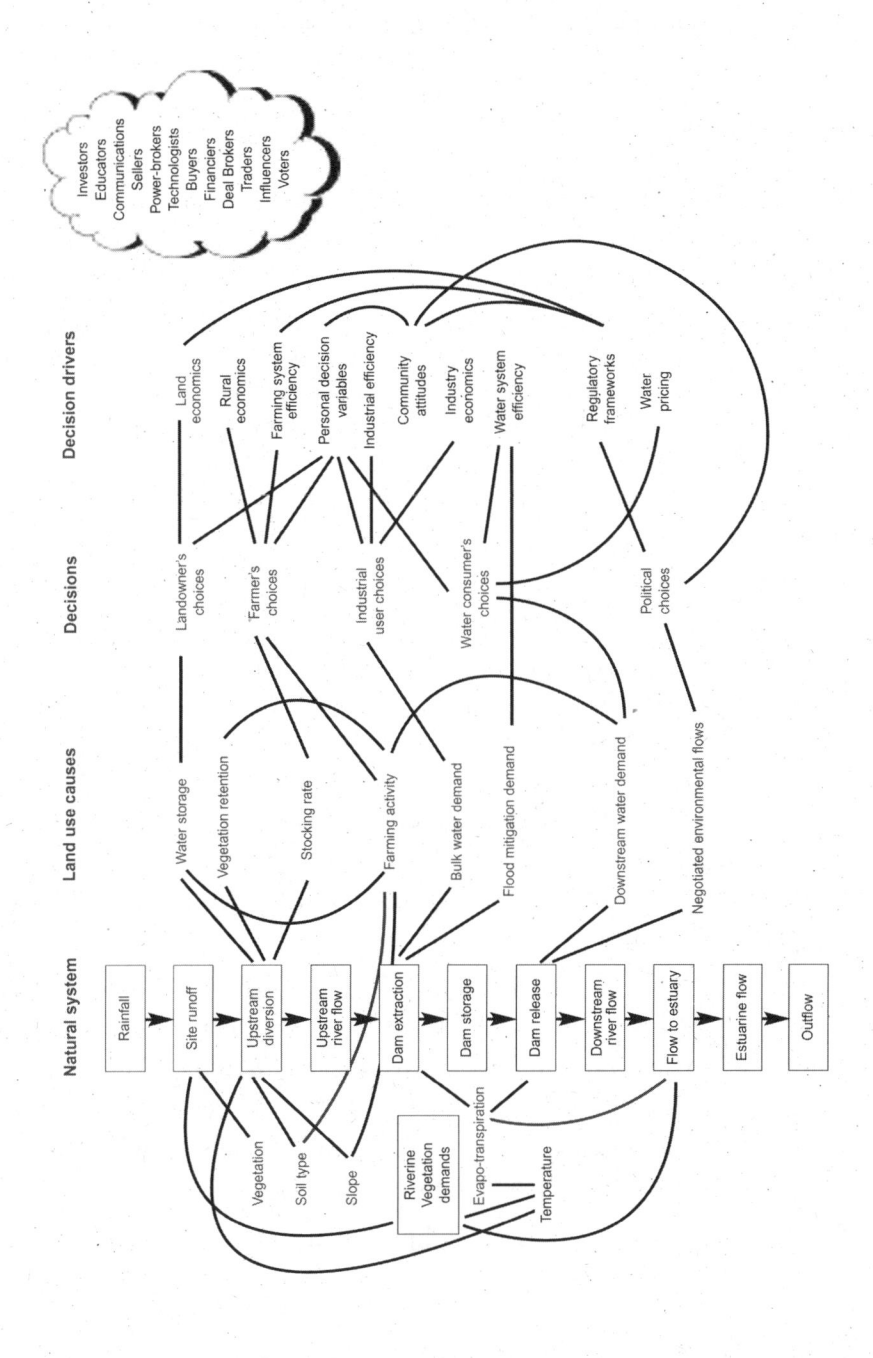

Figure 11.2 Water availability

Process 3: Evaluate policy performance

Outcome
A clear specification of:
- ➢ The behavioural outcomes that are intended by existing policy; and
- ➢ The gaps between those outcomes and what is being achieved.

Specifying the gap between what resource management agencies are achieving, compared with what they are charged with achieving ensures that the strategy being developed is linked to policy that has been endorsed. A failure to frame strategy within formal policy raises the risk that the team's outputs will not be treated as credible by government agencies.

The bulk of the work is preparation. Identifying, collating and evaluating policy instruments and plans that ought to govern natural resource management is a time-consuming task. It can be delegated or conducted as a consultancy. The task of evaluating outcomes from policy implementation can be conducted by the team in a day if the preparation is sound.

A good systems map should make it a relatively simple step to identify which public or private sector organisations are relevant sources of policy, and which government actors are relevant.

Stage 1: Define the strategy boundaries

Without clear boundaries, the strategist will end up trying to cope with excessive complexity. The project is likely to become unmanageable. The team should define:

- The biophysical or social challenges that the strategy is intended to address (see Process 1);
- Any geographic boundaries to the scope of the project (that is, regional, State, national or international); and
- The organisations and government agencies whose roles or activities should be taken into account.

Boundary definition should be simple if the basis of the project has been carefully set.

Stage 2: Clarify the policy aims

To be credible, a sustainability strategy should be 'grounded' in already endorsed or legislated policy. It should be targeted at achieving well-defined, measurable policy aims. Performance measures are rarely clearly stated for natural resource management policy or legislation, but it is possible to infer these.

There is a hierarchy of authority, from mandatory (required by law) to advisory. The strategists need to convert mandates into tangible measures of implementation and effectiveness.

The tasks are:
- Identify all statutory requirements. Review all relevant laws (federal, State or local), which impose an obligation on the identified actors in relation to the issues. This will include Acts governing the agencies or relevant organisations but also any laws that the agency or organisation is required to comply with or administer. List these legally-binding responsibilities.
- List all mandatory plans and policies (federal, State, local or corporate) governing the relevant agencies or organisations. This includes government-endorsed management plans (which have the formal authority of governing the work of agencies). This list represents the managerially-binding responsibilities.
- List the advisory plans and policies (federal, State, local or corporate) that are relevant to the issues. This list represents 'best management practice' advice to agencies and organisations concerned.

Most of this work will have been done in Process 2, Step 1. For each of the instruments, the team should ask 'if this policy principle were being applied, what implementation behaviours or outcomes would be objective proof?' They should do this for every responsibility identified. This will lead to an extensive list of performance criteria that the agencies ought be meeting.

For example, if an agency is expected to apply the precautionary principle, one would expect that agency to have processes that define and apply this in specific decisions. One would expect that any threatened area or species would have some form of protective program in place. If these indicators are not present, then it is reasonable to infer that the law or policy is not being implemented effectively. It is not difficult to turn a broad mandate into some testable indicators of implementation.

Once each management principle has a set of inferred tests of performance. These should be consolidated into objective tests that can be applied across each agency. This provides the basis to link the strategies that are developed by the team to existing policy frameworks.

Stage 3: Evaluate the outcomes (historical and projected)

With broad statements converted into measurable indicators of implementation, it is possible to evaluate implementation of policy. There are two types of evidence, operating at two levels:

- Biophysical and social outcomes which align (or not) with the mandatory or advisory standards. Whether or not these outcomes are being achieved will provide an objective test of effectiveness; and
- Activities and processes that demonstrate management implementation (but not necessarily effectiveness) of policy. If these are not present then it is reasonable to infer that concerted action is not being taken to satisfy the requirements on the agency.

For both, it is necessary to consider:

- Current performance (the state of the environment and the state of management process); and
- The future state, projected on the basis of pressures on the organisation and on the environment, and historical trajectories.

The evidence is likely to be a mixture of scientific data showing biophysical outcomes and projections, market or other social research, and management research of the agencies and organisations concerned. The process of assembling this will be a mixture of desk research (for example, scientific evidence of biophysical outcomes) and fieldwork (for example, market research and evaluation of agency processes and activity measures).

This information can be usefully presented in a table that summarises:

- The management principle and its source;
- The management process tests for demonstration of its implementation;
- The evidence of the existence of these processes;
- The biophysical or social outcomes that would test effectiveness of that implementation; and
- The outcome evidence of effectiveness of implementation.

Stage 4: Evaluate the performance gap

Armed with measurable performance indicators and objective information about outcomes and management process, the team can now identify specific gaps between what ought to be and what is occurring or likely.

To move from problem finding to problem solving, the strategists need to have specified clearly why these gaps exist. To say that *the harm-doing incentive is too great*, or *natural resources are under-valued* provides little guidance to action. However, to say that *the chief executive does not have a sustainability performance measure in their contract* provides a more actionable explanation. Specific, achievable identification of causes will allow the team to begin to look at what might be amenable to change.

Causes will typically be found in:

- Failure of specific control instruments (often attributable to resourcing, transaction costs, or agency incentives);
- Specific perverse incentives in markets;
- The pattern of information signals that is shaping the behaviours; or
- The framework of beliefs and decision-making approach within decision-making organisations.

With clarity about the policy instruments, and the shortfalls in their implementation, the strategy team can now commence its evaluation of the system issues, to form the basis of a strategy.

Process 4: Pick where to intervene

Outcome:

Decisions by the team about the focus of its strategy, based on:
> The points of intervention in the system it wants to change;
> The pressures, for and against, sustainable resource use; and
> The effects of the existing instruments and institutions in furthering or slowing sustainability.

Before the strategists can consider what instruments might suit their purposes, they should focus on the parts of the system where they believe they can have the greatest impact. This involves a judgment about points of intervention to be targeted. Depending on the quality of the preparation and the complexity of the issues, such a focusing session should take between one and two days to complete. It may be possible to break up the process and spread the task over a longer period, providing more opportunities for team reflection.

Stage 1: Identify the pivotal transactions

This is an expansion of the outcomes of the systems mapping from Process 2. The strategists move their attention to getting behind the transactions that are taking place which eventually impact on the environment. A transaction is any exchange or interaction that takes place between actors in the system (for example, a purchase, or an act of policing), or between an actor and the natural system (for example, placing a pump in a river, or putting out the garbage).

The systems map and background information should be reviewed. The team should select a small number of transactions that they consider are pivotal in shaping the impacts on the environment. This is an exercise of judgment, based on the experience and knowledge of the team (which is another reason for ensuring team completeness).

Some of these transactions may be distant in time and place from the effects on the physical environment. As you would have seen from Figure 11.2, water consumption is dictated by the decisions of corporations about their research and development priorities, or by politicians about infrastructure investment, to at least the same degree as it is by a teenager's decision to take an extra-long shower! An industrial corporation's decisions may be made months ahead and in a different country than the moment when the action is taken to implement a conserving but more costly manufacturing process. An individual's water-use practice may be the result of far earlier choices by an architect in designing their home. The strategists need to decide where they expect to have the greatest impact for their limited efforts.

Stage 2: Evaluate what shapes these transactions

Each transaction reflects the impacts of incentives, signals, decision-structures and transaction dynamics. The strategists should dissect these transactions, so that they understand what shapes them.

- What are the specific economic or social incentives that shape this transaction? For multi-party transactions, analysis should be done for each party to the transaction (see Stage 3 below).
- What are the signals and information that inform (or could inform if received) this transaction?
- What decision-making processes and beliefs shape the decisions?
- What are the transaction costs and filtration effects that can be found in this transaction and how do they impact on the outcome?
- What are the technologies that are in use and how do they shape the outcome?

Stage 3: Understanding transaction forces

Force field analysis is used in business for developing negotiation, marketing and political strategies. It can give insights into why people may be acting the way that they are and how influence might be applied. It causes the strategist to think about what drives decision-making. It usually serves to increase the range of possible interventions that are considered.

This is a five-step process.

Step 1: Select the actor(s) the team wants to understand better (for example, the domestic water consumer, the industrial user, or the rural producer).

Step 2: Identify the behaviour that a sustainability strategy might demand from this actor (for example, shorter showers, or implement water saving technology, or capital investment in improved technology). The more precise the team's specification of the behaviour they want, the greater the likelihood that the process will come up with useful results.

Step 3: Write this down in the middle of the page, at the top. Then beneath on the left hand side write 'Forces towards' and on the right 'Forces against'.

Step 4: Brainstorm and write down all of the forces the strategists can identify that might press the actor towards the behaviour you want from them.

Step 5: Do the same for the forces that prevent or discourage them from carrying out the desired behaviour.

Having done this analysis for the suite of parties, and for the important transactions, the strategists will have a comprehensive assessment of the behaviours that need to be changed, and the possible drivers of (or counter to) change. It can be useful to prioritise the forces for and against change, in terms of the power of that influence, and also on the basis of the capacity the strategist has to change that influence. This will assist the team when they come to strategy-making.

A simplified example

ACTOR: DOMESTIC CONSUMER
AIM: TURN OFF TAPS

Forces for	Forces against
Conservation desire	Ignorance of impact
Price of water (costs $)	Price of water (too cheap)
New technologies	Existing stock of taps

Stage 4: Evaluate existing instruments

With understanding of the transactions, and the behaviour of the actors, the next process is to review the management instruments being used, and to evaluate their effect (and effectiveness). Instruments refers to regulatory, market, incentive or other interventions used to shape the behaviours in the system. While the strategy focus is on sustainability, the team should consider the impact on other policy goals, such as improved productivity or economic development. The instruments to pursue these goals may be incidentally countering endeavours to support sustainability (as discussed in Part 2, when considering the perverse effect of protection subsidies).

The steps in the review process are largely based on the RCDM (see Chapter 2 to review). As the concepts are already exhaustively explained, for the sake of brevity the steps will be only briefly described.

Step 1: List the instruments being used to promote or manage resource use. Identify the purpose that each instrument is meant to serve. Consider the extent to which this purpose is, or could be made, consistent with the sustainability goals being pursued.

Step 2: Evaluate the economic or social incentives the instrument creates, and the behaviours it therefore promotes or discourages. For transactions involving a number of parties the analysis should be done for each party, to provide a comprehensive understanding of the incentives. Consider the extent to which these incentives are, or could be made, consistent with sustainability goals.

Step 3: Identify the information which triggers or is necessary for the application of the instrument. Consider the ways in which this information is generated and captured for decision-making, and the transaction costs and inefficiencies that impact on decision-making. The strategy team should consider ways in which this information flow could be altered to improve the likelihood of pro-sustainability decisions.

Step 4: Consider the ways in which the decisions required by the instrument are made, including the process and the ways in which values are applied. The team should consider how environmental values could be better reflected in that decision-making.

Step 5: The team should consider the transaction costs and filtration effects that shape the effectiveness of this instrument and how they impact on sustainability. The team should consider how these aspects of decision-making might be reformed to better support sustainability.

Step 6: Finally, the team should consider the technologies embedded in the management approach and whether they contribute to the natural resource outcomes. For example, a policy instrument to aid farm productivity could be designed to support any kind of farming activity (sustainable or not) or it could be designed to support only more environmentally-efficient production methods.

Stage 5: Review the institutions

Chapter 1 considered the impact of institutions. This stage of the process ensures that the team understands the institutions relevant to the possible strategies. Institutional reform is typically a large scale, long-term endeavour, which is likely to be outside of the scope of a natural resources management team. However, sensitivity to institutional influences can cause a team to modify strategies to better suit a given institutional context.

Step 1: Identify relevant institutions

Revisit the system map (Process 2). Use brainstorming to identify institutions with a direct relationship to the decision-makers the team has identified. These may be authoritative, where an organisation has some power to direct or control, or is directed or controlled by the decision-maker; or they may be advisory, with an information-provision relationship. Relevant institutions do not have to be primarily concerned with natural resource management. For example, banks, local councils, political organisations or even churches, all shape attitudes and behaviour in ways that may be relevant to the operation of a natural resource use system. Having identified the relevant institutions, the team then canvasses the impacts they may be having on the system, and possible ways to better align the effects of that institution with the sustainability objectives.

Step 2: Evaluate intangible institutions

Using a similar approach, identify any intangible institutions which impact on the resource consumption system the strategists are concerned with. These may be:

- Forms of social organisation (for example, peer group or family influence);
- Conventions about relationships (for example, friendship obligations, or accepted responses to power);
- Accepted modes of behaviour (for example, acceptance of modes of behaviour, caution in criticism); or
- Patterns in how resources are transacted and managed (for example, the role of legal documentation, or collaboration).

The team is now nearly ready to consider possible instruments that could change resource use behaviour.

Stage 6: Review possible leverage points

The preceding analyses will ensure that the strategy team is thoroughly briefed and has a clear understanding of behavioural objectives and of the system they have to manage. They will have explored the causes of the behaviours exhibited by actors in that system, from the perspective of forces at work, including the institutions and the management instruments used to pursue policy objectives.

With all this information, the team may risk becoming overwhelmed by complexity. It is necessary that the team decide where to concentrate its efforts. This is a subjective judgment. The quality of facilitation, the quality of the strategy team, and the quality of interpersonal relationships, are all important in ensuring a good outcome that is well supported by team members.

Step 1: Brainstorm points for intervention

Using the systems map as a focus, brainstorm where in the system intervention is likely to be most effective. In doing this, the team participants are likely to move loosely between identification of particular transactions, actors, or instruments as possible points of focus. It is not necessary to constrain this exploration. The aim is to get ideas flowing and to encourage discussion. A team which has been active in the preceding stages may be able to move very quickly to specify possible intervention points. However, in other cases this may require a lot of time.

Step 2: Narrow the focus

Through informal debate the team must decide where they believe intervention would be most powerful, and what type of intervention would be required. Then they are asked to consider where intervention is most feasible, and what form that intervention would need to take to be both feasible and effective. In some teams, a consensus will rapidly emerge and in others the process will be exhaustive.

Step 3: List five fundamental transactions

The third step is for the team to identify up to five fundamental transactions that they believe their strategic intervention should target. These should be listed (usually on butchers' paper) and kept in front of the team. This selection may involve some negotiation.

Step 4: List five primary actors for each transaction

The team should identify up to five actors (people or organisations) who should be the priority targets for behaviour change for each of these fundamental transactions. These should be listed and also kept in front of the team. On completion of this step it is possible that there will be a list of up to 25 actors of significance in the behaviour of the system. What is more likely is that some key actors whose role effects a number of important transactions will emerge as key targets for the strategy, bringing this list down to a more manageable level. The team may wish to refine the list to as much smaller number. The facilitator should ensure that the team questions whether this is a sound judgment about how best to reshape the system, or merely an attempt to disengage from complexity or reduce effort.

Step 5: Identify shaping forces

Take the list of actors and, for each, identify what instruments and institutions most powerfully shape their behaviour in relation to the transactions. This provides greater clarity about the influences which need to be managed. This step may be broken down into project teams to accelerate progress.

Step 6: Negotiate strategic priorities

The team should now negotiate its set of priorities for the possible solution. These should be expressed as:

- What is the problem the team proposes to solve?
- What are the priority transactions the team needs to change?
- Who are the priority actors whose actions are vital to solving the problem?
- What are the key shaping forces for their actions?

These specifics should be documented each on a separate page as a 'Problem Specification' for the team to focus upon. Armed with this, the team is able to begin to consider possible instruments that may have an impact on the problem. Ideally the priorities should be presented in a hierarchy.

Process 6: Designing possible intervention

Outcome:

A preliminary set of ideas about the ways in which a strategy might intervene in the system.

This process assumes that the team participants understand the range of possible natural resource management instruments. With a less-informed group, their ability to canvass instrumental alternatives will be constrained.

It is likely that these processes will be more effective as a series of sessions, focusing in sequence upon particular priority problems (as defined in Process 5), moving towards integration in a focus session. The preceding processes and preparatory work will mean that most of the issues have been canvassed by the strategy team.

Stage 1: Brainstorm and discuss each priority problem

The Problem Specifications should be addressed in priority order. The process below applies for each distinct problem.

Step 1: Generate solutions

After review of the problem specification (and with that specification in front of each participant in the session), begin with this question: 'If it were my problem to fix, where and how would I intervene?'

Elicit ideas from the group, documented on a whiteboard.

After there are at least six possibilities, discuss why a particular intervention might be chosen, compared to some other possible intervention. Allow the discussion to range for some time. Add new possibilities if they emerge. When strategy themes begin to emerge, document them on the white board.

Step 2: Uncover the hidden hypotheses

Once the group has refined the list, test each possibility by asking: 'If this is what we believe might work, what is the underlying hypothesis about how best to manage behaviour that could explain why? Do we believe that this hypothesis is valid?'

The aim is to ensure that the team is focused upon behaviour, and have had to question and debate their beliefs about how behaviour can be managed and changed. This can lead the team to reject some of their own proposed strategies as naïve.

For example, if the team's suggestion is 'tighten regulation to change behaviour', the hidden hypotheses about behaviour might be:

Regulation will be effective because:
- Voluntary compliance is normal; or
- Effective policing is feasible; or
- Regulation will lead to social pressure for compliance.

Once exposed, these hypotheses can be debated and questioned. If the team does not believe all or any of these are robust, then they should reject regulation as a strategy.

The team should decide whether the hypothesis is valid, invalid, or valid only under certain conditions. These conditions should be noted. They may be things like:

Voluntary compliance is normal only if:
- The behaviour does not cost much;
- The regulation is consistent with existing beliefs in the community; and
- Adequate information is provided to those whose behaviour is to be affected.

If (as is likely) it emerges that the simple hypothesis about effectiveness is not sufficient to explain why a strategy may or may not work, then the team is on the path to considering what complementary actions may be needed to support the strategy it finally decides to pursue. Core strategies (such as regulation) may have to be supported by other tactics (such as education, public relations, or improved use of monitoring technologies).

Do not allow issues of practicality (that is, the resources needed to intervene) to exclude ideas at this stage. What seems impractical may emerge as feasible once you have explored the instruments that are available.

For each problem there ought to be many possibilities for intervention. There is no right solution, but many potential solutions to be made 'right' by the people who implement them. This process is designed to focus effort on a subset most likely to pay off from the effort invested. The team should now develop a list of institutional and instrumental change needed to implement the possible solutions that have been proposed.

Stage 2: Refine the possible solutions for each problem

The aim of this stage is to take the possible solutions for each problem, and the team's refined understanding of what is needed to make the behavioural hypotheses valid, and to refine them. In doing so, the team will also draw together their work on instruments and institutions.

Step 1: Expand the instruments for implementation

Specify the instrumental changes needed to give effect to the strategies that have been proposed. Aim to generate around ten instrumental possibilities for each of the solutions proposed. Address questions such as:

- What possible ways might you adjust existing markets, including restructuring subsidies or taxes?
- What rights instruments might be created, or adjustments to existing rights?
- What changes should (or might) be made to regulation, including more effective implementation of existing regulations?
- What supportive information like education and marketing programs could have an impact?
- What short-term incentives, such as subsidies, would help?

This sounds like an impossible task, until you begin to implement it. The team will rapidly arrive at a diverse set of possibilities that can be used to implement the desired strategies. This is important because only a limited range of possibilities will be feasible, given politics and resource limitations.

Step 2: Identify institutional changes

Identify the institutional changes that may be necessary to make preferred instrumental changes effective. This will require the team to consider:

- What flows of information may be necessary to ensure that the instrument is effective;
- What resourcing will be needed;
- Changes that may be necessary to how decisions are made; and
- If any relevant changes to beliefs, values and cultures are required.

The team should then consider what institutional reforms are needed to satisfy these requirements. This step may rule out some possible strategies as unrealistic.

Step 3: Identify complementary actions

The team should then identify what complementary actions are needed to ensure that the behaviour of the key actors is shaped towards the needs of the sustainability strategy. This requires consideration of what information they will need (and what information will be required from them), the resources that will have to be made available and the ways of managing any adverse resourcing impacts on these actors. The team will have to address means to ensure that the actors have the decision-making abilities to do what is wanted of them, and consider how to resolve issues of beliefs and culture that could diminish the effectiveness of the instrumental approaches that are proposed.

Stage 3: Consolidate the options for intervention

The team now has a menu of well-considered possible strategies. They must now recombine these elements, seeking a smaller set of strategies that each addresses a number of the priorities. The aim is to find synergy, and to identify the manageable set of interventions that will have the greatest total impact.

Looking over the material generated from Stage 1 and 2, the team should decide which options are synergistic, or have commonalities in how they impact within the system. The facilitator should ensure that the team remains energetic. The team should try to avoid early rejection of ideas that may (with further work) be made viable, but at the same time reduce the investment of real effort into possibilities that are unrealistic.

Once these strategies have been narrowed and refined, the facilitator should document these groups as 'Strategy 1', 'Strategy 2' and so forth. Give each a tag line. For example, one might be 'Changing the purchaser's approach' or another 'Giving producers reasons to change'. Aim for a small number of strategies made up of different combinations of interventions.

Step 1: Brainstorm the implementation

For each of the strategies, the team should document what complementary initiatives will be required to ensure that the actors are able to implement what is expected of them. This may, for example, highlight the need for training, information, resources or support. This will require that the team address the related marketing and information provision aspects, any financial or resourcing support, and any initiatives that will have to be taken to better equip actors with a role in the strategy to fulfil that expectation.

Step 2: Evaluate possible social impacts

Almost any strategy that changes resource access has the potential to have adverse effects on some groups in society. It is important that the team consider what these impacts might be, and how any serious inequities or other ethical considerations can be addressed within the strategy.

The team should ask where and how the strategy will impact on resource access or the cost or price of access. This should be documented, and the groups who may be adversely impact listed. Based on this, the team will consider whether this raises major social equity or ethical considerations.

The team then should consider the same issues from the perspective of possible structural changes that might result, such as changes to market activity or transfers of power. Where these secondary impacts raise ethical considerations, these should also be noted.

Armed with this information, the team should clearly specify the social or ethical considerations and brainstorm possible means to manage these. Decisions should be added back into the specification of the strategy before selection of a preferred approach.

Process 6: Selecting strategies

Outcome:

Agreed team recommendations about the strategies for sustainability which are to be pursued.

The next stage is to filter and prioritise the strategies the team has generated. One aim is to ensure that the strategists have considered the ramifications of the strategies and amended them to improve their potential to work.

Step 1: Develop evaluation criteria

The team should document the objective criteria against which they intend to evaluate the strategies. These criteria might be factually objective (for example, that the strategy must be fully implementable within the scope of a particular government agency or level of government), or they may be more subjective (for example, judged to be politically feasible), or consist of a mix of these types. The more objective the criteria, the more apparently precise is the evaluation. However, some caution should be exercised because the application of measurable criteria often requires a great deal of additional work to fully specify the strategy so that the tests can be applied.

A team should generate its own criteria. Suggestions to consider for criteria include:

- Can we overcome the barriers to adoption: What is the size and power of its opponents?
- Is this a strategy that can generate widespread support: Can excitement, interest, energy be created?
- Is this approach consistent with ethical responsibility: Does it affect social equity?
- Can it be made practical within accessible resources?
- Can we use this approach to trigger other actions or base it on other actions? Can it be leveraged?
- Can we implement it without too much risk? Is there a possible exit?

To these can be added other considerations relevant to the team, or the organisations which have sponsored the work of the team.

Step 2: Define 'Must', 'Should' and 'Could' criteria

Prioritise the criteria as those which must be satisfied, and then those which 'could' or 'should' be met. The set of proposals should be tested to remove those which will not satisfy the 'must' criteria, or for modification (if this is possible) so that the must criteria are able to be met. This approach allows the strategists to quickly cull strategies that will not prove viable, leaving a feasible sub-set to further develop.

Step 3: Evaluate

Evaluation can be unstructured, using debate and negotiation within the team to agree the preferred approach. A more structured approach is to use a 'weighted attribute' analysis. This can be particularly useful if debate becomes bogged down, if the team may have to justify its proposals, or if the process of translation into action will require others to be comfortable explaining the reasons for the choices made.

Under this approach, a table is created (see below). Each criteria is given a weighting score of importance. Then each possible strategy is listed and given a point score for each of the criteria. The total score for each is the sum of the *score x weight* for each criteria.

Template 3: Weighted attribute evaluation

Criteria	Weighting	Strategy A' score	"A" score x Weight	Strategy 'B' Score	"B" Score x weight
1st criterion	10	3	3x10 = 30	6	6 x 10 = 60
2nd criterion	20	4	4 x20 = 80	2	4 x 20 = 40
3rd criterion	15	6	6 x 15= 90	7	7 x 15 = 105
Totals			= 200		= 205

While the process is mechanical, its real function is to make the team's reasoning more transparent. It is not unusual (nor bad) for the team to proceed to change its criteria, weightings, or scores until they all agree the right strategy to follow. This means debating and refining judgment about the proposals and the criteria, and redesigning strategies as necessary.

Process 10: Prepare for endorsement

Outcome:
A well specified and documented proposal for endorsement and then implementation.

The final stages (prior to implementation plans) ensure that the strategy is comprehensive and complete, and endorsed for implementation

Stage 1: Preliminary endorsement of the strategy

Before moving on to the detailed work of developing an implementation program, the strategy must be endorsed by the key stakeholders. This can be done by workshops and by drafts and discussion papers. The strategy team should ensure that they are clear about who has the authority to ratify the strategy and the process and criteria that will lead to this.

There can be a temptation to 'sell' the strategy, downplaying the contentious parts like penalties or mandatory requirements, or possible costs to some stakeholders. Caution should be exercised, for if the program as presented for endorsement differs from the program once implemented, then trust and goodwill will be damaged. Honesty and directness are valuable, not to be sacrificed in favour of expedience.

Once endorsed, the next stage is extension of the conceptual design into a complete program.

Stage 2: Extension of the strategy

Before implementation, it is worthwhile revisiting the maps of the resource-use system. This ensures that all the actors and the transactions that need to be managed for the proposed strategy to be effective have been comprehensively considered.

Ask the following questions:

- How will we address resource flows and incentives in our implementation program?
- How will we address information flows?
- What values systems issues are relevant, and what will we do about them?
- What decision-making approach issues will we have to deal with and how will we deal with them?

Much of this work has been carried out in the earlier processes, and so this detail should be drawn from the background work and then extended into a practical approach. This step will add tasks to the project plan but reduce the risks of overlooking important activities.

Stage 3: Project planning

Project planning is a discipline in itself. It involves decisions about all the activities, their timing and relationship, and their resource demands. While these issues are not dealt with here, it is worthwhile to embrace this type of discipline to ensure that the project is genuinely budgeted and that all those who are expected to play a part are 'locked in' to their role.

VOICE OF EXPERIENCE: RURAL BEHAVIOURS

Tony Gleeson from Synapse Consulting[5] in Queensland knows about change management and the rural sector and what is needed to assist the move towards sustainable agriculture. He has been working in this field for over 30 years, both in practice and through action research projects.

We asked him: 'If we asked you to advise on how to assist farmers to adopt a new sustainability practice, like more active management of the nutrient balance, what are the key things you would have us think about?

First, we need to get some attention on the practices of land managers – this is what needs to be 'managed', not the nutrient balance per se. And hence it is very important to avoid a narrow approach, to avoid too early a fixation on the construction of the 'problem'. The solution might lie in helping the land manager to envision and move to a different future rather than in adjusting a particular agricultural practice. If your thinking gets too narrow, too fast, you will accept existing practice, existing land use rather than questioning the fundamentals. We have to begin with a careful evaluation of what we need to achieve and to do this we need to understand and take into account the values of those who are directly affected, and also of the broader community who have a stake in the issues. You cannot develop this without dialogue.

Some people think this means investing a lot in formal market research. It does not. The best way to go about it is to get the right people around the table, and begin to talk about the beliefs and values issues. You have to be careful to ensure that this is not driven from the idea that the problem is owned by those who are currently in control of the resources. They are part of the issue, and important, but theirs is only one of the perspectives. If you make them too central, or give them absolute control, then it is possible that you will never consider the more fundamental issues.

How are projects like this set up?

Unfortunately, a lot of the time projects begin with timeframes and specifications that are too restrictive to deal with the real issues, and to have the type of dialogue that is needed to develop understanding. This is a false economy. It also prevents more fundamental questioning about issues like 'why do we do this?' or 'is there a totally different approach we could take?' Social, political issues – in fact the whole gamut of institutional issues – have to be part of the project itself, not pre-defined by someone at a desk. If not, they will never be properly considered.

We also need to be realistic about the outcomes that can be achieved. Our expectations of fast, measured results leads us towards particular kinds of solutions, and measures of success. Yet in changing people, the most important changes may be in behaviour, in a preparedness to change, in a preparedness to have a dialogue.

---

5 See <www.synapseconsulting.com.au>.

If you go for the quick fixes, the changes are likely to be incremental, insufficient to meet the challenge.

What stops change happening, apart from people feeling uncertain?

Institutions – the laws, the norms and customs, the organizations, the markets – are important in understanding change. Frequently they act as constraints on the possible solutions, because they grow up supporting things that may now be barriers to change. In agriculture, many of the R&D and political institutions are embedded in the commodity view of the world, and are culturally attuned to supporting what may be an unsupportable view of the world. Farmer organisations can't face this challenge in trying to work for change, when most of their members do not trust that it is desirable or possible. You may have to begin a process that enables institutional change because the existing institutions are likely to be a major part of the problem.

How can you get people involved?

Inspiration, energy, trust and intellectual honesty. You just cannot do without them. We have to emphasise that 'it can happen'. With the longer-term framework of problem definition and reconstruction it might be useful to pick some easily achievable goals, especially if it is done in an adaptive management context. One example is Landcare groups, where too often the pursuit of a technical solution takes power away from the local people and hands it to technical experts. It can take forever, and you lose excitement. In one instance, it is ten years since a group wanted to remove some weeds, and still no one has agreed on the perfect solution. It would have been better to have let them bulldoze the weeds, and spend the next few years sorting out the problems they may have created. At least they would have been involved.

We can too easily over-complicate the technical issues. We then over-invest resources and energy into them, and leave people out. It is important to keep a sense of proportion about the goals and use resources with this in mind. As I said at the start, the main goal is about people, not about things. You can paralyse people with a tortured process.

You have to aim for some early 'wins' in the process, even if these are only small. It is important to get energy into it, and get something happening (even if it is not always the exactly right thing with hindsight). Too often we get tied up in spending all our energy on trying to find the right technical solution, and we lose sight of just how important it is to create opportunities for people to act and to get involved. This type of task has to be understood as being about changing or working with people, not about things. If you lose sight of this, you will make basic mistakes. Too often we allow technical issues to take control, because they hold out the promise of solutions, but generally it is the people issues that will make all the difference.

What technology is important?

We do need technology, but it has to be appropriate, that is, it needs to be as sophisticated as is needed to achieve the objective, no more. We need fast data capture, easy assessment and (most important) conversion of data and information into something that people can act on. Data are too easily substituted for meaningful information and information for knowledge when we rely on technical people to drive the processes.

Often, someone else has done a lot of the work. We may be better off to get people with similar issues together and let them discuss the situation, define the problem, build off each other, than handing it over to an expert. We can afford to take some technical risk, if it will build social commitment and involvement. We have to be more prepared to make this kind of sensible tradeoff if we are to achieve social change towards sustainability.

But at the end of it all we need to be modest about how much we know about how to move forward – the ones that worry me most are those who 'know' the way forward – or maybe I'm just envious.

References

Alchian, A (1977) 'Some implications of the recognition of property right transaction costs', in Svetozar Pejovich (ed) *The economic foundations of property rights: Selected readings*, Cheltenham: Edward Elgar Publishing, pp 7-28.

Australian Treasury (2002) Intergenerational Report 2002-03, Canberra: Treasury.

Australian and New Zealand Environment and Conservation Council (ANZECC) (2001) Review of the national strategy for the conservation of Australia's Biological Diversity, Environment Australia, Canberra.

Bandura, A (1986) *Social Foundations of Thought and Action: A Social Cognitive Theory*, New Jersey: Prentice-Hall.

Barrett, J and A Scott (2001) *An Ecological Footprint of Liverpool: Developing sustainable scenarios Liverpool*, York: Stockholm Environment Institute, p 121.

Bates, G (2001) *A Duty of Care for the Protection of Biodiversity on Land*, Canberra: Productivity Commission.

Beder S (1995) 'SLAPPs – Strategic Lawsuits Against Public Participation: Coming to a Controversy Near You, *Current Affairs Bulletin*, vol 72, no 3, Oct/Nov, pp 22-29.

Berkes, F (ed) (1989) *Common Property Resources: Ecology and community based sustainable development*, London: Belhaven Press.

Botica, R and White, S (1996) 'Kalgoorlie-Boulder: The Water Efficient City', *Water* September/October, pp 14-17.

Bromley, DW (1991) *Environment and Economy*, Oxford: Blackwell.

Brubacker, E (1995) *Property Rights in Defence of Nature*, London: Earthscan.

Byrne, J and Glover, L (2000) *Climate Shopping: Putting the Atmosphere Up for Sale*, The Australian Conservation Foundation and the Center for Energy and Environmental Policy, Newark: University of Delaware.

Clinch, JP, Convery, FJ et al (1999) *Economic Instruments for Sustainable Development: Improving the External and Working Environment*, Dublin: European Foundation for the Improvement of Living and Working Conditions.

Coase, RH (1960) 'The Problem of Social Cost' *Journal of Law and Economics*, vol 3, no 1, pp 1-44; also in William Breit and Harold M Hochman (eds) (1968), *Readings in Microeconomics*, New York: Holt, Rinehart and Winston.

Cohen H (1982) *You Can Negotiate Anything*, New York: Bantam Doubleday.

Conacher, A and Conacher, J (2001) *Environmental Planning and Management in Australia*, Melbourne: Oxford University Press.

Costanza, R and Segura, O (eds) (1996) *Down to Earth: Practical Applications of Ecological Economics* Washington, DC: Island Press.

Craik, W (2001) *Markets and the Environment The Future of Market Regulation*, Sydney: Australian Museum & NSW Nature and Conservation Council.

Cupit, M (2000) 'Games teach emissions trading lessons' *Environmental finance* (April), pp 25-27.

Decanio, SJ (1997) 'The Economics of Climate Change San Francisco, Redefining Progress', <www.redefiningprogress.org/publications/pdf/ecc.pdf>.

Deni Greene Consulting Services (2001) *A Capital Idea: realising value from environmental and social performance*, Carlton: Environment Australia.

DEST (1997) *Subsidies to the Use of Natural Resources*, Canberra: Department of Environment Sport and Territories.
Doyle, JK (1997) 'The cognitive psychology of systems thinking' *System Dynamics Review* vol 13, no 3, pp 253-265.
Driessen, DM (2003) *The Economic Dynamics of Environmental Law*, Cambridge Mass: MIT Press.
Dunlop, M, Foran, BD et al (2001) *Exploring Solutions to Australia's Long-term land and Water Problems using Scenario Modelling*, Canberra: CSIRO.
Emery, F (1962) 'Heuristic Models of the Marketing Process', in *Human Relations* 1962/9, pp 62-76.
EPA (2000) *State and Local Government Pioneers: How state and local governments are implementing environmentally preferable purchasing practices* Washington: US EPA.
Fijalkowski, A and Fitzmaurice, M (eds) (2000) *The Right of the Child to a Clean Environment Programme on International Rights of the Child*, Hants: Dartmouth Publishing Company Limited.
Foran, B and Poldy, F (2002) *Dilemmas Distilled: A summary and guide to the CSIRO technical report – Future Dilemmas: Options to 2050 for Australia's population, technology, resources and environment*, Canberra: CSIRO.
Foran, B and Poldy, F (2002) *Future Dilemmas: Options to 2050 for Australia's population, technology, resources and environment*, Canberra: CSIRO.
Gibbs, CJ and Bromley, DW (1989) 'Institutional Arrangements for Management of Rural Resources: Common Property Regimes' in F Berkes (ed), *Common Property Resources: Ecology and community based sustainable development* London: Belhaven Press.
Gittins, R (2002) 'We fiddle while our home burns' *Sydney Morning Herald*, 28 May.
Hawken, P, Lovins, A, Hunter-Lovins, L (1999) *Creating the Next Industrial Revolution; Natural Capitalism*, New York: Little Brown.
Hobbs, B (2000) *What kind of Australia do you want?* Sixteenth Brodie Hall Address, Canberra: Australian Resources Research Centre (ARRC).
IPART (2002) *Sydney Water Corporation: Operational Audit 200/2001 Final Report* Sydney: Independent Pricing and Regulatory Tribunal of NSW.
James, D (1997) *Environmental Incentives: Australian Experience with Economic Instruments for Environmental Management* Canberra: Environment Australia.
Karoly, DK, Risbey J, Reynolds A (2003) *Global Warming contributes to Australia's Worst Drought*, Australia: World Wildlife Fund for Nature.
Kuhn, A (1974) *The Logic of Social Systems: A Unified, Deductive, System-Based Approach to Social Science*, San Francisco: Jossey-Bass.
Krockenberger, M, Kinrade, P et al (2000) *Natural Advantage: a Blueprint for a Sustainable Australia* Sydney: Australian Conservation Foundation.
Leahy, T (2000) *Waiting For the End of the World: Popular Responses to Environmental Issues in Australia*, Newcastle: University of Newcastle.
Lenzen, M (2002) *An input-output model*, Canberra: Australian Bureau of Statistics.
Loh, J (ed) (2000) *Living Planet Report 2000*, Gland, Switzerland: World Wildlife Fund for Nature.
Lazarus, Richard J (2004) *The Making of Environmental Law*, Chicago: University of Chicago Press.
Luhmann, N (1984) *Social Systems*, Stanford: Stanford University Press.

Marceau, J, Manley, K et al (1997) *The High Road or the Low Road: Alternatives for Australia's Future*, Sydney: Australian Business Foundation Limited.

Martin, P and Verbeek, M (1998) *National Materials Accounting Strategy: A path to competitive advantage for Australian industry*, Sydney: Profit Foundation Pty Ltd.

Martin, P and Verbeek, M (2002a) *Fifty Million Australians: Can this be sustainable?* Canberra: Land & Water Australia.

Martin, P and Verbeek, M (2002b) 'Property rights and property responsibility' in *Property: Rights and Responsibilities: Current Australian Thinking*. Canberra: Land & Water Australia.

Martin, P and Verbeek, M (2002c) *Rights, Institutions and Sustainability: How can we make it work* in Wilson, A, and Curtis, A (eds) *Agriculture for the Australian Environment*, Albury Johnstone Centre, Charles Sturt University.

Martin, P (2001) *Showcasing the Environmental Industries*, Canberra: Department of Industry Science and Technology.

Martin, P and Verbeek, M (2000) *A Cartography for Natural Resource Law: Finding new paths to effective resource regulation*, Canberra: Land and Water Australia.

McKenzie-Mohr, D and Smith, W (1999) *Fostering Sustainable Behaviour*, Gabriola Island B.C. Canada: New Society Publishers.

Meltz, R (1995) *The Property Rights Issue*, Washington: The Committee for the National Institute for the Environment.

Mercer, D (2000) *A Question of Balance: Natural Resources Conflict Issues in Australia*, Sydney: Federation Press.

Moyer, R (1982) 'Strategic Planning for the Small Firm', *Journal of Small Business Management*, July, p 8.

Moxnes, E (2000) 'Not only the tragedy of the commons: misperceptions of feedback and policies for sustainable development' *System Dynamics Review*, vol 16 (Winter), pp 325-348.

National Centre for Environmental Economics (2001) *The US Experience with Economic Incentives for Protecting the Environment*, Washington: Office of Policy, Economics, and Innovation, US Environmental Protection Agency.

National Institute of Economic and Industry Research (NIEIR) (1996) *Subsidies to the Use of Natural Resources – Executive Summary*, Canberra: Department of the Environment, Sport and Territories.

National Land and Water Resources (2002) *Australian Catchment, River and Estuary Assessment 2002, CRC coasts*, Canberra: Environment Australia.

Nelissen, NJM (1998) 'Environmental Policy Instrumentation in the Netherlands: Comments on Three Decades of Development', *Greener Management International* vol 22 Summer, pp 30-45.

Norberg-Bohm, V (1998) 'Stimulating "green" technological innovation: an analysis of alternative policy mechanisms' *Policy Sciences*, vol 32, no 1, pp 13-38.

Ohmae, Kenichi (1982) *The Mind of the Strategist: The Art of Japanese Business*, Columbus, OH: McGraw Hill.

Ojwang, C and J (eds) (1996) *In Land We Trust: Environment, Private Property and Constitutional Change*, ACTS Environment Policy Series, Nairobi: Initiatives Publishers.

Palmer, K and Walls, M (1999) *Extended Product Responsibility: An Economic Assessment of Alternative Policies*, Washington: Resources for the Future.

Pigou, AC (1920) *The Economics of Welfare*, London: Macmillan.
Pilon, R (1995) *Protecting Private Property Rights from Regulatory Takings*, Centre for Constitutional Studies, Cato Institute, Subcommittee on Constitution Committee on Judiciary United States House of Representatives Washington?
Porter, M (1980) *Competitive Strategy*, Harvard: Free Press.
Porter, M and van der Linde, C (1995) 'Green and Competitive: Ending the Stalemate' in R Welford and R Starkey (eds) *Business and the Environment*, London: Taylor & Francis.
Peake, S, (2002) 'The UN SG's Rio-listic Assessment: how well are we doing after 10 years', *Outreach* issue II, 21 March 2002, <www.unedforum.org//news/outreach/pclll/Issue%2021.pdf>
Price Waterhouse Coopers (2001) *The role of Australia's financial sector in sustainability*, Canberra: Environment Australia: 68.
Regier, HA, Mason, RV et al (1989) 'Reforming the use of Natural Resources' in Berkes, F (ed) *Common Property Resources: Ecology and community based sustainable development*, London: Belhaven Press.
Robbins, SP, Bergman, R et al (1997) *Management*, Sydney: Prentice Hall.
Rose, DB (1997) 'Common property regimes in Aboriginal Australia: totemism revisited' in DD Silva (ed) *The Governance of Common property in the Pacific region*, Canberra: NCDS and the Resource Management in Asia-Pacific project.
Rowley, C (1993) 'The Limits of Democracy' in C Rowley (ed) *Property Rights and the Limits of Democracy* Aldershot: Edward Elgar Publishing.
Silva, DD (1997) *Governance of Common property in the Pacific region* Canberra, NCDS and the Resource Management in Asia-Pacific project.
Simons, KL (2000) *Technology Benchmarks for Sustained Economic Growth*, 18th International System Dynamics Conference, Bergen: Norway.
Skinner, BF (2002) *Beyond Freedom and Dignity*, Indianapolis: Hackett Publishing Company.
Smith, PL, Wilson, B et al (2000) *The ecological role of the native vegetation of NSW*, Sydney: Native Vegetation Advisory Council of NSW.
Smith J (2004) "Redesign of Government Sustainability Education Programa for Business Personnel – From Awareness Raising to Changing Behaviour", unpublished PhD Thesis, Armidale: University of New England.
Stavins, RN (2000) *Experience with Market-based Environmental Policy Instruments*, Washington: Resources for the Future.
Thom, B (2002) *State of the Environment 2001*, Canberra: Environment Australia.
Tierney, J (2000) 'A Tale of Two Fisheries' *The New York Times Magazine*, August 27. Text now available from <www.gametheory.net/news/items/052.html>.
Tully, J (1980) *A Discourse on Property: John Locke and his Adversaries* Cambridge: Cambridge University Press.
Usher, PJ (1997) Common property and regional sovereignty: relations between aboriginal peoples and the Crown in Canada, in *The Governance of Common property in the Pacific region*, Canberra: NCDS and the Resource Management in Asia-Pacific project.
von Bertalanffy, L (1968) *General systems theory*, New York: Braziller.

von Clausewitz, K (1832) *On War*, Military Academy: Berlin, cited in R Bruce, *The Entrepreneurs, Strategies Motivations Successes and Failures*, London: Penguin Books, p 3.

von Weizacker, E, Lovins, AB et al (1997) *Factor 4: Doubling wealth – halving resource use: A new report to the Club of Rome*, Sydney: Allen and Unwin.

Wentworth Group (2002) *Blueprint for a Living Continent: A Way Forward from The Wentworth Group of Concerned Scientists*, Sydney: World Wildlife Fund for Nature.

Wilson, EO (1992) *The Diversity of Life*, Cambridge, Mass: Harvard University Press.

Young, M (1997) *Water Rights: An ecological economics perspective* Canberra: Centre for Resource and Environmental Studies, Australian National University.

Zakon, A and Henderson, B (1980) *Corporate Growth Strategy, Handbook of Business Problem Solving*, Columbus, OH: McGraw Hill.

Zann, LP (2002) *State of the Marine Environment Report for Australia*, Canberra: Department of the Environment, Sport and Recreation.

Index

Aboriginal, 36, 44, 79
  control, 147
  council, 157
  interests, 5
  people, 112, 128
  ownership, 148
ABS, 16
Accelerated Depreciation of Environmental Investment Measures, 62
access, 4
  protecting, 5
  rights, 113
Accredited Licensee Scheme, 62
accountability, 4, 36, 75, 111, 196
  environmental, 143
accounting, 41
administrative
  complexity, 4
  law, 160
Adopt-a-Highway Program, 64
advertising, 24, 39
advocacy
  conservation, 212
  groups, 169
  legislation, 171
Africa, 29
agencies, 4, 72, 75
  police, 47
  State, 5
Agenda 21, 79
aging, 17
agricultural
  heartland, 19
land, 77
air
  craft, 60
  emissions, 19
  pollution, 58, 117
Albury, 16
allocation
  fixed, 116
  share, 116
  stepped, 116
Amazon, 33
Asia, 29
American Economic Association, 17
area unit, 20
Aronson, 194
assessment
  stakeholder, 24
attitudes, 29, 44, 180, 218
  cultural, 14
  economic, 14
auction, 118
Australian Conservation Foundation (ACF), 85
Australian Bureau of Statistics (ABS), 13, 95
Australian Stock Exchange, 217
Australian Treasury Department, 20, 21
Awards
  Green Leaf Award, 64
Baltic Sea, 65
bans, 181
behaviour, 209
  adaptive, 30
  Australians', 5
  change, 27-34, 200-203
  competitive, 30
  human, 15
  management, 15
  resource-use, 4
  team, 11
behavioural
  aim, 194
  science, 30
belief, 15, 17, 29, 32-34, 38, 42-45, 70, 193, 196, 207, 216
  price, 84
  property rights, 133, 140
  social, 69
  system, 33-36, 50, 136
benchmark, 100, 102, 123, 192, 214
Bergman, 78
Berkes, 135
best practice, 54, 122, 200
Bible, 13
biodiversity, 35, 129-131
  Aboriginal rights, 147
biogems, 43
biological
  capacity, 20
  reserves, 60
bonds
  mining industry, 65
Boston Consulting Group, 11
boundary, 38
  geographic, 210
  market, 122
  shoreline, 150
  strategy, 238
  system, 30

bounded rationality, 216
boycotts, 36
brainstorming, 233-234, 246, 247
Brazil, 88
Brundtland Commission, 79
Brunei, 152
budget
  balanced, 20
bureaucracy, 59
Bushcare, 184
business, 5
  groups, 21
Business Council of
  Australia, 43
Byron Bay, 152
Cadbury Schweppes, 62
California, 58
Canada, 65, 110, 145, 147
Canadian Roundtable on the
  Environment and the Economy, 196
Canberra, 16
capability, 43, 97, 200
cap, 2
  consumption, 113-114
  discharge, 114
  incentive, 190
  pollutant, 113
  resource, 115
capitalism, 71, 132
  market, 2
capitalist, 2, 136
carbon
  bonds, 60, 147
  credits, 45
  dioxide (CO_2), 110
  trading, 138
Cartesian revolution, 148
catchment
  committees, 5
Catchment Management Authorities, 73,
  129-131
CATO Institute, 114
Centre for Energy and Environment
  Policy, 17
Certifiable Tradable Offsets (CTO), 60, 147
Chamber of Commerce NSW, 95
change, 183-203, 256
  behavioural, 17
  voluntary, 81
Change Agent Network, 54
Changing Streams Pollution Reduction
  Project, 200
Chile, 120
China, 90

civil
  action, 157
  law, 154-166
    barriers to use, 162-164
  framework, 70
  liability, 156
  litigation, 209
  rights, 136
class action, 157
Clean Up Australia day, 196, 215
climate
  change, 17, 73
Council of Australian Governments
  (COAG), 83, 93
coastal
  environment, 42
  management, 72
  shoreline, 150
Coastcare, 184, 188
Coca Cola, 197
Code of environmental Practice, 99
cognitive
  skills, 32
  system, 38, 216
Coles, Ian, 218-219
Columbia, 58, 68
commercial
  culture, 8
  innovation, 7
  organisation, 15
common law, 58, 133, 143, 154-164
  negligence, 102, 143
  nuisance, 143
  property, 135, 147
community
  participation, 73
  values, 131
Community Right to Know program, 99
compensation, 116, 132, 140-144
competition, 30, 94-95, 192
  resource, 36-37
compliance, 58, 63, 167, 175-177
  cost, 50
conflict, 1, 2, 7, 8, 36, 79
  legal, 166
conservation
  behaviour, 20
  cost, 208-210
  energy, 21
  promotion, 40
  reserve, 147
  resource, 5, 21
  trust, 146
  zone, 185

Conservation Reserve Program, 64
consumer, 12, 16, 21, 59
  domestic, 15
  international programs 97-98
  preference, 16
  urban, 13
consumption, 50
  capital cost, 92
  capping, 113-115
  decision, 58
  demand, 75
  focused, 183
  oil, 68
  pressure, 110
  resource, 78
  tax, 103
container deposit legislation (CDL), 103, 219
context, 12
  social, 17, 72
  economic, 17
contract, 45, 125, 133, 154
cooperation, 36
Cooperative Research Centes (CRCs), 185
Copernican revolution, 143
corporate governance, 98
corporations law, 98,99
cost, 70, 84-85, 209
  administrative, 59
  compliance, 50
  court, 159
  effectiveness, 103
  management, 73
  search, 45, 73
  social 107, 121
  transaction *see* transaction costs
Costa Rica, 60, 147
Council of Australian Governments, 83
courts, 34, 72, 140. 154-164. 174
  civil, 126
  decisions, 157
  system, 165
covenants, 169
conservation, 65, 129
credits
  mitigation, 145
  programs, 110
  trading, 59
CSIRO, 17, 85
culture, 1, 80, 97
  beliefs, 42
  commercial, 8
  consumption, 39
  custodial, 8
  innovative, 78

cultural
  attitudes, 14
  environment, 12
  patterns, 208
custodial, 2
  culture, 8
  payment scheme, 145-146
  roles, 147
custodianship, 5, 6, 8, 36, 143, 146, 159
  Indigenous, 147
Darwin, Charles, 148
data pockets, 232
decision, 15, 29, 37
  consumption, 30, 58
  individual, 30
  making, 31-33
  organisation, 30
  pattern 30
  society, 30
decision-makers, 3, 32, 33, 38, 50
decision-making, 35, 42, 63, 179, 193, 196
defamation, 163-164
demand, 76, 83-84, 110
  embodied water, 13
  water, 13
democracy, 1, 16, 71
  goals, 77
Deni Greene Consulting Services, 88
Denmark, 91, 95
Denver, Colorado, 119
Department of Education Science and Training, 44
depletion, 3
  environmental, 14
  resource, 21, 76
derivative, 137
  instruments, 118
Dillon Reservoir, 68
direct water, 13-14
discharge cap, 114
distributional effect, 79
Dunphy, Dexter, 52-54
duty, 148-9
  of care, 155
Earth Sancuaries Limited (ESL), 146, 217
Easter Island, 134
Eastern Europe, 69
Ecofund, 65
eco-labelling, 63, 97
ecological, 138
  impacts, 47
  responsibility, 144
  services, 21, 50
  sustainability, 21, 99

economic
  attitude, 14
  concepts, 75
  environment, 12
  exploitation, 8
  growth, 21, 76, 210
  institution, 71
  instruments, 58
  literature, 57
  output, 91
  paradigm, 25
  returns, 118, 141
  signals, 42
  system, 28
  value, 3
economy, 44
  agrarian, 1
  brain, 20
  command, 69
  industrial, 1
  monetary, 20
  physical, 20
EcoRecycle Victoria, 218
ecosystem, 24-5, 28, 85-86, 138
  function, 68
  services, 41-42, 85
Ecuador, 58
education, 22, 24, 32, 63, 181, 193-203, 209
  energy, 67
  industry, 53
  investment, 78
  program, 37, 57, 59, 183, 215
    failure, 66
effluent, 45
ejido, 110
elements
  intangible, 70
  system, 28, 38
  tangible, 70
Elizbethan, 88
embodied water
  definition, 13
  demand, 13
Emery, 197
emissions
  levels, 8
  rights, 138
  trans-boundary, 65
emotions, 15
employees, 36
energy
  conservation, 21
  content, 20
  education, 67

industry, 106
  star rating scheme, 97
  use, 16
enforcement, 181
  regulation, 179
Enlightenment, 48
entitlement, 83, 133
  structures, 116
  volume, 116
entrepreneur, 7, 112, 187, 208, 211
  environmental, 172
Environment Australia, 43, 57, 95
Environmental Management System (EMS), 101
environmental, 11
  capital, 3
  cost, 14
  depletion, 14
  degradation, 168
  disaster, 21
  harm, 4, 21
  management, 5,
  resilience, 77
  trust, 185
Environmental Accounting Project, 63
environment planning statements (EISs), 69. 127, 178
Environment Protection Acts, 168
Environment Protection Agency (EPA)
  agency, 167
  NSW, 60
  US, 23, 57, 59, 60, 62, 63, 65
environmentalist, 21, 43
equifinality, 68, 70
equity, 4, 79, 103,155, 160
  social, 21, 72, 77, 111, 128, 139, 208, 210
estuary, 79, 80-82
  management, 72
ethical investment sector, 99
Europe, 29, 39, 48, 76, 105
European, 98, 107, 112
  monarch, 29
European Community, 29
European Foundation for the Improvement of Living and Working Conditions, 91
evaluation issues, 231
exploitation, 91, 116, 139
  capped, 114
  economic, 8
  environment, 36, 44
  resource, 41, 76
extended product responsibility (EPR), 102-105
externalities, 89-91, 149
  unpriced, 54

INDEX

farmers, 13, 41, 64, 94, 124, 143, 255-257
   lobby, 144
feedback, 43, 196
   loops, 33, 213
fees, 58-59, 61-62, 90-92, 145
   advantage, 91
filtration, 34, 38-42, 51, 193
finance mechanisms, 111
fines, 110
   non-compliance, 62
fiscal
   instruments, 89-92
fishers, 38, 41, 49, 79, 110, 120
fit, 38
Florida, 61
   Game and Fresh Water Fish Commission, 145
   Fish and Wildlife Habitat Trust Fund, 145
   Mitigation Park Program, 145
flows
   economic, 208, 235
   information, 12, 29, 32-33, 45, 72, 87, 190, 235
   material 17. 20, 77
   systems, 28
   minimum, 120
   nutrient, 42
   physical, 235
   resource, 29, 31, 45, 52, 190, 217
   waste, 218
flux analysis, 101
food
   genetically-modified, 35
forest, 85-86, 115
   old-growth, 42
Fostering Sustainable Behaviour, 67
Fox River, 117
France, 61, 90
freedom, 156, 208
   exploit, 71
   innovate, 78
free-market, 49, 69, 112
French Revolution, 73, 148
friction, 29, 33-34
Fuji-Zerox, 52
future, 5, 13. 118
   generations, 8, 21
   needs, 209
Future Dilemmas, 20, 36, 77
futures, 137
game theory, 115
GDP, 16, 41
Georges River Foreshore Improvement Program (GRFP), 191

German, 59
   Avoidance of Packaging Waste Ordinance, 59, 104
   government, 47
Germany, 53
Gleeson, Tony, 255-257
globalisation, 49
goals, 5, 15, 224, 226-227
   national, 77
   social, 107
   sustainability, 23
Gordon, Angus, 151-153
government, 3, 6, 13, 15, 24, 36
   Canadian, 65
   Commonwealth, 20
   contracts, 5
   control, 69
   Dutch, 62
   federal, 22
   Italian, 58
   local, 21, 22, 73, 167
   NSW, 14, 191
   New Jersey, 64
   organisation, 15
   policy, 20
   regional, 59, 68
   South Australian, 91
   State, 21, 22
   Victorian, 62
Great Barrier Reef marine park Authority, 119
Green and Clean Week, 64
Green Dot, 59, 104, 180
green
   consumer, 97
   offsets, 54, 124
   products, 98
   purchasers, 96
greenhouse
   emissions, 17. 20, 147
   gases, 107
Greenhouse Challenge, 99
Greenhouse Gas Emission Reduction Trading (CERT), 110
Gunningham, Neil, 181-182, 214
harm
   diffuse, 122
   doers, 6, 123
High Court, 165
Horticulture Australia, 102
Hunter Valley, 60, 121
Ikea, 63
immunity, 149
impact level levy, 91

implementation, 4, 72, 214
  legislation, 171
  regulation, 173, 179
incentives, 4, 15, 29, 59, 62, 129, 130-131, 137, 181, 209, 214, 244
  cash, 184
  capital, 185
  economic, 78
  financial, 6
  investment, 20
  market, 57
  opportunity, 184
  public recognition, 184
  programs, 23, 184, 213
  regulatory, 57
  social, 78
    reward, 184
  types, 184
Indigenous
  communities, 6
  custodianship, 147
  groups, 156
individual, 31
  decisions, 30
  rights, 155
Individual Transfer Quotas (ITQ), 110, 120
Industrial Revolution, 48, 73
inequity, 4, 112, 211
information, 12, 31, 63, 181, 192-203
  consumer, 97-98
  costs, 130
  flows, 15, 29, 32-33, 51, 72, 85, 109, 190
  insitution, 71
  passive, 194
  programs, 99
  structuring, 29
  systems, 97
Initiative of Joint Implementation, 60
innovation, 4, 6, 21, 48-51, 53, 57, 76, 77-78, 106, 172, 208
  capped resource, 115
  commercial, 7
  logistic, 127
  tecnological. 20, 48-49, 68
  system, 15
institutions, 1, 2, 8, 244-245
  defined, 28
  economics, 71
  information, 71
  knowledge, 71
  law, 71, 165
  marriage, 70
  motorcar, 16
  legal, 1, 69
  politics, 71
  public, 208
  social, 70, 211-212
institutional, 80, 255
  arrangements, 140
  barriers, 106
  change, 5, 72
  reform, 5, 70
  design, 6
  structure, 2, 5, 7, 129-130
instrument, 57-82, 243-244
  choice, 7, 66, 70-75
  derivative, 118
  economic, 69
  failure, 68
  fiscal, 89-92
  market, 1, 4, 5, 8. 17, 60, 69, 137, 213
  rights, 113-125
  voluntary, 4
  regulatory, 1, 4, 5, 8, 69
  sustainability, 69
  trading, 60
insurance, 111, 118
intangible, 70
integrity, 4, 8
interest
  groups, 171
  non-tradeable, 115
Intergenerational Report, 2
intergenerational equity, 162
international
  competitiveness, 8
  frameworks, 15
  treaty, 133
International Organisation for Standardisation (ISO), 101
  ISO 14000, 101, 102
intervention, 247-251
invasive
  species, 72
investment, 20
Ireland, 108
irrigated crops, 13
irrigators, 13
Italy, 58
Japan, 53
jurisprudence, 133
judges, 16, 166
Kalgoorlie-Boulder, 186
knowledge, 15, 70, 193
  institution, 71
  scientific, 71
Koran, 13
Korean
  residents, 26
Kyoto Protocol, 17

INDEX

labour, 48
lag, 76
land
  banks, 146
  ownership, 129, 138
  reform, 110
  use, 168
Landcare, 184, 188, 196, 215
law, 15, 27, 256
  administrative, 155, 160
  consumer, 157
  equity, 155
  institution, 71
  marriage, 70
  private, 154
  property, 133
  tort, 154
  violator, 65
lawyers, 141, 165, 166
legal
  barrier, 187
  conflict, 160
  community, 174
  costs, 52
  institutions, 1
  principles, 72
  protection, 129
  regulatory structures, 6
  rights, 155
  standing, 163
  system, 28, 143
legislation, 133
  creation, 169-172
  explotion, 73
levies, 61-62, 90, 110
liability, 102, 149
  tracing, 148-49
licences, 59, 109, 121, 168-172, 181, 210
Life Cycle Analysis, 25, 100-1, 185, 217
litigation, 156, 165
Living Planet Report, 20
local
  authorities, 63
  government, 5, 21, 73, 80, 167
Louisiana, 94
Maori, 134
marine park, 119
markets, 79, 83-131, 209
  boundary, 122
  capitalism, 2
  competition, 1
  creation, 106
  free, 69
  globalising, 7
  instrument, 1, 4, 5, 8, 17, 57, 68, 137

  mechanisms, 1
  property rights, 134
  real, 83-108, 110
  schemes, 59
  social cost, 14
  structure, 114
  support, 3
  system, 17
  world, 7
marketing, 15, 66, 82
  mode, 197
Marks, Bob, 107-108
Maximum Available Control Technology (MACT), 117
mechanisms, 209
  control, 114
  funding, 5
  market, 1
  structuring, 32
media, 64, 82, 169
Melbourne, 85, 219
Memorandum of Understanding (MOU), 60, 145
Mexican Revolution, 110
Miele, 53
minimum flow, 120
Minnesota Contaminated Property Tax, 104
MIPS, 101, 145
Mitigation Park Program, 61
modelling, 194
monarchy, 1
morality, 13, 79
Mortein, 197
Muan faai, 114-115
Murray Darling Basin, 13
  Salinity and Drainage Strategy, 117
Murray River, 117
National Centre for Environmental Economics, 23
National Centre for Environmental Economics, 57, 69
National Companies Code, 75
National Competition Policy, 75
National Fund for Environmental Protection and Water Management, 61
National Party, 144
national park, 60, 79, 146, 147, 168
National Institute of Economic & Industry Research (NIEIR), 92
National Pollution Inventory, 99
National Strategy for the Conservation of Australia's Biological Diversity, 147
natural
  capital, 3, 21
  gas, 19

natural (cont)
  inheritance, 12
  resource, 4, 5, 8, 75
    governance, 211
    management, 72, 220
    use, 15, 28
    strategy, 221
    systems, 6
Natural Capitalism, 41
negawatts, 106
negligence, 154-155
Netherlands, 61, 62
  environmental law, 168
New Jersey, 64
New Zealand, 134
Nobel Laureates, 17
Nolan ITU, 24-26
non-point source, 119
non-tradeable interest, 115
Nordic, 52
norms, 80, 256
North America, 98
Northern Cod Fishery, 76
offsets, 124
  advantages, 124
Oil Spill Liability Trust Fund, 65
Ontario, 110
open system, 29-30, 68
options, 137
Organisation for Economic cooperation and Development, (OECD), 13, 16, 181
open system, 29. 31
Ozone Protection And Synthetic Greenhouse Gas Management Act 1989, 59
Parc National Des Volcans, 61
path dependence, 15, 207, 213-217
pastures, 13
peer group, 111, 194
penalties, 15, 58, 59, 91, 180
performance
  discount, 65
  gap, 240
Performance Track, 62
Permanent Cover Program (PCP), 145
permit
  point source, 119
  system, 119
  tradeable, 59
  wood stoves, 60
Perth, 16
perverse
  incentives, 53
  subsidies, 3, 93
Pigouvian tax, 90

Plastics and Chemical Industry Association, 99
point source, 119
Poland, 58, 61-62, 65, 90
policy 1, 3, 4, 72, 170
  aims, 238
  gaps, 72
  framework, 5
  implementation, 72
  issues, 207-219
  performance, 238
political
  environment, 12
  institution, 71
  skills, 72
  system, 17
politicians, 173
poll
  opinion, 22
pollution, 149
  air, 58
  charges, 62
  emissions, 77
  noise, 61
  regulators, 172
  trans-boundary, 65
  water, 61
Pollution Discharge Elimination System, 119
Pooling, 121-122
population, 3, 19-23
  Australia, 19
  global, 77
  Sydney, 14
  Western Europe, 48
power. 11, 13, 88, 149
precautionary principle, 159
price, 84-85, 107-108, 110-111
  farm products, 13
  reform, 110
  regulation, 177
Price Waterhouse Coopers, 98, 99
pricing sustainability, 107-108
private
  action, 155
  conservation, 146
  law, 154
  markets, 110
  organisation, 15
  property, 13, 66
  regulation, 126, 154-166
  sector, 60
    initiative, 126
  transactions, 69
  use, 146

privatisation, 86-87, 112, 133
privilege, 148-149, 175
Profit Foundation Pty Limited, 96
property
  common, 135
  interest, 79
  non-property, 135
  ownership, 136
  personal, 69
  private, 13, 67, 134, 135
  rights, 27, 69, 83, 87, 107-108, 112, 117, 132-153
  State, 135
psychology, 15, 27
public
  disclosure, 98
  good, 146
  regulation, 125, 167-182
  relations, 25
Purchase and Development Rights, 145
quota, 123
Quito, 58
quality
  cycle, 196
  systems, 4
Queensland, 65, 126
Redford, 43
recycling, 25, 43, 59
  centres, 49
  EPR. 102
reform, 5
  institutional, 70
Regier, 138
regulation, 4, 57-58, 73
  environment, 213
  explosion, 74
  implementation, 173
  price, 177
  private, 58
  public, 58, 209
  system, 114
regulator, 123
regulatory, 79
  cost, 177
  drafting, 173
  design, 180-182
  failures, 66
  instrument, 1, 4, 5, 8, 37, 49, 57, 69
  requirement, 66
religious
  framework, 70
remedies, 179
Responsible Care, 63

resource, 11
  allocation, 8, 12, 72, 167
  available, 14
  banks, 146-147
  conservation, 5
  conserving, 2
  consumption, 6, 24, 78
  custodianship, 5
  dependent, 6
  depleting, 21, 76
  flows, 29, 31, 190, 217
  owner, 71
  policing, 4
  priced, 3
  security, 157
  state of, 5
  structures, 15
  sustainable, 3
  traditional, 79
  use, 4, 5, 11, 13, 19, 70
  yield, 76
Resource Consumption Decision Model, 30
Resource Consumption Decision Model (RCDM), 30
Resources for the Future, 57
revolution
  Cartesian, 148
  Copernican, 148
  French, 73, 148
  Industrial, 1
  technological, 6
reward, 64, 87
  pattern, 31
  pursuit, 29
  systems, 8, 62
rights, 72, 148
  banking, 122
  holder, 118, 127, 139, 187
  individual, 155
  instruments, 109-110, 132
  markets, 109-131
  property, 83
  owners, 45
risk, 65, 135, 165, 175
  civil law, 155-156
  management, 111
    plan, 72
  weighted cost, 149, 209
Robbins, 78
Robinson, Les, 80-82
role models, 81
Rwanda, 61
safety net
  regulatory, 3

San Jose, 58
Scandinavia, 53
science
  behavioural, 30
Schmigal, Peter, 24-26, 230
Sea level
  rise, 73, 150
Second World War, 16
Sector Facility Index, 63
security, 8
  national, 21
segment, 198-199
self-interest, 2, 71
self-regulation, 65, 75, 100
signals, 32, 215
silos, 24
Simons, 77
Singapore, 64
Small and Medium-sized Enterprises (SMEs), 101, 102
Smith, Jodi, 67, 76, 88, 186, 194, 200-203
social
  belief, 69
  capital, 78
  change, 48-50
  comfort, 8
  costs, 112, 121, 208-212
  decisions, 30
  expectations, 15
  goals, 107
  institution, 72
  marketing, 195, 196
  objectives, 5
  reform, 68
  system, 13, 24, 70
  wellbeing, 16
Social Cognitive Theory, 43, 184
Socially Responsible Investment (SRI), 88, 98
sociology, 15, 27
South Australia, 91, 103-4, 108, 181, 215
South East Fishery of Australia, 110
Southern Bluefin Tuna fishery, 119
Special Environment Levy, 68
stakeholder, 72, 173, 202, 221
  assessment, 24
standards, 57, 214
  Australian, 95
  performance, 101
  personal, 43
  wood fire, 59
Standards Australia, 95
State
  agencies, 5
  government, 21
  property, 135
  regulation, 58
State of the Environment 2001 (SoE 2001), 12
State of the Environment Reports, 64
Supreme Court, 165
statistics
  Adopt-a-Highway Program, 64
  advertising, 40
  area unit, 20
  attitudes, 95
  Conservation Reserve Program, 64
  energy, 16
  industrial, 13
  irrigation, 13
  population, 20
  regulations, 57
  subsidies, 44, 92
  urban, 13
  water, 13
stocks
  systems, 28
Strategic Lawsuit Against Public Participation (SLAPP). 164
strategy
  behavioural, 17
  boundaries, 238
  choice, 66
  definition, 11
  formation, 221-257
  instrument-based, 1
  multi-faceted, 25
  objective, 220
  selection, 251-253
  sustainability. 15, 17, 30, 51, 207-208, 243
  traditional, 211
strict liability, 174
structures
  entitlement, 116
  institutional, 7
  systems, 28
structuring
  mechanisms, 32
subsidies, 3, 54, 61, 92-94, 185-187
  benign, 94
  costs, 188-189
Supplemental Environmental Projects, 65
supplier, 59, 102
supply, 76, 83-84, 110
sustainability,
  defined, 78
  initiatives, 73
  principles, 159

problem
  defined, 75
  strategy, 15
  strategist, 71
swaps, 118, 137
Sweden, 58, 62, 63, 90, 91
Switzerland, 58, 91
Sydney, 14, 61
Sydney Airport, 61, 160
Sydney Water Board, 68
Sydney Water Corporation, 14
system
  boundary, 30
  defined, 28
  complex, 29
  economic, 12, 28
  innovation, 15
  legal, 28
  map, 233, 236, 241
  market-based, 30
  natural, 70
  open, 29, 31
  operation, 29-30
  resource-use, 13
  reward, 8
  river, 19
  quality, 4
  social, 12, 13, 24, 70
synergy, 69
tangible, 70
target, 198-199
  environmental, 63
  group, 194
tariffs, 7, 192
taxes, 20, 58-59, 169
  advantage, 91
  environmental, 81, 181
  green, 91
  leaded fuel, 90
  petroleum, 65
  Pigovian, 90
team
  behaviour, 11
  formation, 223, 225
  gaps, 228
  goals, 226-227
  principles, 228
technical tracing, 149
technological
  change, 48-50, 77
  environment, 12
  innovation, 20, 211
  revolution, 6

technology, 48, 50, 61, 70, 73, 76, 139, 180, 218, 256
  farm, 13
  sustainable, 22
Telluride, 60
Texas, 64
Thailand, 114
Tic Tac, 197
time
  lag, 35, 76
  limited rights, 117
  messages, 199
  tourism
  inbound, 20
tipping point, 82
tool, 66
  management, 58
trade, 17
  export, 20
tort, 154, 160
tradeable
  interest, 118
  permit, 59
trading, 83, 210
  weather, 89
transaction, 28, 84, 109, 241, 242
transaction costs, 4, 6, 34-35, 45-47, 49, 73, 75, 79, 100, 121, 126-131, 163, 180
transferable quotas, 119, 189
treaty, international, 133
triple bottom line, 99, 211
un-attenuated rights, 132
uncertainty, 2, 137
Uniblanco, 88
United Kingdom (UK) 94, 146
United Nations, 77
United Nations Convention on Biological Diversity, 147
United National Conference on Environment and Development, 79
United States (US)
  Constitution, 155
  EPA, 23, 57, 59, 60, 62, 63, 65, 117, 179
  Initiative on Joint Implementation (USIJI), 147
  investors, 88
  Kyoto Protocol, and, 17
  private sector, 60
  Trust Company, 88
  War of Independence, 140,
University of Delaware, 17
University of Newcastle, 40
unpriced externalities, 54

user pays, 72
University of Technology Sydney (UTS), 54
values, 42
  choices, 79
  community, 131
  economic, 105
  environmental, 58
  habitat, 60
  non-tangible, 139
  personal, 34
  service, 105
  social, 57
Vehicle registration, 16
Victoria, 62, 219
Victorian Farmer's Federation, 102
Visy, 53
volume entitlements, 116
voluntary
  action, 22, 64, 214
  change, 81
  choices, 80
  code, 100
  conservation, 146
  contol, 59
  custodianship, 146
  instrument, 4, 57
  programs, 191
  work, 187-188
volunteers, 5
Volvo, 63
Walden Asset management, 88
Wallis Lake, 160
Washington, 57
waste, 14, 42, 49
  accumulated, 52
  disposal, 52, 58
  flow, 218
  reduction, 52-54
Waste management Association of Australia, 218
Waste Reduction Grants, 189
water
  allocation, 83
  availability, 237
  catchment, 13
  charge, 58, 68
  consumption, 13, 24-26
  demand, 13
  direct, 13-14
  efficiency, 186
  embodied demand, 13
  harvesting cap, 113
  licenses, 45
  market, 84
  pollution, 61
  purification, 42
  quality, 61
  ration, 114
  right, 120, 138
  rural, 13
  storage, 42
  supply, 85
  use, 8, 13, 15
Water Reform Framework, 83
wealth, 5, 6, 88, 208, 211
  production 5
  structures, 16
weather
  trading, 89
Western Australia, 186
Western Mining, 43
wetland, 60, 61, 173
Wetlands Mitigation Banks, 145
Wetlands Reserve Program, 60
whitegoods, 15
Winemaker's Federation of Australiam 102
wood fires, 60
World Wildlife Fund (WWF), 93
Young, Mike, 44, 129-131
zoning
  laws, 49, 145

Statutes

Aircraft Noise Levy Act 1996 (Cth): 61
Beverage Container Act 1975 (SA): 104
Clean Air Act 1990 (US): 59
Environment Protection Act 1993 (SA): 104, 160
Environment Protection and Biodiversity Conservation Act 1999 (Cth); 99, 148
Environmental Planning and Assessment Act 1979 (NSW): 161
Farm Bill 1996 (US): 60
Native Title Act 1993 (Cth); 162
Ozone Protection And Synthetic Greenhouse Gas Management Act 1989 (Cth): 59
Surface Mining Control and Reclamation Act 1977 (US): 66
Trade Practices Act 1974 (Cth): 157, 175

Cases

Armidale City Council v Alec Finlayson Pty, [1999] FCA 330: 161
Bannister Quest Pty Ltd v Australian Fisheries Management Authority, (1997) 77 FCR 503: 159
Byron Environment Centre v Arakwal People, (1998) 3 AILR 16: 162
City of Botany Bay Council v Minister for Transport and Regional Development, FCA 1495: 160
Donoghue v Stevenson, [1932] AC 562: 155
EM & ES Petroleum Pty Ltd v Shimden Pty Ltd, (unreported, NSWSC 1995, No 2483/92): 161
John Bulun Bulun v R & T Textiles Pty Ltd [1998] FCA 1082: 157
Lockhart River Aboriginal Council v Cook Shire Council, QPELR 344: 157
Mabo v Queensland (No 2) (1992) 175 CLR 1: 156, 157
McKennan v Holden [1999] SAERDC 83: 160
Minister for Urban Affairs & Planning v Rosemount Estate Pty Ltd (unreported, NSWCA, Handley JA, Sheller JA, Cole JA, 14 August 1996): 160
Nicholls v Director General of National Parks and Wildlife (1994) 84 LGERA 397: 159
Qantas Airways Ltd v Mascot Galvanising (Holdings) (unreported NSWSC, 17 December 1998, No 3610/96): 160
Randwick City Council v Minister for the Environment [1999]FCA 1494: 160
Ryan v Great Lakes Council, [1999] FCA 177: 160, 161
van Son v Forestry Commission of NSW, (unreported, NSWSC, Cohen J, 3 February 1995): 160
Yanner v Eaton [1999] HCA 53: 157

ALSO AVAILABLE FROM THE FEDERATION PRESS

Environment and Sustainability Policy

Creation, Implementation, Evaluation

Stephen Dovers

Dovers argues that better public policy is the key to creating a more sustainable environment and shows what this might involve. This is an intensely practical book, intellectually original and rigorous, and written in a concise and accessible style.

He melds a deep knowledge of traditional public policy with a close understanding of the sustainability problems and an appreciation of the complex institutional systems which make up modern civil society. As well as establishing an operational framework for policy analysis and prescription, he provides ways of fulfilling key elements of an effective policy process:

- Problem framing – social debate, monitoring environmental change, handling uncertainty, analysing existing policy, scaling and framing policy problems.
- Policy framing – policy principles, the policy statement, policy goals.
- Policy implementation – policy instrument choice, implementation and communication planning, resources, enforcement and compliance, embedding policy monitoring.
- Policy monitoring and evaluation – ongoing monitoring, evaluation and review, extension and adaptation.
- Inclusion in public policy – coordination and integration, public participation, transparency and accountability, communication mechanisms.
- Institutional settings and reform for effective policy.

Dr Stephen Dovers, a senior fellow at the Australian National University, is widely recognised as one of Australia's leading scholars of environmental policy. He has co-authored two previous books, edited seven and written numerous reports and articles in leading refereed journals.

2005 • ISBN 1 86287 540 5 • paperback • 208 pages • $49.95

ALSO AVAILABLE FROM THE FEDERATION PRESS

Environmental Law Toolkit – NSW

A community guide to Environmental Law in NSW

5th edition

Environmental Defender's Office (NSW)

> Environmental Law Toolkit – NSW *is an invaluable resource ... The complexity [of the modern world], whilst daunting, can be successfully negotiated by having access to accurate and comprehensive information geared to the public interest. Here is where the* Environmental Law Toolkit – NSW *comes into play, use it well.*
>
> Peter Garrett MP

This well-established book written primarily for community groups in New South Wales, is a practical resource on how to use the law to protect the environment. Now in its third edition, it covers the NSW law on:

- environmental planning and assessment
- natural resource management
- pollution management
- biodiversity conservation
- natural and cultural heritage.

It also includes a chapter on environmental advocacy focusing on: submissions, letters and petitions * using the media * access to information * defamation law and safe speech * incorporating an environmental group * corporations and environmental advocacy * environmental protest and criminal law * seeking legal advice and representation.

The *Environmental Law Toolkit* is a publication of the Environmental Defender's Office (NSW), a non-profit community legal centre specialising in public interest environmental law.

2005 • ISBN 1 86287 554 5 • paperback •352 pages • $49.95

ALSO AVAILABLE FROM THE FEDERATION PRESS

Managing Australia's Environment

Stephen Dovers & Su Wild River, editors

Managing Australia's Environment is a report card of unprecedented scope, examining Australia's resource and environmental management institutions and policies against the requirements of ecologically sustainable development. The contributors engage with policy, management and legal issues at all levels of government, across a diverse range of sectors including forests, oceans, the arid zone, water, regional development, the Indigenous domain and environmental protection. The result is a rich source of recommendations for purposeful and adaptive policy and institutional responses to the great challenge of sustainability.

Managing Australia's Environment is written by leading researchers and practitioners, including:

Ian Lowe
Robyn Eckersley
Tim Bonyhady
Clive Hamilton
Ronnie Harding
Gerry Bates
Stephen Dovers
John Dore
Sarah Ewing
Mark Stafford-Smith

Given the size and scope of Managing Australia's Environment, almost any reader with an interest in environmental management should be able to find something of relevance.

Rural Society

This book examines Australia's resource and environmental management institutions and policies against the requirements of ecologically sustainable development. The contributors engage with policy, management and legal issues at all levels of government, across a diverse range of sectors including forests, oceans, the arid zone, water, regional development, the indigenous domain and environmental protection. The result is a rich source of recommendations for purposeful and adaptive policy and institutional responses to the great challenge of sustainability.

The Planet Earth

2003 • ISBN 1 86287 447 6 • paperback • 576 pages • $75.00

ALSO AVAILABLE FROM THE FEDERATION PRESS

'A Question of Balance'

Natural Resources Conflicts Issues in Australia

3rd edition

David Mercer

The book provides detailed case studies of the forest, minerals, tourist and agricultural industries. Mercer's reading is wide and he has drawn on his source material to produce a readable synthesis of some very complex issues. There is considerable factual detail on particular problems and this has been enhanced by a critique of remedial measures. The book provides a wealth of information and analysis ...

Bogong (Canberra & South-east Region Environment Centre)

Avoiding either extreme of the environmental debate, from technological optimism to pessimistic doomsday predictions, Mercer produces a well-researched, scientifically based analysis of the state of natural resources in Australia.

Monash News, November 2000

Well-researched, clear and unrelenting in its criticism of unplanned or poorly planned development.

Annals of Tourism Research

An invaluable reference for anybody involved in or concerned about the management, control and selling price of Australia's natural resources.

Environment South Australia

2000 • ISBN 1 86287 342 9 • paperback • 384 pages • $45.00

ALSO AVAILABLE FROM THE FEDERATION PRESS

Renegotiating the Environment

The power of politics

Jenny Stewart & Grant Jones

Renegotiating the Environment challenges the common perception that politics is the enemy of the environment. It argues that environmental conflict in fact creates opportunities for creative environmental governance; that managers can learn to acknowledge, understand and use politics to achieve more consensual and sustainable solutions. For managers, scientists and activists, this is a compelling possibility.

Stewart and Jones support their case through detailed case studies and offer practical guidance for implementing governance-based responses to environmental problems.

> *This book is a 'must read' for anyone involved in natural resources: politicians, public servants and community leaders, and every student of natural resources, agriculture and the environment. It is a refreshingly honest analysis of the roles that politics, power, leadership, governance and conflict play in decision-making.*
>
> Leith Boully, Chair, Community Advisory Council, Murray-Darling Basin Commission

> *... an original book, with important messages about how to implement change.*
>
> Professor Peter Cullen, Chair, Wentworth Group of Concerned Scientists

> *[A] sensible, persuasive and informed perspective on environmental management, policy and politics. The nine compelling case studies, encompassing aspects of water management, forestry and urban development, give the analysis a thoroughly practical and contemporary flavour. ... clearly written and reassuringly uncluttered by ideological presumptions. I recommend it strongly ...*
>
> Professor Andrew Parkin, Editor, Australian Journal of Political Science

> Renegotiating the Environment *is a new and different way of approaching environmental problems. It is a 'must read' for anyone involved in natural resources: politicians, public servants, managers, scientists, community leaders, activists and students of planning and environment.*
>
> Claudia Baldwin, Australian Journal of Environmental Management

2004 • 1 86287 473 5 • paperback • 192 pages • $39.95